Instructional Survival in the Midst of the Perfect Storm: The Experiences of K-12 Teachers During the COVID-19 Global Pandemic

Instructional Survival in the Midst of the Perfect Storm: The Experiences of K-12 Teachers During the COVID-19 Global Pandemic

EDITED BY

JILL D. SALISBURY-GLENNON
Auburn University

CHIH-HSUAN WANG
Auburn University

AND

DAVID M. SHANNON
Auburn University

emerald
PUBLISHING

United Kingdom – North America – Japan – India – Malaysia – China

Emerald Publishing Limited
Emerald Publishing, Floor 5, Northspring, 21-23 Wellington Street, Leeds LS1 4DL

First edition 2025

British Library Cataloguing in Publication Data

A catalogue record for this book is available from the British Library

ISBNs:
978-1-83708-502-6 HB
978-1-83708-503-3 PB
978-1-83708-504-0 EPDF
978-1-83708-505-7 EPUB

Printed and bound by CPI Group (UK) Ltd, Croydon, CR0 4YY

CONTENTS

PREFACE

Daniel W. Wong and Lucy Wong Hernandez

The COVID-19 novel virus caused a memorable pandemic worldwide. At the national level, it kept us and our families contained in our homes for months and reoriented our relationships with the policymakers, our communities, and even with each other. Schools had closed, and workplaces initiated remote practices to prevent the spread of the coronavirus. Parents and caregivers everywhere struggled to keep their children healthy and occupied. Social-emotional skills are crucial during the formative years for the overall well-being of children and are at the core of all meaningful learning experiences. During these challenging times, while children did not always have access to ideal instruction in their academic subjects, they could still learn essential emotional literacy skills that will serve them their entire lives. The pandemic crisis also presented opportunities for our learning communities and school systems to put into practice more sophisticated and flexible uses of technology, to adjust common approaches to teaching and learning, to re-engineer learning skills and to promote school system changes while expanding education practice to develop a holistic approach to fully engage parents, caregivers, teachers, and all stakeholders.

The strengths and benefits of an edited book such as this are that we have a group of researchers committed to conducting various kinds of evidence-based re-

Instructional Survival in the Midst of the Perfect Storm: :
The Experiences of K–12 Teachers During the COVID-19 Global Pandemic, pages vii–viii.

ISBNs: 978-1-83708-502-6 HB, 978-1-83708-503-3 PB,
978-1-83708-504-0 EPDF, 978-1-83708-505-7 EPUB

search studies in an effort to investigate all factors related to the impact of the pandemic. This research can contribute to our knowledge of how we can improve our learning system to better serve our students, parents, caregivers, teachers, school administrators, policymakers, and all stakeholders. Each chapter of this book represented a well-designed, well-organized presentation of a research product to provide readers with pertinent information about the impact of the pandemic on the educational community at large.

Learning, writing, and editing are a journey that will never end. We hope this book will provide knowledge-based educational information to students, parents, school communities, and all stakeholders to continue improving our students' learning system. We believe our mission will be accomplished if this book facilitates a positive learning experience for the readers.

—Daniel W. Wong and Lucy Wong Hernandez

CHAPTER 1

INTRODUCTION: INSTRUCTIONAL SURVIVAL IN THE MIDST OF THE PERFECT STORM

The Experiences of K–12 Teachers During the COVID-19 Global Pandemic

Jill D. Salisbury-Glennon, Chih-hsuan Wang, and David M. Shannon
Auburn University

Daniel W. Wong
Mississippi State University & University of Southern Maine

Lucy Wong Hernandez
University of Southern Maine

Yan Dai
Auburn University

INTRODUCTORY OVERVIEW

In 2020, many K–12 schools across the world initially planned to shut down for a brief period of time in response to the COVID-19 epidemic. As the Coronavirus

Instructional Survival in the Midst of the Perfect Storm: The Experiences of K–12 Teachers During the COVID-19 Global Pandemic, pages 1–8.

Published under exclusive licence by Emerald Publishing Limited
ISBNs: 978-1-83708-502-6 HB, 978-1-83708-503-3 PB,
978-1-83708-504-0, EPDF, 978-1-83708-505-7 EPUB

began to spread rapidly across the globe, The World Health Organization (WHO) declared this epidemic a pandemic (Mseleku, 2020), and these shut-downs were extended into months and even into entire academic years in an effort to protect students. During these shut-downs, many schools quickly implemented newer modes of instruction for teachers to continue to teach and reach their learners. Specifically, many schools began to implement emergency remote teaching to continue to deliver instruction (Marshall et al., 2022; Trust et al., 2020; Whittle et al., 2020).

These emergency forms of instruction often included Zoom or other forms of on-line distance learning that teachers had to implement quickly, often without the necessary training, guidance and/or technological resources (An et al., 2021; Ferri et al., 2020; Marshall et al., 2022). Ferri et al. (2020) found that this transition to emergency remote learning often resulted in technological, pedagogical and social challenges. As school districts gradually began to approve the in-person return to schools, there was an increase in more hybrid forms of instruction. In some cases, K–12 teachers were expected to teach on-line and in person, often at the same time. In other cases, teachers delivered packets to students who didn't have the technological resources, or the Internet for example, to attend these on-line forms of instruction.

These abrupt shifts to emergency remote and other novel forms instruction in the face of the pandemic often resulted in higher levels of stress and anxiety for K–12 teachers (Hooker et al., 2024; Kim et al., 2022; Pressley et al., 2022). Many considered teachers to be put on the "front lines" (Mosley et al., in press, Ch. 6). Further, much of this instruction took place in isolation. Not only did teachers not have face-to-face contact with their students, but they also lost face-to-face contact with their peer teachers, administrators and other forms of social support in the workplace (An et al., 2022; Leech et al., 2022). In addition, due to stay-at-home orders, many teachers were teaching from home. In many cases, this further caused teachers to experience challenges associated with their work-life balance, as many teachers were tasked with the challenge of teaching their students on-line from their homes, while they also helped their own children to navigate on-line instruction for their teachers (e.g., Marshall et al., 2022; Mutch et al., 2023). This co-edited book serves to elucidate some of the research into both the instructional and the emotional impacts of the COVID-19 global pandemic on K–12 teachers.

BOOK OVERVIEW

The present co-edited book serves to synthesize the research conducted by many scholars with a focus on the many challenges and opportunities that have been experienced by K–12 teachers as the result of the COVID-19 global pandemic. This book will elucidate the various theoretical frameworks, research methodologies, participant populations, research findings, challenges, positive outcomes and future implications for policy and practice based on the results this research.

Instructional and Emotional Impacts of the COVID-19 Global Pandemic on K–12 Teachers

In the second chapter included in this co-edited book, *Instructional Survival: A Qualitative Case Study of Elementary Teachers' Experiences Teaching Remotely and Concurrently During COVID-19*, Ladendorf (Chapter 2), used a qualitative case study methodology to investigate the lived experiences of elementary teachers as they taught both remotely and concurrently during the pandemic. Results were categorized into two themes: instructional and emotional impacts. The instructional impacts of the pandemic directly affected the emotional impacts, as the transition to more remote forms of instruction led to the primary emotions experienced by teachers of shock, fear and isolation. The results of this study imply that when faced with future challenges and crises which are perhaps inevitable, K–12 teachers need to be provided additional instructional resources and training and perhaps equally as important, with the necessary emotional support from administrators, mentors and peer teachers (Ladendorf, Chapter 2).

Teacher Stress, Burnout and Job Dissatisfaction

In the third chapter, entitled *Educators' Job Burnout and Intentions to Leave During the COVID-19 Pandemic*, Camp, Zamarro and McGee (Chapter 3), used nationally representative samples to investigate K–12 teachers' levels of job related burn-out including their thoughts regarding leaving the profession. Results of the analyses indicated that the pandemic was a very challenging time for teachers resulting in large increases in teacher stress, burn-out and even their consideration of exiting the teaching profession. Some of the factors that contributed to these increases included teacher age, the need to change instructional modality, often multiple times; and COVID-related health concerns. Finally, these researchers found that the expressed concerns were actually somewhat different between teachers and administrators suggesting a potential disconnect in the workplace. The results of this study suggest the importance of administrators' awareness of the concerns of K–12 teachers as well as the need to assist teachers with their technological and emotional needs to help retain K–12 teachers.

Somewhat relatedly, in the fourth chapter in this co-edited book, *A Perfect Storm: COVID-19 as a Demotivating Factor Contributing to Teacher Stress, Burnout and Mental Health*, Jones, Kramer and Broadbent (Chapter 4) conducted a mixed methodological study using close to 4000 K–12 teacher participants from across the U.S. to investigate the impact of the COVID-19 global pandemic on teachers' stress, burnout and mental health. Quantitative results indicated that there was a significant increase in teacher stress, burn-out and mental health as the result of the COVID-19 global pandemic. Further, the results of qualitative written responses, focus groups and interviews demonstrated that some teachers chose to leave the profession, while others started to explore other career options. Specifically, some teachers discussed side hustles that they were developing, while others considered going back to school to obtain degrees outside of the field of education. Based on these findings, Jones, Kramer and Broadbent (Chapter 4) suggested that during these challenging times, there is a need for administrators to work toward meeting the needs of teachers and that more resources need to be in place to help teachers such as additional technological and student supports. Finally, the authors concluded that increased incentives for teachers to remain in the profession such as better salaries, student loan forgiveness options, and overall efforts to help make the teaching profession more valued, respected and appreciated could potentially all help to retain more teachers.

Teacher Morale, Mental Health, Mentoring and Social Support

In Chapter 5, entitled *Elementary Teacher Morale and Mental Health Following the COVID-19 Pandemic*, Marshall, Pressley, Schoettler, Trammell, and Smith (Chapter 5) used a theoretical framework of teacher demoralization to explore teacher morale and mental health at the end of the 2021–2022 school year. According to Marshall et al. (Chapter 5), several factors contributed to the fact that the pandemic was incredibly challenging for educators. First, many K–12 teachers were forced to teach using novel online formats for which they had not been properly trained. Further, these online modes of instruction often resulted in significantly less social interaction. These factors as well as others resulted in higher levels of teacher stress, burn-out and job dissatisfaction. Further, Kim et al. (2022) asserted that teacher stress and burnout was at an all-time high when hyflex teaching was introduced (as cited in Marshall et al., Ch. 5). Thus, Marshall et al., conducted an explanatory, sequential mixed methods design (Creswell et al., 2011) using both a quantitative survey as well as focus groups to investigate the effects of the pandemic on elementary teachers' morale and mental health. Results of these analyses indicated that while teacher morale definitely suffered as the result of the COVID-19 global pandemic, such factors as administrative support, parent support and teacher autonomy all positively predicted teacher morale and teacher mental health (Marshall et al., Ch. 5). The authors further suggested that these variables could serve to increase teacher morale in the future. Finally, in line with the research conducted by Jones, Kramer and Broadbent (Chapter 4) these researchers also asserted the need to ensure that teachers receive appropriate compensation for their work.

Mosley et al. (Chapter 6) sought to investigate the positive effects of gratitude and teacher mentoring in their chapter entitled *Social Support and COVID-19: How U.S. K–12 Teachers Were Impacted by Gratitude and Mentoring During the COVID-19 Pandemic*. This study extended the prior research into teacher support using a modified grounded theory methodological approach. Results of multiple triangulation techniques showed three themes that suggested that social support, in particular mentoring and gratitude, were extremely helpful for teachers individually, at the classroom level and at the building level. The results of this study provide additional support for prior research into the numerous benefits of multiple forms of support (Cutrona & Russell, 1990) and yield implications for the importance of supporting teachers during the pandemic years and beyond.

In Chapter 7, *Teacher Self-Efficacy During COVID-19: A Qualitative Study on Experienced High School Teachers*, Conley (Chapter 7) conducted a qualitative study to investigate teachers' self-efficacy experiences during the COVID-19 global pandemic. Specifically, using a qualitative interview study, the researcher investigated how the four sources of self-efficacy: mastery experiences, vicarious experiences, social persuasion and physiological state (Usher & Pajares, 2006) affected the self-efficacy of teachers in the midst of the pandemic. The researcher concluded that all teachers experienced challenges related to all four sources of self-efficacy at some point during this challenging time. However, having a growth mindset served to help teachers to overcome some of these challenges. The researcher further concluded that these self-efficacy influences were dependent upon support from their school and their school leadership.

In Chapter 8, entitled *Impact of COVID-19 on Students with Special Needs and Parental Involvement*, Wood and Wood (Chapter 8), conducted a sequential mixed-methods study with special education teachers in an effort to study teachers' perceptions and concerns regarding the impact of the COVID-19 pandemic on their students with Special Needs. Results of a thematic analysis revealed that these teachers were most concerned about: a lack of academic skills, a lack of available services such as the Internet, a lack of student attendance, and attention and socio-emotional stability since their students' socioemotional needs may not have been met during the global pandemic.

In *Researching the Entangled: Post COVID-19 Cognitive, Psychological and Motivational States*, Ayyildiz and Yilmaz (Chapter 9) conducted a combination design to assess high school students' and teachers', and university students' and teachers' cognitive changes, psychological states and motivational levels as the result of the COVID-19 global pandemic. Results of their analyses of the high school teachers' data revealed that the teachers experienced depression, anxiety and a loss of motivation during the post COVID-19 pandemic period. Further, there was also a correlation between depression and generalized anxiety disorder amongst high school teachers. These findings led the researchers to conclude that the impact of the pandemic affected each teacher somewhat differently and that there is a need to deliver teacher education programs with an even greater emphasis on application in addition to content.

In Chapter 10, *K–12 Teacher Support During the COVID-19 Pandemic*, Menchaca and Garcia (Chapter 10), conducted an historical account to investigate how teachers felt about their preparation to teach in a distance learning format, and to describe the types of distance learning support that teachers received during the COVID-19 global pandemic. Grounded in a theoretical framework of social support systems, the study used a qualitative research design using focus group sessions as well as an online questionnaire. Results of the analyses revealed three themes. First, teachers indicated that they did not feel as if they had received enough preparation for online teaching. Second, these teachers felt a need for additional and continued technological support. And third, teachers expressed a need for more social/emotional support from principals and peers to help them to navigate these challenging times.

In *Attachment, Attention and Achievement during the COVID-19 Pandemic: A Conceptual Literature Review*, Banks, Campbell, Dillard and Torres (Chapter 11) synthesized the existing literature into attachment theory, cognitive load theory, and attention mechanisms to provide a theoretical framework to examine academic achievement under the stressful conditions of the COVID-19 global pandemic. Specifically, these authors sought to: provide an overview of attachment theory and related research, explore cognitive load theory and its implications for attention, and to assess the effects of attachment on attention and academic success during an especially challenging time, the COVID-19 global pandemic. The results of their review of the literature suggested that cognitive load theory may provide a framework to explain the relationships between attachment and attention during stressful times. Further this review suggested that marginalized groups may be more susceptible to cognitive load challenges when faced with highly challenging tasks and events.

CONCLUSION

In closing, we would like to thank the many researchers who came together in an effort to bring our vision to fruition and to further elucidate the instructional and emotional impacts of the COVID-19 global pandemic on K–12 teachers. In some ways, K–12 education as we know it will be forever changed as the result of the COVID-19 global pandemic. This collaborative effort resulted in a vast collection of research conducted in many diverse learning contexts. The present co-edited book presents both the challenges as well positive outcomes as the result of the COVID-19 global pandemic. Finally, this book will conclude with a thematic summary written by Dr. Daniel Wong and Dr. Lucy Wong Hernandez over all of the presented research as well as the implications for teachers during future crises in the K–12 classroom.

REFERENCES

An, Y., Kaplan-Rakowski, R., Yang, J., Conan, J., Kinard, W., & Daughrity, L. (2021). Examining K–12 teachers' feelings, experiences, and perspectives regarding online teaching during the early stage of the COVID-19 pandemic. *Educational Technology Research and Development, 69*, 2589–2613.

An, H., Mongillo, G., Sung, W., Fuentes, D. (2022). Factors affecting online learning during the COVID-19 pandemic: The lived experiences of parents, teachers, and administrators in U.S. high needs K–12 schools. *Journal of Online Learning Research, 8*(2), 203–234.

Ayyildiz, P. & Yilmaz, A. (2025). Researching the entangled: Post-COVID-19 cognitive, psychological and motivational States. In J. D. Salisbury-Glennon, C.-H. Wang &

Shannon, D. M. (Eds.), *Instructional survival in the midst of the perfect storm: The experiences of K–12 teachers during the COVID-19 global pandemic* (pp. 141–165). Emerald Publishing.

Banks, R. F., Campbell, M. B., Dillard, D. M., & Torres, J. A. (2025). Attachment, attention, and achievement during the COVID-19 pandemic: A conceptual literature review. In J. D. Salisbury-Glennon, C.-H. Wang & Shannon, D. M. (Eds.), *Instructional survival in the midst of the perfect storm: The experiences of K–12 teachers during the COVID-19 global pandemic* (pp. 189–210). Emerald Publishing.

Camp, A. M., Zamarro, G., & McGee, J. (2025). Educators' job burnout and intentions to leave during the COVID-19 pandemic. In J. D. Salisbury-Glennon, C.-H. Wang & Shannon, D. M. (Eds.), *Instructional survival in the midst of the perfect storm: The experiences of K–12 teachers during the COVID-19 global pandemic* (pp. 30–48). Emerald Publishing.

Conley, S. M. (2025). Teacher self-efficacy during COVID-19: A qualitative study on experienced high school teachers. In J. D. Salisbury-Glennon, C.-H. Wang & Shannon, D. M. (Eds.), *Instructional survival in the midst of the perfect storm: The experiences of K–12 teachers during the COVID-19 global pandemic.* (pp. 103–122). Emerald Publishing.

Cresswell, J. W., & Plano-Clark, V. L. (2011). *Designing and conducting mixed methods research* (2nd ed.), Sage.

Cutrona, C. E., & Russell, D. W. (1990). Type of social support and specific stress: Toward a theory of optimal matching. In B. R. Sarason, I. G. Sarason, & G. R. Pierce (Eds.), *Social support: An interactional view* (pp. 319–366). John Wiley & Sons.

Ferri, F., Grifoni, P., & Guzzo, T. (2020). Online learning and emergency remote teaching: Opportunities and challenges in emergency situations. *Societies, 10*(4), 86. https://doi.org/10.3390/soc10040086

Hooker, S. A., Olson-Bullis, B., Levin, A., Ziegenfuss, J. Y., Margolis, K. L., & Rossom. R. C. (2024). Depression and anxiety among K–12 teachers in the United States: A systematic review. *School Psychology*. Advance online publication. https://doi.org/10.1037/spq0000666

Jones, D., Kramer, B., & Broadbent, C. (2025). A perfect storm: COVID-19 as a demotivating factor contributing to teacher stress, burnout, and mental health. In J. D. Salisbury-Glennon, C.-H. Wang, & Shannon, D. M. (Eds.), *Instructional survival in the midst of the perfect storm: The experiences of K–12 teachers during the COVID-19 global pandemic* (pp. 49–67). Emerald Publishing.

Kim, L. E., Oxley, L., & Asbury, K. (2022). "My brain feels like a browser with 100 tabs open": A longitudinal study of teachers' mental health and well-being during the COVID-19 pandemic. *The British Journal of Educational Psychology, 92*(1), 299–318. https://doi.org/10/1111/bjep.12450

Ladendorf. K. (2025). Instructional survival: A qualitative case study of elementary teachers' experiencing teaching remotely and concurrently during COVID-19. In J. D. Salisbury-Glennon, C.-H. Wang & Shannon, D. M. (Eds.), *Instructional survival in the midst of the perfect storm: The experiences of K–12 teachers during the COVID-19 global pandemic* (pp. 9–27). Emerald Publishing.

Leech, N. L., Gullett, S., Cummings, M. H., & Haug, C. A. (2022). The challenges of remote K–12 education during the COVID-19 pandemic: Differences by grade level. *Online Learning Journal, 26*(1), 245–267.

Marshall, D. T., Pressley, T., Neugebauer, N. M., Trammell, D. L, & Smith, N. E. (2025). Elementary teacher morale and mental health following the COVID-19 pandemic. In J. D. Salisbury-Glennon, C.-H. Wang & Shannon, D. M. (Eds.), *Instructional survival in the midst of the perfect storm: The experiences of K–12 teachers during the COVID-19 global pandemic* (pp. 69–82). Emerald Publishing.

Marshall, D. T., Shannon, D. M., & Love, S. M. (2022). Teaching during the transition to remote instruction. In D. T. Marshall (Ed.), *COVID-19 and the classroom: How schools navigated the great disruption*. Lexington Books.

Menchaca, V. D., & Garcia, A. (2025). K–12 teacher support during the COVID-19 pandemic. In J. D. Salisbury-Glennon, C.-H. Wang & Shannon, D. M. (Eds.), *Instructional survival in the midst of the perfect storm: The experiences of K–12 teachers during the COVID-19 global pandemic* (pp. 167–187). Emerald Publishing.

Mosley, K. C., McCarthy, C. J., & Gupta, A. (2025). Social support and COVID-19: How U.S. K–12 teachers were impacted by gratitude and mentoring during the COVID-19 pandemic. In J. D. Salisbury-Glennon, C.-H. Wang & Shannon, D. M. (Eds.), *Instructional survival in the midst of the perfect storm: The experiences of K–12 teachers during the COVID-19 global pandemic* (pp. 83–102). Emerald Publishing.

Mseleku, Z. (2020). A literature review of E-Learning and E-Teaching in the era of COVID-19 Pandemic. *International Journal of Innovative Science and Research Technology, 5*(10), 588–597.

Mutch, C., McKnight, H. (2023). "I couldn't do what I needed to do for my own family": Teacher-parents during COVID-19 lockdowns. *Social Sciences & Humanities Open, 7*(1). https://doi: 10.1016/j.ssaho.2023.100401

Pressley, T., Ha, C., & Learn, E. (2021). Teacher stress and anxiety during COVID-19: An empirical study. *School Psychology, 36*(5), 367–376. https://doi.org/10.1037/spq0000468

Trust, T., & Whalen, J. (2020). Should teachers be trained in emergency remote teaching? Lessons learned from the COVID-19 pandemic. *Journal of Technology and Teacher Education, 28*(2), 189–199.

Usher. E. L., & Pajares, F. (2006). Sources of academic and self-regulatory efficacy beliefs of entering middle school students. *Contemporary Educational Psychology, 31*(2), 125–141. https://doi.org/10.1016/j.cedpsych.2005.03.002

Whittle, C., Tiwari, S., Yan, S., & Williams, J. (2020). Emergency remote teaching environment: A conceptual framework for responsive online teaching in crises. *Information and Learning Sciences, 121*(5/6), 311–319. https://doi.org/10.1108/ILS-04-2020-0099

Wood, J. N., & Wood, A. (2025). Impact of COVID-19 on students with special needs and parent involvement. In J. D. Salisbury-Glennon., C.-H. Wang & Shannon, D. M (Eds.), *Instructional survival in the midst of the perfect storm: The experiences of K–12 teachers during the COVID-19 global pandemic* (pp. 123–140). Emerald Publishing.

CHAPTER 2

INSTRUCTIONAL SURVIVAL

A Qualitative Case Study of Elementary Teachers' Experiences Teaching Remotely and Concurrently During COVID-19

Karen Ladendorf
College of DuPage

The COVID-19 pandemic brought about a sudden shift to emergency remote instruction for millions of teachers around the globe. Teachers had to balance their new remote work with the emotional toll of the pandemic. This qualitative case study sought to understand the experiences of elementary school teachers as they navigated both remote and concurrent instruction during the 2020–2021 school year. Three elementary teachers were recruited for this study. Teachers completed two interviews and were observed three times during remote and concurrent instruction. The resulting data was analyzed over three cycles for emergent themes. The impact that COVID-19 had on teachers fell into two categories: instructional and emotional impacts. Instructionally, teachers utilized previously created lessons and adapted them to delivery to a digital video format. Teachers did not incorporate much new technology and relied on teacher-led instruction. The instructional impact was connected to the emotional impact COVID-19 had on these teachers. They experienced

Instructional Survival in the Midst of the Perfect Storm:
The Experiences of K–12 Teachers During the COVID-19 Global Pandemic, pages 9–27.

Published under exclusive licence by Emerald Publishing Limited
ISBNs: 978-1-83708-502-6 HB, 978-1-83708-503-3 PB,
978-1-83708-504-0 EPDF, 978-1-83708-505-7 EPUB

shock, fear, and isolation while having to navigate remote instruction. Teachers focused on instructional survival throughout the year, measuring their success by their ability to survive to the last day of school. Recommendations for remote and blended are explored as well as lessons that can be gleaned from these three teachers' navigation of emergency remote instruction.

Keywords: Elementary Education; Remote Learning; Concurrent Instruction; Online Instructional Strategies

March 2020 is a month that many educators can state exactly where they were, what they were teaching, and how they reacted when they found out schools were closing nation-wide. COVID-19 moved rapidly through the United States, forcing many individual districts and states to make the difficult decision to move to a remote setting for the remainder of the 2019–2020 school year. These same institutions struggled with the decisions on when to reopen, how to do so safely, and what safety protocols to put in place throughout the 2020–2021 school year.

In the middle of the decisions were K–12 students and teachers, who experienced multiple changes and challenges throughout the remote instruction. Remote learning on a large scale had never occurred in United States history. While some higher grade level teachers and students had previous experience with remote instruction, younger grades had very little. COVID-19 brought about a new experience for elementary students and teachers: remote learning followed by concurrent instruction.

This study explored the lived experiences and stories of three elementary teachers as they navigated teaching and ERI from March 2020 through May 2021. The school had a culture of technology integration prior to COVID-19: being fully 1:1 devices with all students for eight years. Students in the 3rd–5th grade were provided with a district-owned MacBook Air laptop device as were the teachers. The state this school was in, closed all schools for the last two months of the 2019–2020 school year. The school district had opted to begin the 2020–2021 school year fully remote and provided the backdrop for the three teachers' stories in this study.

REVIEW OF THE LITERATURE

Remote instruction has been utilized in the United States for multiple decades. Organizations and companies utilized satellites, televisions, and video recordings to share consistent training presentations across the country throughout the 1980s and 1990s (Rozitis et al., 2018). K–12 schools followed suit in the 1990s, looking for ways to provide credit recovery (Vadell, 2013), expand course offerings (Cavanaugh et al., 2004), and reach rural communities (Hannum et al., 2009). Just prior to the COVID-19 pandemic, there were over 400 full-time virtual schools and over 200 blended learning schools throughout the United States (Miron et al.,

2018). However, there was, and continues to be, a lack of teacher training and guidance for remote instruction.

Remote instruction was built into less than 5% of teacher preparation programs (Kennedy & Archambault, 2012). Remote instructors had to develop their skills and knowledge independently, relying on their own experiences in the physical classroom and online. Many remote instructors prior to COVID-19 were full-time traditional teachers supplementing their income with remote work, teachers who had left the traditional classroom for a flexible schedule, or were retired teachers (Archambault & Larson, 2015). Many had advanced degrees, multiple years in education, and went into remote instruction willingly and excited to try something new (Archambault & Crippen, 2009).

Prior to COVID-19, remote instructors felt overall satisfied with their positions, pointing to the flexibility of the position and the ability to personalize learning for individual students (Larkin et al., 2016). Remote instruction provided these teachers with opportunities to try new and innovative instruction, engage with parents at a higher level, and experience teaching without the frustrations of the physical classroom (Archambault & Larson, 2015). They were able to become a facilitator, and not the giver of knowledge, by using problem-based and critical thinking exercises with performance-based assessments (Dietrich et al., 2020). Remote instructions also relied on their knowledge of their content, the technology, their instructional strategies and how the areas combine into their technological, pedagogical and content knowledge (TPACK) to provide engaging instruction online (Koehler & Mishra, 2008).

Remote instruction was not without its challenges. Remote instructors had to be very organized due to the potentially large class sizes (Archambault & Larson, 2015) and accompanying large workload (Larkin et al., 2016). The flexibility of the daily schedule also challenged the work-life balance of many remote instructors (Farmer & West, 2019). They also had expanded roles providing technical support to parents and students (Amro & Borup 2019).

These experiences were limited to remote instructors who had opted for remote work. COVID-19 brought about required remote instruction for 1.7 billion K–12 students globally (Dietrich et al., 2020). Additionally, this was not traditional remote learning. It was known as Emergency Remote Instruction (ERI), or remote instruction occurring due to a sudden emergency or event (Hodges et al., 2020). It was temporary, unanticipated, and a reaction to the emergency at hand (Hodges et al., 2020). All teachers had to navigate both a global pandemic and remote instruction (Demaray et al., 2021) throughout the 2020–2021 school year.

ERI also brought the implementation of concurrent instruction to multiple K–12 school districts. Concurrent instruction, also known as parallel or simultaneous instruction, saw teachers providing instruction to in-person and remote or virtual students at the same time from the physical classroom (Bartlett, 2022). This was a new concept and uncharted territory for K–12 educators.

STATEMENT OF THE PROBLEM AND RESEARCH QUESTIONS

Research is still being gathered on the impact COVID-19 had on K–12 school systems. This study sought to gather the views of the impact COVID-19 had on elementary school teachers as they navigated both remote and hybrid learning. Traditionally remote learning had been limited to high school students (Vadell, 2013). Elementary teachers have been missing from the research on remote learning in general. Their experiences during the COVID-19 pandemic are unique and can be used to gain new insight into remote instruction and teacher needs.

The purpose of this qualitative case study was to understand the lived experiences of elementary teachers teaching remotely during the COVID-19 pandemic. This study was guided by the following research questions:

> RQ_1: How did elementary teachers describe the impact that COVID-19 had on their work in and out of the classroom?
> RQ_2: What observed and described changes did elementary teachers make during remote and concurrent instruction due to COVID-19?

METHODS

A qualitative case study was conducted at the end of the 2020–2021 school year. The school utilized in this study was a K–5 suburban elementary school in the Midwest-Great Lakes region. Three elementary teachers in grades 3–5 were identified and recruited. The teachers had been employed at the same school for a minimum of ten years. The three teachers also had previous experience with technology and curriculum within the school building.

Pseudonyms were used throughout the study. Jennifer taught 3rd grade, Caroline 4th grade and Anita taught 5th grade. Jennifer was the least tech-savvy of the group while Caroline was extremely comfortable with technology and online learning. Anita was the oldest of the group with only four years until her retirement.

School Schedules

The three teachers had experienced multiple schedules throughout the 2020–2021 school year. First, the school began the year with a schedule known as "full remote." Teachers and students began at 8:45am with a combination of 2.5 hours of live video conferencing using the video conferencing app, Zoom, as well as asynchronous learning time. Full class instruction ended at 2:15pm to allow teachers time to work with individual or small groups of students until 3:45pm. Teachers also used the last one and a half hours to collaborate and attend professional development sessions on Mondays, depicted in Table 2.1.

A hybrid schedule was adopted in October 2020 with the goal of having students return safely to the school building, depicted in Table 2.2. Students were divided into two groups: A and B. Each group was comprised of either fully remote or in-person students. Group A met daily 8:45am–11:20am fully in person with their teacher. After travel time, Group A met with exploratory teachers on Zoom, a synchronous video conferencing tool, from home and had additional asynchronous work time. Group B began the day at home with exploratory courses on Zoom and asynchronous work time. Group B met with their teacher on Zoom in the afternoon.

The face-to-face time with the classroom teacher was focused on two content areas: mathematics and language arts. Teachers completed a daily math lesson that lasted approximately one hour. Language arts lessons included grammar, writing, and whole-group read-aloud, lasting approximately one hour and fifteen minutes. The remaining time was allocated for class circles and connections as well as bathroom and movement breaks. Students completed social studies and science work during asynchronous learning time at home.

Finally, the concurrent schedule was developed to allow for more in-person learning time. Students whose families had chosen to attend remotely participated in class while the teacher provided instruction to in-person learners. Table 2.3 depicts the changes made to the daily schedule. Students attended school 8:45am–12:50pm daily. After a lunch break, teachers attended professional development and collaboration sessions on Mondays. Tuesdays-Fridays provided time for teachers to meet with individual or small groups or students.

The face-to-face time with the classroom teacher continued to focus on language arts and mathematics. Students also met with their exploratory teachers during the extended time. In-person students would rotate between music, art, and physical education while remote students rotated art, physical education, and music. The remaining time was allocated for class circles and connections as well as bathroom and movement breaks. Teachers were able to add social studies or science lessons if time was remaining. Otherwise, those subjects continued to be covered asynchronously.

This study occurred while Jennifer, Caroline, and Anita were experiencing concurrent instruction. They had students physically in-person with them as well as remote learners joining in via Zoom for synchronous instruction. The teachers had previously experienced fully remote instruction, beginning the 2020–2021 school year with all of their students in remote instruction.

Each teacher was interviewed twice in-person. Interviews occurred after their teaching time had ended. The first interview focused on the teacher's experiences with ERI during the initial shutdowns in March 2020 through the start of the 2020–2021 school year. The second interview occurred after a class observation to review the lesson and discuss the teachers' perspectives of the end of the 2020–2021 school year. Two interviews were conducted to limit the amount of time teachers were pulled and to respect their plan time or after school hours. Each teacher was also observed three times in a remote or concurrent instructional setting. The teachers also provided access to their Google Classroom spaces as well as Seesaw Learning journals for gathering assignment information.

Data was analyzed in three steps. First, a first cycle coding included finding larger categories and themes through a full read-through of all data. A second cycle was completed diving the data utilizing NVivo and descriptive coding (Saldaña, 2016). A final cycle of pattern coding was completed to find emergent themes (Saldaña, 2016). Analytical memos were written to reflect on the emergent themes and artifacts (Emerson et al., 2011). A focus group was conducted after data analysis to review the findings with the teachers as member checking.

The researcher in this study was a district administrator at the time. She provided multiple professional development sessions with the three teachers in past school years and supported all teachers with technology access and integration. She did not work with the teachers in a supervisory or evaluator role in the past. The researcher entered the teachers' virtual classrooms as a participant observer, connecting with the students, and interacting with the content.

RESULTS

The emergent themes fell into two categories: instructional impacts and emotional impacts of COVID-19 on the elementary teachers. Instructional impacts focused on how the teachers approached their instruction during both remote and concurrent teaching. These themes also explored the types of resources and instructional practices teachers utilized throughout the 2020–2021 school year. Emotional impacts focused on how the teachers reacted emotionally to COVID-19, their teaching situation, and their students.

Instructional Impacts

COVID-19 impacted the three elementary teachers' instruction and planning in multiple ways, the first being a need to create a detailed organizational method. The teachers were forced into a strict daily schedule, no matter if they were teaching remotely, in-person, or concurrently. In a typical school year, the teachers had some "wiggle room" over their daily schedule, being able to extend a lesson a few minutes longer if needed or combine classes for activities. In the immediate response to COVID-19, the district implemented the full remote learning schedule from Table 2.1. Students were logging into class synchronously via Zoom using their district-issued laptops while at home. The three teachers had to make sure the Zoom links were correct, and they were on time to the minute for students to switch between Zoom rooms.

The district worked to bring students back into the school building throughout the school year. Both the hybrid schedule in Table 2.2 and the concurrent schedule in Table 2.3 were implemented later in the school year. Both schedules allowed students and teachers to return to the physical building with very strict safety and health measures put into place. The local health department required the school to contact-trace all students and staff, making notes of who came within 6-feet of individuals if they were sick and tested positive for COVID-19. The safety

TABLE 2.1. Full Remote Schedule

Monday	Tuesday–Friday
8:45am–2:15pm Combination of 2.5 hours of live instruction with asynchronous work and exploratory classes	
2:15pm–3:45pm Teacher professional development and collaboration time	2:15pm–3:45pm Individual and small group instruction time

TABLE 2.2. Hybrid Schedule

Monday	Tuesday–Friday
All Remote 8:45am – 2:15pm	Morning Session 8:45am–11:20am A in person or remote with classroom teacher B remote with exploratory classes
2:15pm–3:45pm Teacher professional development and collaboration time	Afternoon Session 1:10pm–3:45pm B in person or remote with classroom teacher A remote with exploratory classes

TABLE 2.3. Concurrent Schedule

Monday	Tuesday–Friday
8:45am–12:50pm Concurrent instruction	
2:00pm–3:45pm Teacher professional development and collaboration time	2:15pm – 3:45pm Individual and small group instruction time

protocols included allowing only one class in the hallway at a time, no mixing of classes, and no lunch in the school building. The teachers had to leave at an exact minute to take students to the bathroom, exploratory classes, and to exit the building at the end of the day so they would not cross paths with other classes and cross-contaminate students. While the teachers were able to control the students physically in the building, the remote students needed guidance and scheduling.

To stay on time, no matter the day or building schedule being used, the teachers created very detailed daily schedules for the students. The students knew down to the minute how long they were working on activities, which Zoom links to click, and what materials they would need. An example daily schedule from Anita is below in Figure 2.1.

Anita's daily schedule was from a concurrent schedule day. She was teaching students both in-person and on Zoom. Anita needed the detailed schedule as much as her students did. Her in-person students utilized the Zoom links to collaborate with their remote classmates and to see the virtual board clearer. Her remote students needed to switch between Zoom links multiple times throughout the day and the schedule kept them on track.

The detail in the schedules kept the teachers organized as well as assisted the students with their daily tasks. The students were given all the materials and schedules needed to be successful. This also helped the students to develop independence as none of the teachers had to worry about their entire remote groups not logging into Zoom on time. This worry was reserved for individual students, not the entire class.

The safety protocols and strict schedule impacted the teachers as they planned and instructed the students, whether in person or online. Anita described the schedule as constraining:

> I don't like it because you are constrained. You don't have that freedom to go over a little bit more. You know? And it's shorter than normal. So, it really forces you to look at, okay, I don't do [math] fluency. I don't do the [math] application problem. I don't do [math] student debrief. Sorry, I know it's important, but they get [math] concept development and they get the problem set. That's what they get.

The schedule forced her and her colleagues to shorten their instruction, with the priority being staying on time. Anita focused on what could be taught within the short timeframe versus how she should be teaching remotely or concurrently.

The teachers' extensive organizational details also impacted their instructional planning. All three teachers felt they planned more for their remote students than their in-person learners. Jennifer expressed this specifically:

> No, we plan more for our remote. And I don't know if it's because we sent a lot of stuff home. Any pick-up [the school] had, third grade probably sent the most home all year round because we were firm believers that they need to be holding books like the reading books and worksheets and templates and stuff.

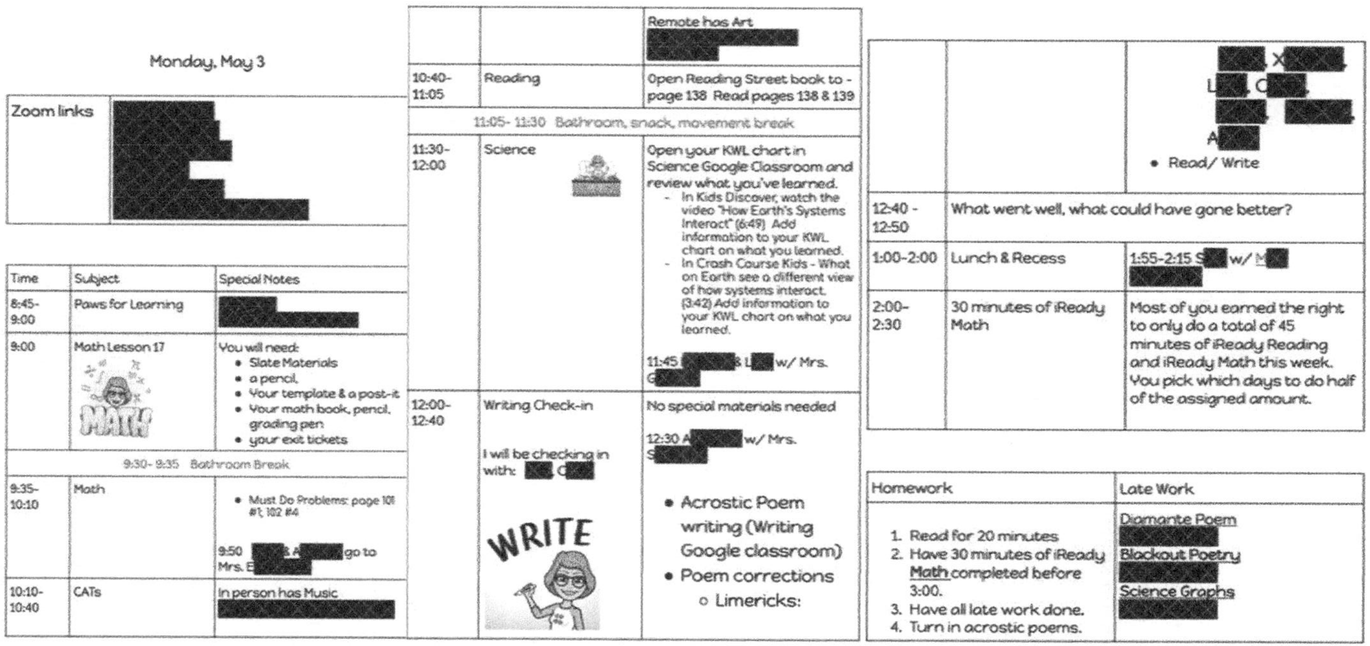

Monday, May 3

Zoom links	

Time	Subject	Special Notes
8:45-9:00	Paws for Learning	
9:00	Math Lesson 17	You will need: • Slate Materials • a pencil. • Your template & a post-it • Your math book, pencil, grading pen • your exit tickets
9:30- 9:35 Bathroom Break		
9:35-10:10	Math	• Must Do Problems: page 101 #1, 102 #4 9:50 & A go to Mrs. E
10:10-10:40	CATs	In person has Music
		Remote has Art
10:40-11:05	Reading	Open Reading Street book to - page 138 Read pages 138 & 139
11:05- 11:30 Bathroom, snack, movement break		
11:30-12:00	Science	Open your KWL chart in Science Google Classroom and review what you've learned. - In Kids Discover, watch the video "How Earth's Systems Interact" (6:49) Add information to your KWL chart on what you learned. - In Crash Course Kids - What on Earth see a different view of how systems interact. (3:42) Add information to your KWL chart on what you learned. 11:45 & L w/ Mrs. G
12:00-12:40	Writing Check-in I will be checking in with: , C	No special materials needed 12:30 A w/ Mrs. S • Acrostic Poem writing (Writing Google classroom) • Poem corrections o Limericks:
		, X , L , C , , A • Read/ Write
12:40 - 12:50	What went well, what could have gone better?	
1:00-2:00	Lunch & Recess	1:55-2:15 S w/ M
2:00-2:30	30 minutes of iReady Math	Most of you earned the right to only do a total of 45 minutes of iReady Reading and iReady Math this week. You pick which days to do half of the assigned amount.

Homework	Late Work
1. Read for 20 minutes 2. Have 30 minutes of iReady Math completed before 3:00. 3. Have all late work done. 4. Turn in acrostic poems.	Diamante Poem Blackout Poetry Science Graphs

FIGURE 2.1. Daily Schedule
Anita's daily schedule from May 3, 202. Black spaces removed live links and student names.

However, the planning was focused more on their pacing of instruction and not the actual instructional activities. Jennifer specifically mentioned sending her remote students' materials each month for the month ahead. She said the students needed all the materials in advance, so she needed to be ready for them. Her planning was focused on the pacing of her instruction, not the specific instruction happening online. Jennifer needed her pacing to stay on time especially during the concurrent schedule. She had one day a month to send home materials, and needed to ensure the remote students had everything they needed to stay on pace with the in-person students when she was teaching concurrently.

The second emergent theme in the instruction was the repurposing of previously created lessons. All three teachers relied on their previous lessons for remote and concurrent instruction. As Jennifer had pointed out previously with her planning, the instruction was based on their previous lessons. The three teachers used the same lessons and simply moved the instruction to a Zoom setting. Anita did move some lessons into the SMART Lumio Suite, a robust online interactive software provided by the school district, for virtual collaboration while Caroline relied on the Google suite for collaboration. Jennifer utilized a combination of Seesaw Learning Journal and Google for collaboration but preferred for students to complete their work independently and on paper if possible.

The teachers acknowledged using previously created materials and lessons and simply adapting the activities to be completed via Zoom within the daily schedule. Jennifer pointed out her past assignments as being helpful to her:

> I mean I've been doing this for a long time. I mean we, my teammate and I, we pretty much got it nailed down to how we plan and stuff. But planning a week or month out and having materials, because we already had things sent home for remote was nice because then we just needed to make certain copies for things for the in-person learners. It was nice.

Jennifer relied on past pacing, activities, and materials for the foundation of her instruction in the remote and concurrent schedules. The previously created materials allowed her to figure out the digital components and navigate remote and concurrent learning without having to recreate her lessons. Caroline agreed with Jennifer, pointing to her usage of previous materials:

> Well, we had so much stuff already. Digitally. I feel like if I didn't, it would have been awful…So if we did not as a district have a lot of those digital components, it would be very hard to teach remotely.

Where Jennifer relied on her past hard-copy activities, Caroline was grateful to have previously created digital activities she was able to utilize. Caroline had gone paperless in her classroom for multiple years, incorporated digital learning tools, and had used the flipped classroom model in years past. She felt ready for the digital shift.

The three teachers were hesitant to incorporate new technology into their instruction, relying instead on just a few tools for ease of planning and technical support for the students. Anita felt incorporating new tools would have been overwhelming. She noted that when multiple districts went fully remote in March 2020, many companies offered free access to their paid platforms. Anita commented,

> The pressure of trying to figure everything out and being inundated, which as a nice inundation, with offers of you can use this platform for free. And it's just like, I don't have time to figure out what I want to try if I want to try anything new. So that was like, it's nice, but I can't try something new right now.

It was easier for Anita to navigate familiar tools than to add new tools to the mix. She opted to dive deeper into tools the school district had for multiple years and to use them to their fullest potential. "How can I maximize? I'm not throwing a lot of technology things at [the students]. I have used Seesaw more this year than I've ever used it before." Even Caroline, the most technology-savvy of the group, opted to use "mostly old tools," due to the ease of use and familiarity for the students.

The teachers did incorporate collaborative gaming sites to engage the students and gather formative data on student learning. While Anita opted for SMART Lumio Suite pre-created games and Google Forms, Jennifer and Caroline used websites such as Kahoot and Quizizz to engage students and gather formative feedback. They also acknowledged the positive of opening email communication for the students, with Anita stating "That has been the best new tool for the students. Please don't take it away."

A final theme within instruction was the task-oriented nature of the instruction. Through the daily schedule, the teachers provided multiple tasks that needed to be completed. Students were given time to complete the work during daily asynchronous learning. Homework in a traditional sense was non-existent.

Anita pointed out the need to teach "to the middle" throughout the 2020–2021 school year.

> A lot of the stuff that we have gotten away from, we went back to. A lot of stand-and-deliver type of teaching. Just because, well, it's easier to deliver it that way than to try to figure out how the logistics of remote and everything else work.

Anita and her colleagues went with the easiest methods to provide students with learning activities, many of which ended up being fully teacher-led or completely independent. While the teachers did attempt to get the students to partner up with each other, it required everyone to be on Zoom whether they were in-person or online. The device became a physical barrier to the students as well as their masks and the required 6 feet of distance between them.

If all work was completed, students were given choice boards with additional tasks to complete. An example choice board from Caroline is in Figure 2.2. Students had to complete each of the five tasks at least once during the week.

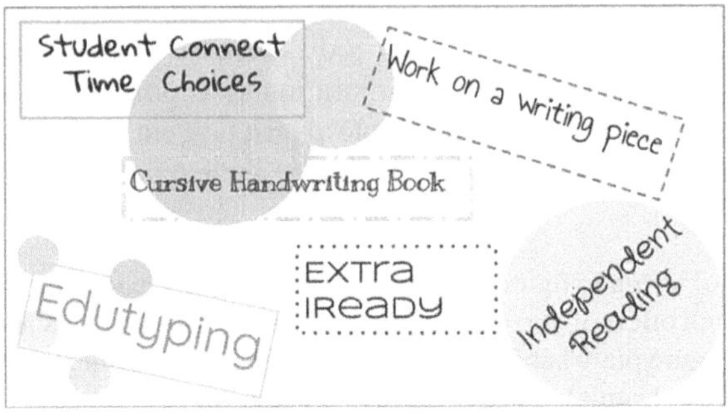

FIGURE 2.2. Choice Board
Choice board includes a paper-based cursive practice book, independent freewriting time, Edutyping for typing fluency practice, additional iReady math and reading personalized lessons, or independent reading on a book of personal choice.

While the teachers relied on tasks, schedules, and checklists to keep students moving through the curriculum, they did look for ways to incorporate collaboration when possible. The concurrent schedule allowed teachers to virtually mix their in-person and virtual learners. Both Anita and Caroline had all in-person learners join their remote classmates on Zoom. They would use breakout rooms for the students to mix and collaborate. Students worked collaboratively on math problems and shared their answers with their teachers via Google Docs or SMART Lumio. Jennifer allowed her in-person students to join the remote students on Zoom by student choice, where Anita and Caroline required it.

Emotional Impacts

COVID-19 had multiple emotional impacts on these teachers. When reflecting on the initial move to ERI in March 2020, all three teachers mentioned shock and denial. Jennifer described the experience in March 2020 as "terrifying," while Caroline said she was "in a constant state of shock." They all said goodbye to their students on a Thursday not knowing they would not be coming back for the rest of the year. The district first extended their spring break to two weeks, then moved to remote learning for the remainder of the school year.

The teachers all turned their thoughts to their students at the end of the 2019–2020 school year. Caroline mentioned,

> …just thinking about my students. Which ones I was more worried about and their emotional state and their home life. Just worried about their [social emotional learning] components, not necessarily worrying about school."

Anita concurred with Caroline, her voice cracking and tears coming to her eyes when she said:

> Yes, that class, I mourn them, you know what I mean? We were a tight group. We got along really well. It was a great class personality. It was really, really sad, when you're like, I'll never see these kids again.

The ERI of March 2020 tore students and teachers away from each other. Over a year later, the emotions were still raw in the three teachers as they thought back to the onset of COVID-19. They wanted to ensure their students were safe while trying to figure out a remote learning model as they taught.

The three teachers had the same feeling at the start of the 2020–2021 school year when they found out less than one day before the opening Institute Day, they would be starting the year fully remote. Jennifer noted,

> I was thinking, oh my gosh, I can't. How am I supposed to start a year doing [remote]? I mean, yes, I ended up doing it, but how do you start with a brand-new group of kids that you've never met and how do you do this?

The teachers found themselves pivoting to remote instruction at the last second yet again. They panicked over pacing their instruction. Anita pointed out she was "freaking out" about math specifically. The math curriculum had a set one-lesson-per-day model.

> I'm not able to do a lesson a day [online]. And they [admin] were like, don't worry about it. But I just kept feeling I was getting a message that we have to make sure we get through the curriculum.

While they had to respond to ERI with a set daily schedule, that schedule and resulting detailed organization caused panic and stress to the teachers.

Emotionally, the teachers felt lonely and distant from their colleagues. They missed walking down the hallway to bounce ideas off each other. They felt isolated at home and wanted time with their colleagues. Anita opted to teach remotely from her classroom and described the experience as "lonely as hell."

> It was lonely as hell. It was lonely because at the beginning of the year [2020–2021], people didn't have to be in the building. They could choose to be in in the building or they could choose to be at home. So, I work better here [in the school]…but nobody else was down in this wing [hallway]. And that's very isolating, you know? It's hard to bounce ideas around.

All three teachers struggled to develop a work-life balance while they were fully remote. Jennifer and Caroline opted to teach from their homes due to having their own children at home. However, they found it difficult to stop teaching and instead would work until all hours of the night. They also had to balance their own children and navigate remote learning as parents. They also felt pressure from their students' parents to be available late into the night for questions and technical support. Jennifer reminisced:

> You just never stopping work because you're at home. We had never done this before so we're trying to be consistent as a team. And then the just the texts and zoom calls throughout the day, into the evening…just never having an ending point. There's always something to do. And then just the balance of being a mom and making sure my first grader at the time was able to log into her Zoom meetings and get through her digital resources.

Jennifer experienced ERI as both a teacher and a parent. She felt her teammates kept her working throughout the evenings with no end in sight. She struggled to create a work-life balance, something her colleague, Caroline, worked very hard to do.

> The parents thought you were on your device all the time and like, "Can you pop on [Zoom]?" Well, no, I can't pop on. It's five o'clock. I was just making sure I was setting those boundaries with parents and with myself. No, I'm not going to be up until 11pm answering parent emails, captive.

Anita pointed out the students were working outside of traditional school hours as well, with a few of her students completing work at 10pm, 11pm, or midnight in the initial ERI of March 2020. The expanded access to class materials beyond the school walls encouraged students and parents to complete work or start communications with the teachers at later hours. It was a difficult balance the teachers had to create, one that Jennifer struggled with while Caroline felt successful.

Finally, the emotional impact of COVID-19 and ERI developed a negative perception of remote learning within the teachers. Anita and Jennifer felt remote instruction was not positive for all students. They noted their remote students being distracted at their homes, not taking their online learning as seriously as the teachers wanted, and families randomly pulling students out of class for errands and family matters.

Jennifer stated many times throughout our interviews, "School is school." She felt students belonged in the physical building:

> I just feel like kids belong in school… I think they need to be in a social place with other children, no distractions. So that way I can be there…Of the five I have at home, two of them are being really successful. The others I wish I could just see them and be able to help them because they're just getting lost at home with the distractions, forgetting to come online, forgetting to come to school.

Jennifer also shared how one of her remote students would not show up to online class because they either overslept, were bored, or had other errands to complete with their parents. It was very frustrating for her to not have some level of control over the student while they were supposed to be attending class online.

Anita agreed with Jennifer, citing the home distractions and lack of engagement from some of her remote learners. "They're distracted by the things at home…at home is where I play and relax and it's really hard mentally then to turn on that switch as be serious with my learning." She also shared a story of one of her students who was not participating well while attending class via Zoom:

> So, I have a kid who was on the [intervention list]. I was like, oh my gosh, we need to get this kid in person. Because he's like this at home *laying back in chair, rotating around, lounging, not looking at me* and he you know he's slouching and he's doing his artwork and he's not able to focus. Like he would legitimately roll out of bed sit in his chair and log on to the Zoom. I mean, didn't brush his teeth, didn't comb his hair, didn't change out of his jammies. You need to tell your brain that you need to be at school…and when he's in the classroom he pays attention. There is something to be said being in the classroom. The mentality of this is where I do work.

Neither Anita nor Jennifer fully embraced remote learning emotionally and developed a negative view of remote learning in general. They felt traditional, in-person learning was more appropriate for their elementary students and for themselves as teachers.

Concurrent instruction also weighed heavily on the teachers. Anita and Jennifer struggled with the scheduling and managing of students both at home and in their classroom. Without an additional adult in the physical or Zoom room, it was difficult to assist students with technical problems while still managing classroom behavior and work completion. They already felt burned out from remote learning and concurrent instruction fried them further.

Caroline did not fully concur with Anita and Jennifer, noting her remote students were successful, attentive, and engaged. She felt they learned as much as her in-person students and as much as in years past. She noted all of her students grew in her benchmark assessments and felt successful themselves throughout the year. Caroline was also one of a few teachers who had originally volunteered to teach remotely if only a few students and families were going to opt for remote learning. The 2020–2021 school year was originally going to have all in-person learning with a full remote option for families until COVID-19 grew and the health metrics forced everyone to be fully remote. Caroline agreed with Jennifer and Anita on concurrent instruction. She felt it was overwhelming and too much to manage with fourth grade students. She preferred teaching just remotely or just in-person, but not combined. Caroline worked through this by treating her in-person students as virtual ones with everyone on Zoom while they were physically with her in the classroom.

Caroline originally told me in our first interview that she would choose to teach remotely in the future if given the opportunity. She liked the format and the schedule. However, she changed her mind for our second interview:

> I've been thinking about [teaching remotely] a lot. I even told my husband I was just really surprised with my answer to that question. Then I was like, I don't know, I love the interaction. The one thing I don't like necessarily about the remote teaching is sometimes the engagement is really hard. Work completion is also really hard and getting them to like either join Zoom or stay on Zoom or follow the schedule can be

> really tricky, especially if you don't have parents who are monitoring. I'd rather you guys [the students] all be in person because then I at least know for this amount of time we're getting stuff done.

Caroline was overall very positive about her remote teaching experience. Yet, she still wanted to be in-person with her students. She missed the emotional side of teaching: interacting with her students.

CONCLUSIONS

COVID-19 and the resulting emergency remote instruction impacted the elementary teachers in a variety of ways. Instructionally, the teachers were forced into a situation they had not been prepared for in their initial training (Kennedy & Archambault, 2012) nor could the school district have anticipated (Tienken, 2020). The impact on teachers manifested in both instructional and emotional ways.

The teachers made very few changes to their instruction. They relied on previously created material, activities, and lessons to get them through the ERI. Their planning was focused on pacing, not necessarily on innovative instructional strategies. The reliance on previously created material left little room for new technology or digital tools beyond Zoom. While they incorporated some collaborative group work and online games for engagement, most of their instruction was teacher-led. Instruction became task-oriented using the detailed daily schedule and asynchronous learning tasks lists to keep students on track. While choice was incorporated, choice was limited to pacing and timing, not for demonstration of learning. Task-oriented and teacher-driven learning was familiar to the teachers and more comfortable than innovative, remote instruction which they felt underprepared for (Lai, 2017).

The teachers' instructional response to ERI was directly tied to their emotional responses to COVID-19. Like many people, the teachers were in initial shock and denial of the global pandemic in March 2020. They grappled with the fear and anxiety of a pandemic while trying to navigate their new remote world. They were further shocked with a sudden shift back to remote learning for the start of the 2020–2021 school year. These changes were in conjunction with their overwhelmed feelings of work-life balance at home. They had to navigate remote instruction while also navigating remote learning as parents (Anderson & Hira, 2020). Furthermore, they were isolated from each other and could not easily give or receive feedback from colleagues. They lost contact with students and families in March 2020, leaving them hoping those families were ok. All this combined to an overall negative view of remote and concurrent instruction (Santos et al., 2021). It was an overwhelming experience, with a large workload, they had never been prepared or trained for (Dietrich et al., 2020).

The emotional toll COVID-19 had on the teachers resulted in their goal for instructional survival. They saw the 2020–2021 school year as a challenge and success was determined by their ability to emotionally survive to the last day of school.

SUMMARY

COVID-19 and the resulting ERI of the 2019–2020 and 2020–2021 school years impacted teachers both instructionally and emotionally. They felt as though they were in a state of "instructional survival" throughout the two years. Their survival to the end of the year was their measure of success.

While this qualitative study cannot speak to a generalized experience of all elementary teachers during ERI, the stories of these three educators can bring multiple lessons to life for K–12 school districts and researchers. Anita, Jennifer, and Caroline's experience showcase the stress and toll COVID-19 had on them and the resulting impact on their instruction. They relied on previously created materials, pacing in advance to send home material, and stand-and-deliver style instruction with only few opportunities for students to collaborate and engage with each other. They struggled to engage students in learning activities that were not game based. They also struggled to get students to attend class online and be in a learning mindset. All three struggled to set boundaries and develop a work-life balance that included time for themselves and other personal tasks such as caring for their own children. The teachers had to battle through these challenges while also handling the fear, anxiety, and shock of the COVID-19 pandemic on the world in general.

Three lessons arise out of our teacher's stories. First, ERI is stressful and requires much preparation and support from the instructor. Without the lead time prior to the 2020 Institute Day and additional preparation time, the teachers fell back on their previously created materials and did not fully adapt to the remote setting. Secondly, the presence and offers of multiple tools and resources can become a burden versus a help in an emergency situation. Too many new digital tools, resources, schedules, and protocols can cause additional stress and anxiety for teachers, which will negatively impact their instructional practices. Last, teachers need to connect emotionally with each other and their students through interactions and engagement. Isolation from each other can limit their ability to collaborate and problem solve with other teachers. It also creates a barrier for teachers when instructing and knowing their students' progress.

IMPLICATIONS FOR FUTURE RESEARCH

While K–12 districts have moved back to a normal sense of school in the years following the COVID-19 ERI of 2020 and 2021, lessons can be learned from these three teachers. It is imperative that K–12 districts not only acknowledge the emotional impact of the pandemic on their teachers but to recognize the impact will last for years to come. Emotional care must be given to teachers. Further, guidance and support for innovative blended instruction that can move between in-person and remote settings should be the focus for professional development. Additional research should be conducted on the successes and challenges upon the return from remote instruction in K–12 schools from the system, administrative, instructor, and student levels. Finally, research should be conducted on how to best support teachers in emergency situations where remote instruction is immediately necessary. The education community now knows it is not a matter of if, but rather when another emergency remote instruction situation will arise. K–12 districts need to be ready to support teachers both instructionally and emotionally.

REFERENCES

Amro, F. & Borup, J. (2019). Exploring blended teacher roles and obstacles to success when using personalized learning software. *Journal of Online learning Research, 5*(3), 229–250.

Anderson, E., & Hira, A. (2020). Loss of brick-and-mortar schooling: How elementary educators respond. *Information and Learning Sciences, 121*(5/6), 411–418. doi: 10.1108/ILS-04-2020-0085

Archambault, L. & Crippen, K. (2009). K–12 distance educators at work: Who's teaching online across the United States. *Journal of Research on Technology in Education, 41*(4), 363–391.

Archambault, L. & Larson, J. (2015). Pioneering the digital age of instruction: Learning from and about K–12 online teachers. *Journal of Online Learning Research, 1*(1), 49–83.

Bartlett, L. (2022). Specifying hybrid models of teacher's work during COVID-19. *Educational Researcher, 51*(2), 152–155. doi: 10.3102/0013189X2110699399

Cavanaugh, C. S., Jo Gillan, K., Kromrey, J., Hess, M., & Blomeyer, R. (2004). *The effects of distance education on K–12 student outcomes: A meta-analysis.* Learning Point Associates.

Demaray, M. K., Ogg, J. A., Malecki, C. K., & Styck, K. M. (2021). COVID-19 stress and coping associations with internalizing problems in 4th through 12th grade students. *School Psychology Review, 51*(5), 1–20. doi: 10.1080/2372966X.2020.1869498

Dietrich, N., Kentheswaran, K., Ahmadi, A., Teychene, J., Bessiere, Y., Alfenore, S., Laborie, S., Bastoul, D., Loubiere, K., Guigui, C., Sperandio, M., Barna, L., Paul, Etienne, Cabassud, C., Line, A., & Hebard, G. (2020). Attempts, successes and failures of distance learning in the time of COVID-19. *Journal of Chemical Education, 97*(9), 2448–2457. doi: 10.1021/jchemed.0c00717

Emerson, R. M., Fretz, R. I., & Shaw, L. L. (Eds.). (2011) *Writing ethnographic fieldnotes.* The University of Chicago Press.

Farmer, T. & West, R. (2019). Exploring the concerns of online K–12 teachers. *Journal of Online Learning Research, 5*(1), 97–118.

Hannum, W. H., Irvin, M. J., Banks, J. B., & Farmer, T. W. (2009). Distance education use in rural schools. *Journal of Research in Rural Education, 24*(3). http://jrre.psu.edu/articles/24-3.pdf

Hodges, C., Moore, S., Lockee, B., Trust, T., & Bond, A. (2020). The difference between emergency remote teaching and online learning. *Educause Review.* https://er.educause.edu/articles/2020/3/the-difference-between-emergency-remote-teaching-and-online-learning

Kennedy, K., & Archambault, L. (2012). Offering preservice teachers field experiences in K–12 online learning: A national survey of teacher education programs. *Journal of Teacher Education, 63*(1), 185–200. doi: 10.1177/0022487111433651

Koehler, M. J., & Mishra, P. (2008). Introducing TPCK. In AACTE Committee on Technology and Innovation (Eds.), *Handbook of technological pedagogical content knowledge (TPCK) for educators* (pp. 3–29). Routledge.

Lai, K. W. (2017). Pedagogical practices of NetNZ teachers for supporting online distance learners. *Distance Education, 38*(3), 321–335. doi: 10.1080/01587919.2017.1371830

Larkin, I. M., Brantley-Dias, L., & Lokey-Vega, A. (2016). Job satisfaction, organizational commitment, and turnover intention of online teachers in the K–12 setting. *Online Learning, 20*(3), 26–51.

Miron, G., Shank, C., & Davidson, C. (2018). Full-time virtual and blended schools: Enrollment, student characteristics, and performance. *National Education Policy Center.* School of Education, University of Colorado Boulder.

Rozitis, C. p., Tomaselli, K. R., & Gyabak, K. (2018). Special Issue: Instructional design in K–12 online and blended learning environments. *Journal of Online Learning Research, 4*(3), 229–231.

Saldaña, J. (2016). *The coding manual for qualitative researchers* (3rd ed.). Sage Publications.

Santos, J. M., De Jesus, L. F., Sealmoy, R. R., & Fajardo, R. R. C. (2021). Online distance learning amidst the pandemic COVID-19. *International Journal of Educational Research and Innovation, 15*, 291–304. doi: 10.46661/ijeri.5271

Tienken, C. H. (2020). The not so subtle inequity of remote learning. *Kappa Delta Pi Record, 56*, 151–153. doi: 10.1080/00228958.2020.1813502

Vadell, K. (2013). Approaching K–12 online education in Pennsylvania. *Online Journal of Distance Learning Administration, 16*(2), 2616–2624.

CHAPTER 3

EDUCATORS' JOB BURNOUT AND INTENTIONS TO LEAVE DURING THE COVID-19 PANDEMIC

Andrew M. Camp, Gema Zamarro, and Josh McGee
University of Arkansas

The 2020–2021 academic year was trying for educators. We use nationally representative samples of teachers and school leaders from the RAND American Educator Panels to document K–12 teachers' and leaders' levels of concern about job-related burnout and stated consideration of leaving the profession. We also study factors associated with teachers' and administrators' high concerns about job burnout and teachers' considerations to leave their jobs. Approaching retirement age (being 55 or older), having to change instruction modes, hybrid teaching, COVID-19 related health concerns, and high levels of job burnout all appear to be important predictors of teachers' probability of considering leaving or retiring from teaching. Health concerns and switching instruction modes were also associated with higher levels of concern about teacher burnout. Interestingly, our results indicate a potential disconnect between factors that affect administrators and those that affect teachers. Leaders, especially those in larger education systems, may not be acutely aware of the

Instructional Survival in the Midst of the Perfect Storm:
The Experiences of K–12 Teachers During the COVID-19 Global Pandemic, pages 29–52.

Published under exclusive licence by Emerald Publishing Limited
ISBNs: 978-1-83708-502-6 HB, 978-1-83708-503-3 PB,
978-1-83708-504-0 EPDF, 978-1-83708-505-7 EPUB

impacts that shifting modes of instruction have on teachers and thus underestimate the stress doing so puts on teachers. Overall, our analysis from the first full academic year in the pandemic raises concerns about potential increases in teacher turnover as a result of high levels of job burnout during the pandemic, which aligns with recent reports of increased teacher turnover entering the third academic year of the pandemic. Surveys like ours could be used to monitor teachers' considerations to leave and levels of job burnout during times of crisis and help inform timely strategies for better-retaining teachers.

INTRODUCTION

Throughout the COVID-19 pandemic, challenges associated with K–12 school staffing and changes in instructional mode received considerable attention from the media and public officials. Following nationwide school closures in the early months of the pandemic, schools reopened in the fall of 2020 using combinations of in-person, hybrid, and remote learning models. Teachers were challenged to adapt their curricula to allow for social distancing in the classroom and provide synchronous or asynchronous remote instruction for students to engage with at home. Administrators had to manage complicated logistics, such as contact tracing, to comply with COVID-19 health guidelines. Even for those teachers and administrators returning to in-person instruction, unexpected quarantines and necessary mitigation measures represented a substantial deviation from schools' normal operations. As a result of these unexpected and challenging working conditions, educators' levels of stress and burnout appeared high throughout the first pandemic school year (Diliberti & Kaufman, 2020; Diliberti et al., 2021; Zamarro et al., 2022), raising concerns about a potential increase in turnover and future teacher shortages (Goldberg, 2021; Lavery, 2020).

Teacher turnover often has negative effects on students (Hanushek et al., 2016), and a teacher shortage might be particularly disruptive in certain subjects, such as STEM and Special Education, or districts (e.g., rural districts) that already struggled to find qualified teachers (Goldhaber, 2021; Nguyen et al., 2020). In addition, higher levels of job dissatisfaction and intentions to leave could harm educators' effectiveness, students' academic progress, and student motivation even if educators do not leave their positions (Madigan & Kim, 2021). Given the large learning losses students experienced during the pandemic, promoting the stability and quality of the teaching workforce is of particular social importance and policy relevance. Therefore, it is important for policymakers and educational leaders to better understand why teachers considered leaving their teaching positions and what factors appear to contribute to burnout of educators so that we might find ways to better support teachers and administrators during current and future challenging times.

We examine this issue using three nationally representative surveys administered through the RAND's American Teacher Panel (ATP) and the American School Leader Panel (ASLP).

LITERATURE REVIEW

Teacher Burnout

Pre-pandemic studies of teacher burnout have characterized the phenomenon as a combination of emotional exhaustion, depersonalization, and decreased professional efficacy (Hakanen et al., 2006; Skaalvik & Skaalvik, 2010). Researchers have typically sought to understand burnout using the Job Demands-Resources model (Demerouti et al., 2001; Hakanen et al., 2006) wherein burnout is the result of increased job demands (e.g., time pressures and low student motivation) without corresponding increases job resources (e.g., professional autonomy and support from administrators). Importantly, research has found that changes in job demands and resources affect teachers' emotional states and motivations to quit almost exclusively through burnout, indicating that identifying burnout in teachers may be crucial in predicting these responses (Skaalvik & Skaalvik, 2020).

Identifying which teachers may be experiencing burnout has important implications for students. Studies of teacher burnout have documented that students with teachers experiencing burnout may have worse academic and behavioral outcomes (Herman et al., 2018) and that burnout is negatively and meaningfully associated with teacher health (Hakanen et al., 2006).

Teaching in the Pandemic

Given that teaching was a high-stress profession before the pandemic, it is concerning that the COVID-19 crisis appears to have exacerbated teachers' levels of stress and burnout. Diliberti et al. (2021) survey a sample of former teachers from the ATP in December 2020. Their sample included both teachers who left the profession in the two years leading up to the COVID-19 pandemic as well as those who left during the first nine months of the pandemic. They find that stress was the most common reason given by public school teachers for leaving the profession both before and during the pandemic, but the COVID-19 crisis appears to have added to that stress. Almost half of the public school teachers who voluntarily left the profession between March and December 2020 said it was because of the COVID-19 pandemic (Diliberti et al., 2021).

According to a separate ATP survey from January 2021, teachers' intentions to leave also appeared elevated early in the pandemic. Steiner and Woo (2021) find that nearly one-quarter of teachers indicated they were likely to leave their jobs by the end of the school year. If realized, this would have represented a 7 percentage point increase in teacher turnover compared with an average national turnover rate of 16% pre-pandemic (NCES, 2019) and lead to significant instability in the teacher workforce.

To some extent, these survey results stand in contrast with the experiences of teachers early in the pandemic. Herman et al., (2021) find that, relative to the fall of 2019, teachers in May 2020 reported lower levels of stress and that teachers who reported confidence in and satisfaction with school leadership in the fall were more likely to report lower levels of stress in the spring. Similarly, Kraft et al., (2021) document the protective role that positive working conditions played in sustaining teachers' sense of success during the spring of 2020. Entering the 2020–21 school year, many teachers continued to report somewhat lower levels of stress during the first month of the school year (Pressley et al., 2021) before increases in stress and burnout later in the fall of 2020 (Diliberti et al., 2021; Steiner & Woo, 2021).

Together, these findings indicate that teachers' level of stress and burnout declined during the first few months of the pandemic followed by sharp increases once the 2020–21 school year was fully underway. While contradictory at face value, this trend is consistent with the job demands-resources model of burnout (Demerouti et al., 2001) which proposes that increasing job demands (e.g., teaching during a pandemic) without corresponding increases in job resources (e.g., supports, planning time, etc.) leads to higher levels of exhaustion and burnout. In this framework, the initial improvement in (Herman et al., 2021) or buffering of (Kraft et al., 2021) teacher's psychological well-being during the spring of 2020 might be understood to some extent as the result of decreasing job demands due to lowered expectations for teachers and students during these initial pandemic months (Malkus, 2020). Once the first pandemic school year was underway and teachers had to provide for in-person and virtual learning alongside pandemic-related health concerns and preventative measures, job demands would likely have increased to levels above that of the pre-pandemic period. In this way, increasing job demands during the 2020–21 school year were accompanied by increased levels of stress and burnout (Diliberti et al., 2021; Steiner & Woo, 2021; Zamarro et al., 2022).

Teacher Turnover During COVID-19

As state-level administrative data became available, an emerging literature documented actual teacher turnover during and after the COVID-19 pandemic. Although evidence from Arkansas, Massachusetts, North Carolina, South Carolina, and Washington indicated stable teacher turnover during the first full school year in the pandemic (2020–2021) and only a slight increase in turnover entering the second pandemic school year (2021–2022) (Bacher-Hicks et al., 2023; Bastian & Fuller, 2023; Camp et al., 2022; Goldhaber & Theobald, 2022), reports show an increase in turnover entering the third pandemic school year (2022–2023). In North Carolina, teacher turnover increased by 4.4 percentage points (39%) during the third pandemic school year, relative to the 2019–20 school year, and much of this increase appears to be driven by teachers leaving mid-year (Bastian & Fuller, 2023), potentially due to high levels of job-related stress. Similarly, teacher turnover in Washington and Arkansas is at its highest levels observed in available administrative data (Camp et al., 2023; Goldhaber & Theobald, 2023).

Post-Pandemic Instability

While less attention has been paid to turnover and staffing challenges in non-instructional positions (e.g., Bruno, 2025; Camp et al., 2023; Goldhaber & Gratz,

2022), there are early indications that these individuals may also have experienced high levels of burnout and fatigue which may result in staffing shortages. Using a nationally representative survey of principals, Woo and Steiner (2022) find that approximately 80% of secondary school principals experienced frequent job-related stress during the first pandemic school year, leading some to suggest an impending crisis among school leaders (DeMatthews, 2021).

The prospect of increased teacher and principal turnover is concerning for schools and students. Replacing teachers is costly and can drain school resources (Barnes et al., 2007; Birkeland & Curtis, 2006; Milanowski & Odden, 2007). Additionally, teacher turnover negatively affects student achievement which could make it more difficult for students to recover from any learning losses experienced during the pandemic (Ronfeldt et al., 2013). While the effects of principals on student outcomes are not as established as the effects of teachers, increased principal turnover may also lead to negative impacts on students' outcomes (Bartanen et al., 2019, 2022).

METHODS

Data

We use three surveys from the ATP and ASLP to study teachers' and principals' considerations to leave the classroom and levels of burnout during the first academic year (2020–21) of the COVID-19 pandemic.

To examine teachers' intentions to leave, we included questions on a 15-minute survey administered to the nationally representative RAND ATP[1] from March 22 to March 31, 2021. Our sample contained 1,045 teachers. Table 3.1 presents descriptive statistics for this nationally representative sample of teachers. Following the composition of the nation's teaching labor force, most teachers in our sample (73%) are female and 86% are white. 29% of teachers in our sample teach in an urban area, 39% teach in the suburbs, and 31% teach in a town or rural area. The ATP and ASLP additionally provide an indicator variable for whether more than 50% of students in each school are from minoritized racial/ethnic groups or qualify for free or reduced-price lunches. In our sample, 49% of teachers work in schools serving a majority of minoritized students or students living in poverty (as indicated by receiving free or reduced-priced lunches).

Using these data, we identify teachers who are approaching retirement age as those who are 55 years old or older[2] (N=170; 16%). Among teachers in our

---

[1] https://www.rand.org/education-and-labor/projects/aep/about.html. RAND American Educator Panels, American Teacher Panel, 2021 ATP Module on Finances, Retirement, and Job Preferences, UAR0421T, RAND Corporation, Santa Monica, CA, April, 2021.

[2] Each state and several municipalities operate their own teacher retirement plans where retirement eligibility ages vary across and frequently within plans. This makes it difficult to determine which age would truly be a teachers first retirement eligibility age. However, although few plans allow teachers to retire at age 55 with full benefits, the full retirement age is not far off in most plans. For more information, see Fuchsman et al. (2023).

TABLE 3.1. Descriptive Statistics for ATP Survey Data (March 2021)

	N	Mean	SD	Min	Max
Female	1024	0.73	0.44	0.00	1.00
Not White	1024	0.14	0.35	0.00	1.00
Age	1022	43.92	10.26	24.00	74.00
Ages 35-44	1045	0.30	0.46	0.00	1.00
Ages 45-54	1045	0.30	0.46	0.00	1.00
Ages 55+	1045	0.16	0.37	0.00	1.00
Elem. Teacher	1045	0.44	0.50	0.00	1.00
Middle Sch. Teacher	1045	0.30	0.46	0.00	1.00
Pr(Infection)	1021	16.37	20.11	0.00	100.00
Pr(Hosp/Die|Infection)	1020	11.81	19.78	0.00	100.00
Has been vaccinated	1029	0.76	0.43	0.00	1.00
Switch Modality	1034	0.71	0.45	0.00	1.00
Number of Mode Switches	1034	2.31	2.95	0.00	20.00
Remote Instruction	1045	0.30	0.46	0.00	1.00
Hybrid Instruction	1045	0.49	0.50	0.00	1.00
Urban	1045	0.29	0.45	0.00	1.00
Suburban	1045	0.39	0.49	0.00	1.00
Town/Rural	1045	0.31	0.46	0.00	1.00
Minoritized/High-Poverty School	1045	0.49	0.50	0.00	1.00
High Job Burnout	1045	0.51	0.50	0.00	1.00
High Outside Burnout	1045	0.14	0.35	0.00	1.00
High Care Responsibilities Burnout	1045	0.27	0.45	0.00	1.00
Did Not Consider Leaving	1024	0.59	0.49	0.00	1.00
Considered Leaving for Any Reason	1024	0.41	0.49	0.00	1.00
Considered Leaving Due to COVID	1024	0.22	0.42	0.00	1.00
Considered Leaving for Other Reasons	1024	0.19	0.39	0.00	1.00

sample, 309 (30%) reported teaching fully remote to most of their students for most of the 2020–21 school year, 509 (49%) reported they taught in a hybrid model, and 220 (22%) reported teaching fully in person. Finally, 71% of teachers in our sample reported they had to switch instructional modes (e.g., transitioning to in-person learning or temporarily switching to remote learning) at least once during the 2020–2021 school year, and the average teacher switched modes twice.

At the time of our survey, teachers were also asked other questions designed by the RAND ATP team that we use in our analysis. We use teachers' responses to a series of questions about burnout. Teachers rated the following challenges on a scale from 1 ("Not a concern right now") to 4 ("A major concern"):

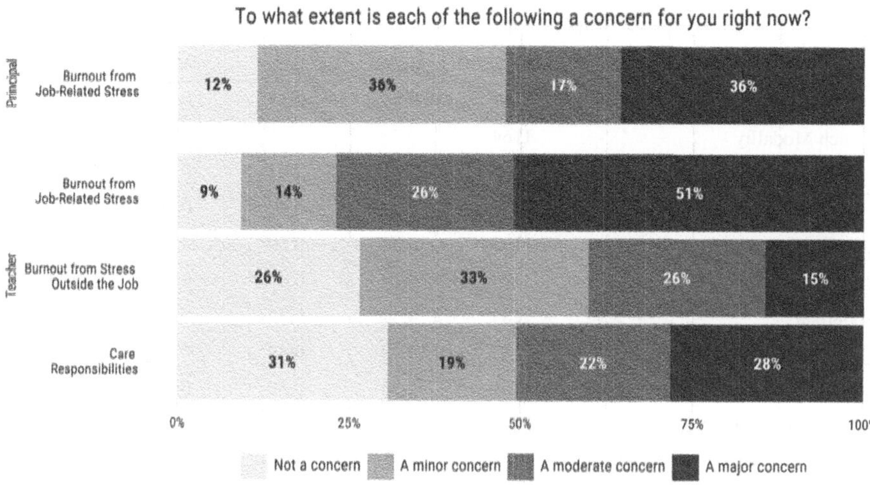

FIGURE 3.1. Teachers' Levels of Concern About Burnout from Job-Related Stress, Burnout from Stress Outside the Job, and Care Responsibilities. Note: Results weighted using ATP-provided sampling weights

- feelings of burnout associated with stress from the job;
- feelings of burnout associated with stress outside the job; and
- responsibilities to care for her children or other loved ones.

For each of these, we created a dummy variable representing high levels of concern if the respondent answered they were a major concern. Teachers who reported they preferred not to say were coded as missing values in our analysis. Figure 3.1 presents the distribution of teachers' responses to these questions. In our sample, 51% of teachers reported that feelings of burnout associated with stress from the job were a major concern, compared with 14% who reported that feelings of burnout outside the job were a major concern and 28% who reported high levels of concern about responsibilities for taking care of their children or other loved ones.

Additionally, we use responses to a pre-pandemic survey of 5,464 teachers[3]. Administration of this survey took place from February 10th to March 16th, 2020, and focused on teachers' retirement knowledge and preferences. Several questions on the 2020 survey were repeated on the 2021 survey, allowing us to study how teachers' attitudes may have changed through the pandemic.

Finally, we examine differences between teachers' and principals' reported levels of concern about job burnout using a similar survey of 1,183 school-level

[3] RAND American Educator Panels, American Teacher Panel, 2020 ATP Survey on Finances, Retirement, and Job Preferences, UAR0120T, RAND Corporation, Santa Monica, CA, April 2020.

TABLE 3.2. Descriptive Statistics for ASLP Survey Data (March 2021)

	N	Mean	SD	Min	Max
Has been vaccinated	1141	0.84	0.37	0.00	1.00
Switch Modality	1164	0.76	0.43	0.00	1.00
Number of Mode Switches	1164	2.08	2.01	0.00	20.00
Remote Instruction	1183	0.20	0.40	0.00	1.00
Hybrid Instruction	1183	0.56	0.50	0.00	1.00
Urban	1183	0.27	0.44	0.00	1.00
Suburban	1183	0.32	0.47	0.00	1.00
Town/Rural	1183	0.39	0.49	0.00	1.00
Minoritized/High-Poverty School	1159	0.55	0.50	0.00	1.00
High Job Burnout	1183	0.34	0.47	0.00	1.00

leaders (e.g. principals) administered through the ASLP from March 22nd through March 26th, 2021[4]. Table 3.2 presents descriptive statistics for this nationally representative sample. Due to data limitations, we are unable to match gender, race, or age information for principals in this sample, as this information is not provided by RAND in the publicly available files. However, we are still able to examine the relationship between principals' feelings of job-related burnout, considerations of leaving their position, vaccination status, urbanicity, primary learning mode, and if their school had to change mode of instruction during the 2020–21 school year.

For both teachers and principal survey responses, we construct variables indicating considerations of leaving their current position or the profession during the 2020–21 academic year. For teachers, our survey asked if they had "considered leaving or retiring from your current position as a teacher in the last year" with separate options available to indicate if they had considered due to COVID, for other reasons, or not at all. For principals, the closest question available asks them to indicate whether it was likely they would "leave [their] job by the end of the current school year (2020–21)." Variable definitions are summarized in the supplementary table located at the end of this chapter.

Empirical Approach

We first present descriptive trends on the teachers' commitment to remaining in the profession during the first academic year of the pandemic as well as teachers' and principals' concerns about job burnout. We then use statistical logit

[4] RAND American Educator Panels, American School Leader Panel, 2021 Spring COVID-19 Distance Learning Survey, CRS0421S, RAND Corporation, Santa Monica, CA, Spring 2021. https://www.rand.org/education-and-labor/projects/aep/surveys/items/COVID-19-response-survey-crs-spring-2021.html

models to study factors associated with the overall probability of teachers and principals having considered leaving or retiring from the profession in the last year with a logistic regression model following specification (A):

$$
\begin{aligned}
&Prob\left(ConsiderLeaving_i\right)\\
&\quad = \Lambda(\beta_0 + \beta_1 Vaccinated_i + \beta_2 SwitchedMode_i\\
&\quad + \beta_3 TeachingMode_i + \beta_4 Urbanicity_i\\
&\quad + \beta_5 MinoritizedHighPovSchool_i\\
&\quad + \beta_6 HighJobBurnout_i)
\end{aligned}
\qquad (A)
$$

Where our outcome variable, *ConsiderLeaving*, takes value 1 if the teacher reports having considered leaving or retiring from their current position during the past year or if the principal indicates they are likely to leave their position by the end of the year at the time of the March 2021 survey.

Explanatory variables in this specification include a binary variable which takes a value of 1 if the respondent indicates having received at least one dose of a COVID-19 vaccine at the time of the survey, as it may capture an increased sense of personal safety from that vaccination. Additionally, we include three indicator variables capturing the instructional modes used in each school. The first, *SwitchedMode*, indicates if a respondent reports having changed instructional mode at least once during the school year, while *Remote* and *Hybrid* represent if a respondent has taught primarily via a remote or hybrid modality. We additionally include variables to account for differences by urbanity[5] and the student body (majority minoritized or high-poverty) of the school. The final variable in this specification indicates if respondents report high levels of job-related burnout as described in the previous section. We estimate (A) separately for principals and teachers.

Next, we study factors associated with the separate probabilities of teachers' considering leaving or retiring because of COVID, for other reasons, or not considering leaving at all using a statistical multinomial logit model. This analysis builds upon the logit model specification (A) and includes additional explanatory variables to account for demographic differences, grade-level differences, differences in perceived health risk, and high concerns about other forms of burnout. Specifically, the set of controls includes self-reported gender, whether the teacher identifies as non-White, and three dummies for teacher age ranges (ages 35–44, ages 45–54, and ages 55+). We also include two dummies to capture the grade

[5] We use NCES classifications for urbanity. See https://nces.ed.gov/programs/edge/docs/LOCALE_CLASSIFICATIONS.pdf for more details.

level of teaching (elementary grades, middle grades), with high school grades as the reference category.

$$\begin{aligned} Prob(Y_i = j \mid X_i) \\ &= \Lambda(\beta_0 + \beta_1 Vaccinated_i + \beta_2 SwitchedMode_i \\ &+\beta_3 TeachingMode_i + \beta_4 Urbanicity_i \\ &+\beta_5 MinoritizedHighPovSchool_i \\ &+\beta_6 HighJobBurnout_i + \beta_7 Demographics_i \\ &+\beta_8 GradeLevel_i + \beta_9 CovidRisk_i \\ &+\beta_{10} HighNonJobBurnout_i \\ &+\beta_{11} HighJobBurnout_i \times HighNonJobBurnout_i \\ &+\beta_{12} HighCareBurnout_i) \end{aligned} \qquad \text{(B)}$$

where

$$j = \begin{cases} 1 \; Considered\ Leaving\ Because\ of\ COVID \\ 2 \; Considered\ Leaving\ for\ Other\ \text{Re}asons \\ 3 \; Did\ Not\ Consider\ Leaving \end{cases}$$

We use two variables to capture teachers' reported COVID risks (*CovidRisk*$_i$). First, we include the average of teacher-reported probabilities that they will get COVID, either at their job or outside of that job, in the next three months. Second, we also include the teacher's reported probability that, if infected, they will end up in the hospital because of COVID or die. To explore if self-reported burnout captures a distinct factor from these other controls, we first estimate (B) without any burnout variables before estimating with variables representing high levels of job burnout, non-job burnout, and burnout stemming from care responsibilities, as previously described. To explore the additive effects of job and non-job burnout, we also include the interaction of these variables in this extended specification.

While we expect burnout to explain a large portion of considerations or intention to leave, we also expect that other factors, such as perceived health risks, may also explain these outcomes independently of burnout. Similarly, factors distinct from those related to intending to leave could explain reported burnout. As teacher burnout may have negative effects on student outcomes regardless of actual turnover, we explore the relationship between factors and reported job burnout using logit models with control variables as in specifications (A) and (B) and with *HighJobBurnout* as the outcome variable.

In all models, we use sampling weights included with the ATP to maintain a nationally representative sample of educators. To aid interpretation, we present our estimates as average marginal effects.

RESULTS

Teachers' Intentions to Leave Have Increased

Using surveys from March 2020 and 2021, we compared responses to questions asking teachers about their long- and short-term commitment to the profession. In March 2020, 74.2% of teachers indicated that they planned to work as a teacher until retirement while 16.5% of respondents were unsure and 9.3% of respondents indicated that they did not plan to do so. In March of 2021, a year after the start of the pandemic, teachers' commitment to the profession decreased as 69% of teachers indicated that they planned to work as a teacher until retirement. Teachers appear to have become more uncertain as only 9.5% of respondents indicated that they would not work as a teacher until retirement while 21.5% indicated that they were uncertain.

As illustrated in Figure 3.2, teachers' reported probability of leaving their current state or the profession within the next 5 years increased from 24% on average in March 2020 to 30% in March 2021. This change was due to a reduction in the percentage of teachers reporting a zero-percent probability. We observe similarly reported probabilities regardless of instructional mode.

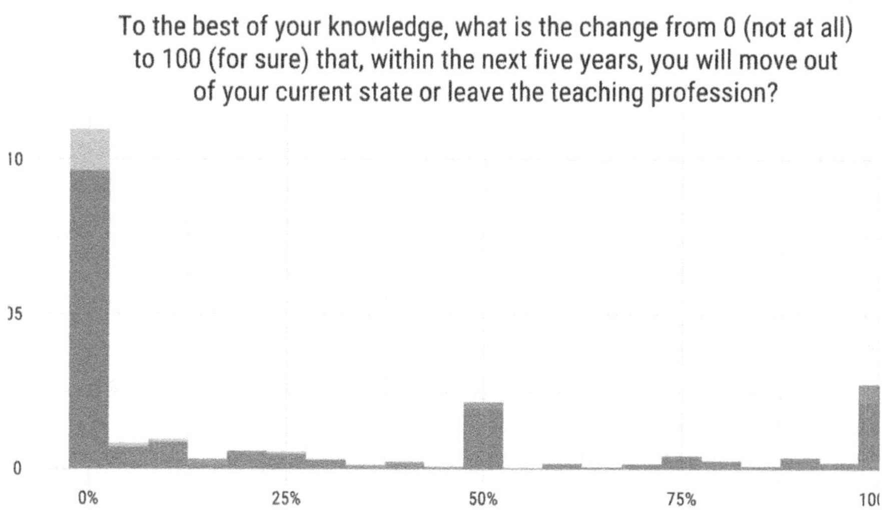

FIGURE 3.2. Teachers' Reported Probability of Leaving their Current State or the Profession in the Next Five Years. Note: Results weighted using ATP provided sampling weights

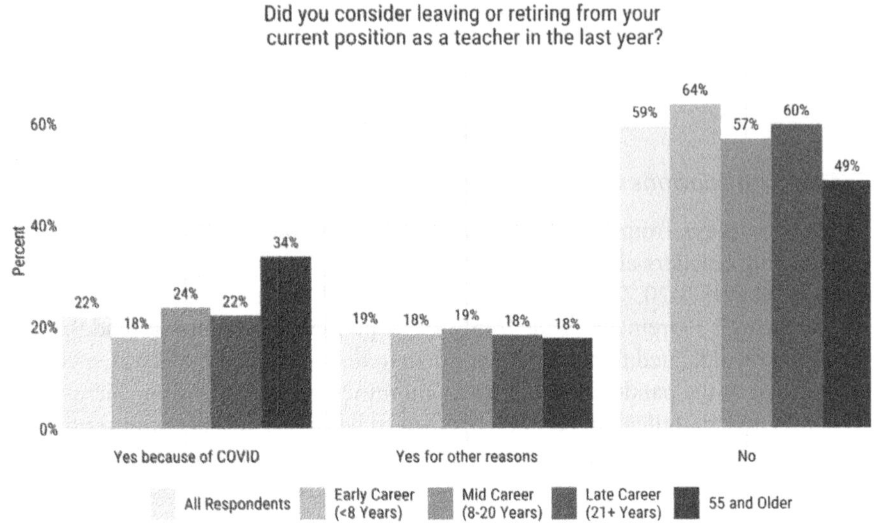

FIGURE 3.3. Teachers' Consideration of Leaving or Retiring from their Current Position. Note: Results weighted using ATP-provided sampling weights

We also asked teachers if they considered leaving their current positions within the last year and, if they did, whether the COVID-19 pandemic was motivating this decision. Teachers' responses to this question are presented in Figure 3.3. Overall, 41% of teachers declared that they have considered leaving or retiring from their current position during the last year. Of these, 22% indicated that the COVID-19 pandemic was the primary reason for their consideration while 19% of respondents indicated that the consideration was caused by other reasons. While we do not observe significant differences in responses to this question by the level of teacher experience, those approaching retirement considered leaving at higher rates. 34% of teachers aged 55 and older declared they were considering leaving or retiring because of COVID-19 as compared to 18–24% of respondents across experience levels.

Multiple Factors Predict Intending to Leave

We further investigated factors associated with the probability of teachers' consideration to leave their current position within the last year. Our estimates following the empirical models described in (A) and (B) above are presented in Table 3.3. Examining the results from specification (A), reported in columns 1 and 2, we see that high levels of job-related burnout are the largest predictors of considerations of leaving for both teachers and principals. All else equal, reporting that job-related burnout was a major concern was associated with a 23 and 31 percentage point increase in reporting considerations of leaving for principals

TABLE 3.3. Factors Related to the Probability of Considering Leaving or Retiring

	(A)		(B)		
	Principal	**Teacher**	**Because COVID**	**Other Reasons**	**Did Not Consider**
Has been vaccinated	-0.036	-0.053	0.002	-0.061**	0.059
	(0.029)	(0.036)	(0.033)	(0.029)	(0.038)
Switch Modality	0.003	0.093**	0.032	0.058*	-0.090**
	(0.028)	(0.036)	(0.033)	(0.031)	(0.036)
Remote Instruction	0.061	-0.037	0.063	-0.108***	0.045
	(0.038)	(0.046)	(0.043)	(0.038)	(0.047)
Hybrid Instruction	0.055*	-0.023	0.079**	-0.100***	0.021
	(0.030)	(0.040)	(0.037)	(0.031)	(0.041)
Suburban	0.013	-0.047	-0.021	-0.017	0.037
	(0.028)	(0.038)	(0.032)	(0.034)	(0.038)
Town/Rural	0.011	0.004	-0.006	0.021	-0.016
	(0.029)	(0.041)	(0.035)	(0.033)	(0.041)
Minoritized/High-Poverty School	-0.026	0.007	-0.032	0.035	-0.003
	(0.023)	(0.032)	(0.027)	(0.027)	(0.032)
High Job Burnout	0.234***	0.310***	0.195***	0.111***	-0.306***
	(0.022)	(0.024)	(0.029)	(0.027)	(0.029)
Female			0.023	-0.031	0.008
			(0.032)	(0.030)	(0.037)
Not White			0.060	-0.068	0.008
			(0.039)	(0.043)	(0.049)
Ages 35-44			-0.009	-0.032	0.041
			(0.036)	(0.033)	(0.041)
Ages 45-54			-0.003	-0.018	0.021
			(0.036)	(0.034)	(0.042)
Ages 55+			0.115***	0.006	-0.121**
			(0.041)	(0.041)	(0.052)
Elem. Teacher			-0.054*	0.016	0.038
			(0.030)	(0.029)	(0.035)
Middle Sch. Teacher			-0.043	0.013	0.030
			(0.030)	(0.030)	(0.036)
Pr(Infection)			0.000	0.001	-0.001
			(0.001)	(0.001)	(0.001)
Pr(Hosp/Die|Infection)			0.002**	-0.001	-0.000
			(0.001)	(0.001)	(0.001)
High Outside Burnout			0.076	0.077	-0.153*
			(0.077)	(0.077)	(0.083)
Job X Outside Burnout			-0.112	-0.029	0.141
			(0.085)	(0.085)	(0.096)
Care Burnout			0.044	-0.013	-0.031
			(0.030)	(0.030)	(0.036)
Observations	1,118	1,024	1,020	1,020	1,020
Pseudo R^2	0.158	0.102	0.116	0.116	0.116

Note: .01 - ***; .05 - **; .1 - *; Results displayed as average marginal effects. Heteroskedastic robust standard errors reported. ATP-provided sampling weights used.

and teachers, respectively. These estimates are significant at the 99% confidence level. Interestingly, having switched modalities, as compared with teaching using the same instructional mode all year, was associated with a 9 percentage point increase in the likelihood of teachers' considering leaving their position but no statistically significant effect for principals. This indicates that the experiences, and stressors, of principals and teachers, may have been substantially different from each other during the 2020–21 school year.

The results of our multinomial logit[6], reported in columns 3–5 of Table 3.3, highlight significant differences in how factors in our model are associated with teachers' reasons for considering leaving their position or the profession. Interestingly, teachers aged 55 or higher, as compared with teachers ages 34 and lower, were 12 percentage points more likely to report considerations of leaving due to COVID but no more likely to report considerations of leaving for other reasons. Relatedly, having been vaccinated is associated with a 6-percentage point reduction in the probability of teachers reporting that they considered leaving for reasons other than the COVID-19 pandemic, significant at the 99% confidence level. Looking at teachers' health concerns, compared to teachers who report a zero percent chance of being hospitalized or dying because of COVID-19, those who think they have a 50% chance are 10 percentage points more likely to have considered leaving or retiring because of COVID.

We also find evidence that instructional modality is associated with teachers' considerations of leaving. All else equal, teachers who report having taught most of the school year via a hybrid modality were 8 percentage points more likely to report having considered leaving due to COVID and 10 percentage points less likely to report having considered leaving for other reasons as compared to teachers who taught the majority of the year in-person. These estimates are significant at the 99% confidence level. Similarly, teachers who taught primarily via a remote modality were 11 percentage points less likely to report having considered leaving as compared to teachers who taught the majority of the year in-person. Switching modality appears to have been particularly difficult for teachers as teachers who switch modality at least once during the year, as compared to those who taught via the same modality for the whole year, were 9 percentage points less likely to report that they did not consider leaving and 6 percentage points more likely to report considering leaving for other reasons. These estimates are significant at the 99% and 90% confidence levels.

Consistent with the results reported in columns 1 and 2, the largest factor associated with teachers' considerations of leaving their position appears to be self-reported job-related burnout. All else equal, reporting high levels of concern about job-related burnout, as compared with reporting lower levels of concern,

[6] We have also examined the relationships between these factors and any considerations of leaving using a logit model, however we prefer the multinomial model to highlight statistically significant differences in how each factor relates to different reasons for having considered leaving their position. Logit regression results available upon request from the authors.

was associated with a 20 percentage point increase in the likelihood of having considered leaving due to COVID, an 11 percentage point increase in the likelihood of having considered leaving for other reasons, and a 31 percentage point decrease in the likelihood of not having considered leaving. These estimates are significant at the 99% confidence level.

Differences Between Teachers' and School Leaders' Experiences

As self-reported burnout both captures unique variation in teachers' considerations to leave and is the largest single factor explaining these considerations, we next examine factors associated with teachers' and administrators' reported level of burnout. Additionally, we believe that a comparison of teachers' and administrators' feelings of burnout may reveal important differences in the experiences of these two roles. We first estimate two separate logit models for teachers and administrators that have the same dependent variable and shared explanatory variables similar to specification (A). Second, we estimate a logit model using high levels of teacher concern about job-related burnout as our dependent variable, following the more extensive model described in (B) above. Results for these analyses are shown in Table 3.4.

Beginning with the paired analysis of teacher and school leader burnout, we see that urbanity levels are the only factors that are significant at the 95% confidence level or higher for both teachers and school leaders. All else equal, suburban and town/rural school leaders were between 9 and 11 percentage points less likely to report high levels of concern about job-related burnout. While switching mode of instruction is a significant predictor of high levels of job burnout for teachers in our model in column (2), this does not seem to be the case for administrators. Mostly teaching in a hybrid mode appears associated with high concerns about job burnout among administrators with an increased probability of about 8 percentage points. But this effect is only marginally statistically significant at the 90% confidence level.

Examining the results in column 3, we see that multiple factors appear to be significant predictors of teachers' high levels of concern about job burnout. Holding all else constant, female teachers are 18 percentage points more likely to report that job-related burnout was a major concern than male teachers. This estimate is significant at the 99% confidence level. Although teachers approaching retirement age (Age 55+) were more likely to consider leaving or retirement as reported in Table 3.3, we do not find a positive association between approaching retirement age and higher concerns about job burnout. While the perceived risk of serious COVID-19 complications is only marginally significant, the perceived risk of infection appears to predict teachers' high concerns about job burnout. Teachers who think they have a 50% chance of getting infected with COVID are 15 percentage points more likely to report high levels of concern about job burnout than teachers perceiving a zero chance of getting COVID.

TABLE 3.4. Factors Related with High Concern about Feelings of Job Burnout

	(A)		(B)
	Principal Burnout	**Teacher Burnout**	**Teacher Burnout**
Has been vaccinated	-0.020 (0.044)	0.029 (0.038)	0.060 (0.039)
Switch Modality	-0.013 (0.038)	0.083** (0.037)	0.076** (0.036)
Remote Instruction	0.079 (0.054)	-0.048 (0.051)	-0.059 (0.051)
Hybrid Instruction	0.077* (0.042)	0.049 (0.044)	0.040 (0.044)
Suburban	-0.088** (0.042)	-0.045 (0.041)	-0.041 (0.040)
Town Rural	-0.107** (0.042)	-0.107** (0.044)	-0.095** (0.044)
Minoritized/High-Poverty School	-0.049 (0.033)	-0.000 (0.034)	-0.010 (0.034)
Female			0.177*** (0.037)
Not White			0.011 (0.047)
Ages 35-44			-0.017 (0.045)
Ages 45-54			0.006 (0.046)
Ages 55+			-0.052 (0.053)
Elem. Teacher			-0.065* (0.036)
Middle Sch. Teacher			-0.013 (0.037)
Pr(Infection)			0.003*** (0.001)
Pr(Hosp/Die|Infection)			0.001 (0.001)
Observations	1,118	1,029	1,020
Pseudo R^2	0.012	0.015	0.054

Note: .01 - ***; .05 - **; .1 - *
Results displayed as average marginal effects. Heteroskedastic robust standard errors reported. ATP-provided sampling weights used.

Having to switch modes of instruction is associated with higher levels of teacher concern about job burnout. Holding all else constant, teachers who have switched modes of instruction at least one time are 7.6 percentage points more likely to report high levels of concern for job burnout than those who have consistently taught via the same mode of instruction. This estimate is significant at the 95% confidence level. Interestingly, teaching in a town or rural school, as compared with a city school, is associated with a 9.5 percentage point decreased probability of reporting high levels of concern for job burnout. This estimate is significant at the 95% confidence level.

CONCLUSIONS

The 2020–2021 academic year was a trying year for teachers and, as a result, teachers reported large increases in stress and burnout along with a diminished sense of success (Diliberti et al., 2021; Kraft et al., 2021; Steiner & Woo, 2021). In our analysis, we find that teachers also conveyed high concerns about job burnout and an increased self-reported probability that they may leave the profession relative to before the pandemic. Importantly, these increases were not uniform across all teachers. We find four factors that are possible explanations of these results. First, a larger proportion of those approaching retirement age reported having considered leaving or retiring because of COVID, independently of concerns about job burnout. These increased considerations of leaving the profession are understandable given the elevated risk that the pandemic posed to older individuals. However, the loss of these more experienced teachers would be problematic for schools as they might lose their more effective teachers (Harris & Sass, 2011; Wiswall, 2013).

Secondly, we find that most teachers had to change instructional mode at least once and many experienced multiple disruptions during the year. Having to change instructional modes was associated with both an increased probability of considering leaving or retiring and, according to studies of administrative data, increases in actual teacher turnover (Camp et al., 2023). Third, teaching in a hybrid model appeared to be especially challenging for teachers as it was associated with increased consideration of leaving because of COVID, potentially due to the added stress that teachers faced when managing both synchronous and asynchronous classes. Finally, COVID health concerns were also an important factor associated with an increased probability of considering leaving and reporting high levels of concern about job burnout. Although these health concerns probably declined with the availability of vaccines, such vaccines were unavailable for much of the 2020–21 school year and this lack of effective prophylactics may have contributed to the stress teachers felt.

Comparing concerns about job burnout among teachers and administrators, as reported in Table 3.3, our results indicate that administrators may have been relatively less affected by the factors we considered and that affected teachers' concerns about job burnout. For instance, changes such as shifting instructional modes were associated with higher levels of concern about job burnout for teachers but not administrators. Leaders, especially those in larger education systems, may not be acutely aware of the impacts that shifting modes of instruction have on teachers and thus underestimate the stress doing so puts on teachers. Alternatively, leaders who are actively involved in the decision-making process could feel some sense of control over these factors which attenuates the stress that teachers felt. Together, our results provide evidence that teachers and administrators not only had difference experiences during the COVID-19 pandemic but also that the working conditions and characteristics of teachers are predictive of both intentions to leave and self-reported burnout. These findings have important implications going forward as the teaching profession may face increased turnover due to lasting impacts of the COVID-19 pandemic.

Our analysis of the first full academic year of the pandemic raises concerns about a potential increase in teacher turnover because of high levels of job burnout during the pandemic. Although teacher turnover remained relatively stable during the first two pandemic school years, recent reports for several states show an uptick in teacher turnover entering the third pandemic academic year 2022–2023 (Bacher-Hicks et al., 2023; Bastian & Fuller, 2023; Camp et al., 2022, 2024; CERRA, 2022; Goldhaber & Theobald, 2022, 2023). The lasting impacts of any changes in teacher turnover are yet to be seen; however, even small rates of teacher turnover could be problematic if concentrated in areas with teacher shortages (e.g., rural areas or in certain fields like math, science, or special education) (Dee & Goldhaber, 2017). Finally, higher levels of job dissatisfaction could affect teacher effectiveness and could harm student academic progress even if teachers decide not to leave (Madigan & Kim, 2021).

Teachers are the largest school-based factor contributing to students' academic success (Gershenson, 2021). Teachers are also the school personnel most often tasked with implementing interventions and new programs. Throughout the pandemic, American students experienced significant learning losses relative to what we would have expected them to learn (Goldhaber et al., 2022). Given the importance of teachers in ensuring student's academic success and emerging evidence that limited staff capacity may be hampering efforts to address COVID-19 related learning losses (Carbonari et al., 2024), the uncertainty surrounding the stability of the teacher workforce documented in existing research is concerning.

IMPLICATIONS FOR THE FUTURE

Our results highlight the importance of considering how different working conditions might relate to the experiences of individuals within the education sector. Individuals who perceive themselves to be more at risk, such as older teachers in the context of COVID-19, may be more likely to report high levels of burnout or increased considerations of leaving the profession. Similarly, the disconnect between administrator's and teacher's feelings of burnout may be found in contexts other than the COVID-19 pandemic. While our analysis does not directly examine teacher turnover, these findings do inform efforts by educational leaders and policymakers seeking to address turnover stemming from educator stress and burnout. Given the disconnect between administrator's and teacher's feelings of burnout, it will be important that any efforts to address the specific concerns of teachers include the voices of teachers themselves so that their input, informed by the specific job demands and resources they face, can be considered.

Moving forward with continued uncertainty, our results indicate that educational leaders should be attuned to these differing individual experiences and that targeted efforts, such as additional instructional support for teachers, may be needed to address these concerns and promote both teacher and principal retention. The use of surveys, like ours, to monitor teachers' considerations to leave and levels of job burnout, and factors associated with those considerations, could be a timely source of information for school leaders, districts, and policy makers, to help inform the design of timely potential interventions and strategies to help retain teachers in those circumstances.

In this respect, research has highlighted the importance of supporting working conditions to help retain teachers. Kraft et al. (2021) document how schools with strong communication, targeted training, meaningful collaboration, fair expectations, and authentic recognition for their teachers helped them maintain their sense of success during the beginning of this pandemic. Finding ways to help close the disconnect between what affects teachers' levels of job burnout and what affects administrators, using for example surveys like ours, could help administrators find ways to develop supportive work environments that would help retain teachers.

SUMMARY

Educators faced many challenges during the COVID-19 pandemic. We use nationally representative samples of teachers and school leaders from the RAND American Educator Panels to document K–12 teachers' and leaders' levels of concern about job-related burnout and stated consideration of leaving the profession. We also study factors associated with teachers' and administrators' high concerns about job burnout and teachers' considerations to leave their jobs. Approaching retirement age (being 55 or older), having to change instruction modes, hybrid teaching, COVID-19 related health concerns, and high levels of job burnout all appear to be important predictors of teachers' probability of considering leaving or retiring from teaching. Health concerns and switching instruction modes were also associated with higher levels of concern about teacher burnout.

Interestingly, our results indicate a potential disconnect between factors that affect administrators and those that affect teachers. As a result, leaders (especially those in larger education systems) may not be acutely aware of the impacts that shifting modes of instruction have on teachers and thus underestimate the stress doing so puts on teachers. Overall, our analysis from the first full academic year in the pandemic raises concerns about potential increases in teacher turnover stemming from high levels of job burnout during the pandemic, which aligns with recent reports of increased teacher turnover entering the third academic year of the pandemic.

Despite the importance of the teaching profession, there is a shocking lack of ongoing efforts to monitor teachers' working conditions and perceptions. The lack of data surrounding teachers' experiences early in the pandemic presented a significant challenge for policymakers and educational leaders attempting to prevent increased school staffing challenges. Our analysis complements studies of realized teacher turnover by identifying factors associated with teachers' increased concerns about burnout and considerations of leaving their position or profession. Surveys like ours could be used to monitor teachers' considerations to leave and levels of job burnout during times of crisis, might be helpful to close the disconnect between teachers' and principals, and help inform and tailor timely strategies to better retain teachers.

SUPPLEMENTARY TABLE: VARIABLE DEFINITIONS

Variable	Description
$ConsiderLeaving_i$	A binary indicator variable that takes a value of one if respondents indicate that they considered leaving or retiring from their current position in the past year (teachers) or if they stated it was likely they would leave their job by the end of the 2020-21 school year (leaders) and zero otherwise.
$Vaccinated_i$	A binary variable taking a value of one if respondents report having received at least one dose of a COVID-19 vaccine and zero otherwise.
$SwitchedMode_i$	A binary variable taking a value of one if respondents report having switched modes of instruction (e.g., from remote to hybrid) at least once during the 2020-21 school year and zero otherwise.
$TeachmingMode_i$	A set of two binary indicator variables taking values of one if a respondent reports teaching the majority of the school year via remote or hybrid instruction (with majority in-person instruction as the omitted reference category) and zero otherwise.
$Urbanicity_i$	A set of two binary indicator variables taking values of one if a respondent teaches in a suburban or rural/town school (with urban school as the omitted reference category) and zero otherwise. Urbanicity classifications are made by the National Center for Education Statistics (NCES).
$MinoritizedHighPovSchool_i$	A binary indicator variable taking a value of one if a respondent teaches in a majority non-white school or teaches in a school where more than 50% of students qualify for free or reduced-priced lunch and zero otherwise.
$HighJobBurnout_i$	A binary indicator variable taking a value of one if a respondent indicates that "feelings of burnout associated with stress from [their] job," is "a major concern," and zero otherwise.
$HighNonJobBurnout_i$	A binary indicator variable taking a value of one if a respondent indicates that "feelings of burnout associated with stress outside of [their] job," is "a major concern," and zero otherwise.

Variable	Description
$HighCareBurnout_i$	A binary indicator variable taking a value of one if a respondent indicates that "responsibilities to care for [their] own children or other loved ones," is "a major concern," and zero otherwise.
$CovidRisk_i$	A set of two continuous variables that represent (1) respondent's self-reported probability of being infected with COVID-19 in the next three months and (2) respondent's self-reported probability that, if infected, they will be hospitalized or die.
$GradeLevel_i$	A set of two binary indicator variables that take a value of one if a respondent teaches elementary (K-5th grade) or middle school (6-8th grade) with high school (9-12th grade) as the omitted reference category.
$Demographis_i$	A set of five binary indicator variables that take a value of one if (1) a respondent reports their gender as female, (2) if a respondent identifies as non-white, (3) if a respondent is aged 35-44 years old, (4) if a respondent is aged 45-54 years old, and (5) if a respondent is aged 55 or older with respondents under the age of 35 serving as the reference category.

ACKNOWLEDGEMENTS

We thank the Walton Family Foundation and the Equable Institute for financial support. We have no conflicts of interest associated with this work to disclose.

Correspondence should be directed to: Andrew M. Camp, Annenberg Institute at Brown University, Box 1985, Providence, RI, United States. Email: andrew_camp@brown.edu

REFERENCES

Bacher-Hicks, A., Chi, O. L., & Orellana, A. (2023). Two years later: How COVID-19 has shaped the teacher workforce. *Educational Researcher, (52)4*, 0013189X2311536. https://doi.org/10.3102/0013189X231153659

Barnes, G., Crowe, E., & Schaefer, B. (2007). *The cost of teacher turnover in five school districts: A pilot study*. National Commission on Teaching and America's Future. https://eric.ed.gov/?id=ED497176

Bartanen, B., Grissom, J. A., & Rogers, L. K. (2019). The impacts of principal turnover. *Educational Evaluation and Policy Analysis, 41*(3), 350–374. https://doi.org/10.3102/0162373719855044

Bartanen, B., Husain, A. N., & Liebowitz, D. D. (2022). *Rethinking principal effects on student outcomes*. https://doi.org/10.26300/R5SF-3918

Bastian, K. C., & Fuller, S. (2023). *Educator attrition and hiring in North Carolina Public Schools During the COVID-19 pandemic* (EPIC Insights). Education Policy Initiative at Carolina. https://epic.unc.edu/wp-content/uploads/sites/1268/2023/02/Educator-Attrition-and-Hiring-in-NC.pdf

Birkeland, S. E., & Curtis, R. E. (2006). *Ensuring the support and development of new teachers in the Boston Public Schools: A proposal to improve teacher quality and retention*. Boston Public Schools.

Bruno, P. (2025). Pandemic-era school staff shortages: Evidence from unfilled position data in Illinois. *Education Finance and Policy,* 1–45. https://doi.org/10.1162/edfp_a_00450

Camp, A., Zamarro, G., & McGee, J. B. (2022). *Changes in teachers' mobility and attrition in Arkansas during the first two years of the COVID-19 pandemic.* (EdWorkingPaper: 22-589). Annenberg Institute at Brown University. https://doi.org/10.26300/KHRG-KF39

Camp, A., Zamarro, G., & McGee, J. (2024). Looking back and moving forward: COVID-19's impact on the teacher labor market and implications for the future. *Educational Evaluation and Policy Analysis, 01623737241258184. https://doi.org/10.3102/01623737241258184*

Carbonari, M. V., Davison, M., DeArmond, M., Dewey, D., Dizon-Ross, E., Goldhaber, D., Hashim, A. K., Kane, T. J., McEachin, A., Morton, E., Muroga, A., Patterson, T., & Staiger, D. O. (2024). The impact and implementation of academic interventions during COVID-19: Evidence from the Road to Recovery Project. *AERA Open, 10,* 23328584241281286. https://doi.org/10.1177/23328584241281286

CERRA. (2022). *South Carolina annual educator supply & demand data tables, 2022–23.* Winthrop University. https://www.cerra.org/uploads/1/7/6/8/17684955/supply___demand_data_tables_2022-23.pdf

Dee, T., & Goldhaber, D. (2017). *Understanding and addressing teacher shortages in the United States* (Policy Proposal No. 2017–05; The Hamilton Project). Brookings Institution. https://www.brookings.edu/wp-content/uploads/2017/04/es_20170426_understanding_and_addressing_teacher_shortages_in_us_pp_dee_goldhaber.pdf

DeMatthews, D. E. (2021, October 21). We're facing a looming crisis of principal burnout. *Education Week.* https://www.edweek.org/leadership/opinion-were-facing-a-looming-crisis-of-principal-burnout/2021/10

Demerouti, E., Bakker, A. B., Nachreiner, F., & Schaufeli, W. B. (2001). The job demands-resources model of burnout. *Journal of Applied Psychology*, *86*(3), 499–512. https://doi.org/10.1037/0021-9010.86.3.499

Diliberti, M. K., & Kaufman, J. H. (2020). *Will this school year be another casualty of the pandemic?: Key findings from the American Educator Panels Fall 2020 COVID-19 Surveys.* https://www.rand.org/pubs/research_reports/RRA168-4.html

Diliberti, M. K., Schwartz, H. L., & Grant, D. (2021). *Stress topped the reasons why public school teachers quit, even before COVID-19.* RAND Corporation. https://doi.org/10.7249/RRA1121-2

Fuchsman, D., McGee, J. B., & Zamarro, G. (2023). Teachers' willingness to pay for retirement benefits: A national stated preferences experiment. *Economics of Education Review*, *92*, 102349. https://doi.org/10.1016/j.econedurev.2022.102349

Gershenson, S. (2021). *Identifying and producing effective teachers.* (EdWorkingPaper: 21–351). Annenberg Institute at Brown University. https://doi.org/10.26300/RZSY-7158

Goldberg, E. (2021, April 7). As pandemic upends teaching, fewer students want to pursue it. *The New York Times.* https://www.nytimes.com/2021/03/27/us/covid-school-teaching.html

Goldhaber, D. (2021, May 18). Analysis: COVID-19 raised fears of teacher shortages. But the situation varies from state to state, school to school & subject to subject. *The 74 Million.* https://www.the74million.org/article/analysis-COVID-19-raised-fears-of-teacher-shortages-but-the-situation-varies-from-state-to-state-school-to-school-subject-to-subject/

Goldhaber, D., & Gratz, T. (2022). *School district staffing challenges in a rapidly recovering economy* (CALDER Flash Brief No. 29–0122; CALDER Flash Brief). National Center for Analysis of Longitudinal Data in Education Research. https://caldercenter.org/publications/school-district-staffing-challenges-rapidly-recovering-economy

Goldhaber, D., Kane, T., McEachin, A., Morton, E., Patterson, T., & Staiger, D. (2022). *The consequences of remote and hybrid instruction during the pandemic* (No. 30010). National Bureau of Economic Research. https://doi.org/10.3386/w30010

Goldhaber, D., & Theobald, R. (2022). Teacher attrition and mobility in the pandemic. *Educational Evaluation and Policy Analysis*, 016237372211392. https://doi.org/10.3102/01623737221139285

Goldhaber, D., & Theobald, R. (2023). *Teacher turnover three years into the pandemic era: Evidence from Washington State* (No. 32–0223; CALDER Policy Brief). Center for Analysis of Longitudinal Data in Education Research. https://caldercenter.org/sites/default/files/CALDER%20Policy%20Brief%2032-0223.pdf

Hakanen, J. J., Bakker, A. B., & Schaufeli, W. B. (2006). Burnout and work engagement among teachers. *Journal of School Psychology, 43*(6), 495–513. https://doi.org/10.1016/j.jsp.2005.11.001

Hanushek, E. A., Rivkin, S. G., & Schiman, J. C. (2016). Dynamic effects of teacher turnover on the quality of instruction. *Economics of Education Review*, *55*, 132–148. https://doi.org/10.1016/j.econedurev.2016.08.004

Harris, D. N., & Sass, T. R. (2011). Teacher training, teacher quality and student achievement. *Journal of Public Economics*, *95*(7–8), 798–812. https://doi.org/10.1016/j.jpubeco.2010.11.009

Herman, K. C., Hickmon-Rosa, J., & Reinke, W. M. (2018). Empirically derived profiles of teacher stress, burnout, self-efficacy, and coping and associated student outcomes. *Journal of Positive Behavior Interventions, 20*(2), 90–100. https://doi.org/10.1177/1098300717732066

Herman, K. C., Sebastian, J., Reinke, W. M., & Huang, F. L. (2021). Individual and school predictors of teacher stress, coping, and wellness during the COVID-19 pandemic. *School Psychology*, *36*(6), 483–493. https://doi.org/10.1037/spq0000456

Kraft, M. A., Simon, N. S., & Lyon, M. A. (2021). Sustaining a sense of success: The protective role of teacher working conditions during the COVID-19 pandemic. *Journal of Research on Educational Effectiveness*, *14*(4), 727–769. https://doi.org/10.1080/19345747.2021.1938314

Lavery, L. (2020, December 19). The pandemic is causing teachers to flee the profession. *Salon*. https://www.salon.com/2020/12/19/the-pandemic-is-causing-teachers-to-flee-the-profession/

Madigan, D. J., & Kim, L. E. (2021). Does teacher burnout affect students? A systematic review of its association with academic achievement and student-reported outcomes. *International Journal of Educational Research*, *105*, 101714. https://doi.org/10.1016/j.ijer.2020.101714

Malkus, N. (2020). *Too little, too late: A hard look at spring 2020 remote learning*. American Enterprise Institute. https://www.aei.org/wp-content/uploads/2020/10/Malkus-Too-Little-Too-Late.pdf?x91208

Milanowski, A. T., & Odden, A. R. (2007). *A new approach to the cost of teacher turnover* (Working Paper No. 13). School Finance Redesign Project, Center on Reinventing Public Education.

NCES. (2019). Table 210.30. Mobility of public elementary and secondary teachers, by selected teacher and school characteristics: Selected years, 1987–88 through 2012–13. In *Digest of Education Statistics*. https://nces.ed.gov/programs/digest/d19/tables/dt19_210.30.asp

Nguyen, T. D., Pham, L. D., Crouch, M., & Springer, M. G. (2020). The correlates of teacher turnover: An updated and expanded meta-analysis of the literature. *Educational Research Review, 31*, 100355. https://doi.org/10.1016/j.edurev.2020.100355

Pressley, T., Ha, C., & Learn, E. (2021). Teacher stress and anxiety during COVID-19: An empirical study. *School Psychology*, *36*(5), 367–376. https://doi.org/10.1037/spq0000468

Ronfeldt, M., Loeb, S., & Wyckoff, J. (2013). How teacher turnover harms student achievement. *American Educational Research Journal*, *50*(1), 4–36. https://doi.org/10.3102/0002831212463813

Skaalvik, E. M., & Skaalvik, S. (2010). Teacher self-efficacy and teacher burnout: A study of relations. *Teaching and Teacher Education, 26*(4), 1059–1069. https://doi.org/10.1016/j.tate.2009.11.001

Skaalvik, E. M., & Skaalvik, S. (2020). Teacher burnout: Relations between dimensions of burnout, perceived school context, job satisfaction and motivation for teaching. A longitudinal study. *Teachers and Teaching, 26*(7–8), 602–616. https://doi.org/10.1080/13540602.2021.1913404

Steiner, E. D., & Woo, A. (2021). *Job-related stress threatens the teacher supply: Key findings from the 2021 State of the U.S. Teacher Survey*. RAND Corporation. https://doi.org/10.7249/RRA1108-1

Wiswall, M. (2013). The dynamics of teacher quality. *Journal of Public Economics*, *100*, 61–78. https://doi.org/10.1016/j.jpubeco.2013.01.006

Woo, A., & Steiner, E. D. (2022). *The well-being of secondary school principals one year into the COVID-19 pandemic*. RAND Corporation. https://doi.org/10.7249/RRA827-6

Zamarro, G., Camp, A., Fuchsman, D., & McGee, J. B. (2022). *Understanding how COVID-19 has changed teachers' chances of remaining in the classroom*. (EdWorkingPaper: 22-542). Annenberg Institute at Brown University. https://doi.org/10.26300/2Y0G-BW09

CHAPTER 4

A PERFECT STORM

COVID-19 as a Demotivating Factor Contributing to Teacher Stress, Burnout, and Mental Health

Denisha Jones
Sarah Lawrence College

Brianne Kramer and Clint Broadbent
Southern Utah University

In this chapter, we pull data from the second phase of a mixed-method study examining the impact of COVID-19 on teachers. In a two-month period at the end of 2021 and the beginning of 2022, we administered a survey to 3,982 participants. Following the survey, we conducted nine focus groups and 25 semi-structured interviews. The survey consisted of the Oldenburg Burnout Inventory (OBI), Perceived Stress Scale (PSS), and PHQ-8 (Patient Health Questionnaire depression scale).

Our investigation into how COVID-19 impacted teachers' mental health indicates a significant rise in teacher stress, burnout, and mental health. Data from the PHQ-8 indicated moderate levels of depression across the participants, while data from the OBI found above-average levels of burnout within both subscales of disengage-

Instructional Survival in the Midst of the Perfect Storm:
The Experiences of K–12 Teachers During the COVID-19 Global Pandemic, pages 53–71.

Published under exclusive licence by Emerald Publishing Limited
ISBNs: 978-1-83708-502-6 HB, 978-1-83708-503-3 PB,
978-1-83708-504-0 EPDF, 978-1-83708-505-7 EPUB

ment and exhaustion and a moderate rise in stress levels from the PSS. Data from qualitative questionnaires, focus groups, and interviews support these findings, with participants identifying the following factors as contributing greatly to their mental health: unmanageable increases in workload, inconsistency in school/district policies, decreases in teacher autonomy, and lack of support for students' mental health.

To say that teaching is a stressful profession would be an understatement. Researchers have examined the day to day stresses of teaching and the growth of cumulative stressors brought on by various policy and reform efforts (Burke & Greenglass, 1996; Evers et al., 2004; Harmsen et al., 2018; Johnson et al., 2005; Kyriacou, 2001; Wiley, 2000). Though teacher stress is not a new phenomenon, it did increase greatly in the three years following the onset of the COVID-19 global pandemic. As schools across the country closed and switched to remote, virtual, and hybrid formats, teachers were forced to adapt to new teaching environments, to embrace new safety protocols including masking and social distancing, and to continue educating students while living with the fear that they or their family could get sick and die.

During the first year of the pandemic, 2019–2020, some teachers reported higher levels of stress and reduced levels of well-being (Chan et al., 2021), while other studies found less reports of stress during the lockdown and higher levels of coping which may be attributed to the lack of in-person teaching (Herman et al., 2021). In the spring of 2020, new sources of stress developed as schools globally closed and instruction shifted to remote formats including concerns on being a caregiver during remote instruction, worrying about students and their families, and the uncertainty regarding the future of teaching (Hirshberg et al., 2023; Parthasarathy et al., 2022; Pressley et al., 2021). These new stressors differed from previous sources of teacher stress including feeling ineffective with students (Blase, 1982) and low support from parents and the community (Grayson & Alvarez, 2007) which often coincided with a correlation between high levels of burnout and exhaustion.

The 2020–2021 school year saw a resurgence in teacher anxiety and stress as school plans for reopening changed rapidly and teachers' concern over their health and the health of their families were often at odds with expectations that were needed a return to normal. As some schools moved forward with plans to reopen but were then forced to enact hybrid models because many teachers refused to return to in-person teaching, the public support for teachers in the spring 2020 quickly dissipated as the public blamed them for not wanting to do their job (Nerlino, 2023). Given how COVID-19 was transmitted, teachers had an increased risk of infection. Based on a CDC definition, 42% to 54.1% "of all school employees met the CDC definition for being at increased risk for severe COVID-19..." and 63.2% to 71.9% lived with someone at high risk for severe COVID-19 if infected (Selden et al., 2020, p. 6). Teacher safety had been a growing concern due to the rise in school-based gun violence (Fink, 2018; Gewertz, 2022); however, the global pandemic forced teachers to fear placing their loved ones in danger if they were exposed in the classroom.

STATEMENT OF THE PROBLEM

In this chapter, we propose a framework for understanding how the working conditions for teachers associated with COVID-19 increased teacher stress, which lead to higher levels of demotivation, and an increase in teacher shortages across the country. We argue that the stress of teaching and living during a global pandemic was akin to adding a heavy burden on top of an already unsustainable profession, resulting in the crumbling of an infrastructure barely held together. Moreover, we seek to not only contribute to the growing literature on teacher stress, burnout, and mental health, but to produce new narratives that expand our understanding of these well-studied phenomena. Though most research focuses on teacher burnout as something within their locus of control to correct through self-care and setting better boundaries, we discuss how the pandemic led to a host of external factors that altered the working conditions and context of teaching causing demoralization (Santoro, 2018) and demotivation (Dörnyei & Ushioda, 2021).

As teachers and educators, we are committed to exploring strategies for recruiting, preparing, and retaining excellent teachers. As scholars, we recognize a host of factors that make teaching challenging and that impact the likelihood that all students will spend each year of compulsory schooling working with a competent and dedicated adult. Thus, we remain troubled by the increase in teacher attrition and the appearance of a mass exodus of teachers in the aftermath of a global pandemic. We use our findings from a two-phase mixed methodological study on the impact of COVID-19 on teachers to generate a theory on how an increase in stress and burnout from COVID-19 impacted teachers' motivation and contributed to the growing teacher shortage.

REVIEW OF THE LITERATURE

To ground our study in the current literature, we begin with an exploration of how teacher stress and burnout developed prior to the global pandemic. By examining earlier work on job satisfaction and motivation, we seek to provide a clear understanding of the context of teaching and the impact that it had on teachers' mental health and decisions to leave the profession. We then examine current research findings on teacher stress and anxiety during the initial onset of the pandemic and the first year of pandemic teaching. Next we review the research on motivation and demotivation in relation to traditional models of teacher burnout to explore how the concept of demoralization may provide a more nuanced framework for understanding the role of COVID-19 in pushing teachers out of the profession. We argue that an inherently stressful job combined with an increase in an unsustainable workload, decrease in autonomy, and new health and safety fears created the perfect storm forcing many teachers to evacuate the field of education.

Job Demands and Resources

Burnout was originally conceived as a process where workers feel incapable of achieving a sense of accomplishment as a result of experiencing high levels of emotional exhaustion and becoming detached and cynical (Demerouti et al., 2001; Maslach et al., 1996). Despite believing that burnout was limited to those working in human services, Demerouti and her colleagues (2001) expanded the JD-R (job demands-resources) model to other stressful professions that included high job demands and limited job resources. The JD-R model explores how an increase in job demands (i.e., workload, contact with recipients, and the physical environment) leads to exhaustion while simultaneously job resources (i.e., rewards, security, and support) are depleted leading to disengagement (Demerouti et al., 2001; Skaalvik & Skaalvik, 2015, 2018). "The JD-R model assumes that job demands are most predictive of feelings of exhaustion, whereas lacking job resources is most predictive of disengagement from work" (Demerouti et al., 2001, p. 502).

Skaalvik and Skaalvik (2018) examined the relationship between perceived job demands and job resources on teacher motivation to leave the profession, teacher well-being, and engagement in 760 teachers from Norway. Three measures of job demands were: time pressure, discipline problems, and low student motivation. Job resources included supportive colleagues, supervisory support, collective school culture, and value consonance. Emotional exhaustion, depressed mood, and psychosomatic responses were used to measure teacher well-being. Engagement and motivation to leave the teaching profession were measured directly with established scales. To determine the association between job demands, job resources, engagement, and motivation, on teacher well-being, they analyzed two models with demands and resources as primary and secondary factors. "Analysis of job demands and job resources as second order factors…revealed that the job demands included in the study strongly predicted lower teacher well-being, whereas the job resources that we included moderately predicted higher well-being. The job resources were also directly associated with engagement" (Skaalvik & Skaalvik, 2018, p. 1267).

Their findings were supportive of prior research that job demands were more strongly related to teacher well-being than job resources. When job resources and demands were analyzed as secondary factors, teacher well-being was mediated through an association between engagement and job demands. Skaalvik and Skaalvik (2018) offer the following reasoning for why teacher engagement is important for teacher well-being.

> A possible explanation is that job demands or stressful working environments lead to increased emotional exhaustion, depressed mood, and psychosomatic responses which again deprive teachers of their engagement. Underlying this examination is the understanding that it is not job demands in themselves that deprive teachers of

> their engagement, but job demands that the individual teacher is not able to cope with. (p. 1267)

Job resources and demands were analyzed as primary factors to explore which had a stronger association with engagement, teacher well-being, and desire to leave the profession. Of the job demands, time-pressure greatly predicted lower levels of teacher well-being while student motivation and discipline had a weak relationship, supporting their previous findings that emotional exhaustion more often resulted from time-pressure than behavior issues.

Skaalvik and Skaalvik (2018) previously defined value consonance as an alignment between the teacher's values and the norms of the school. In the primary factor model, only value consonance and relationships with colleagues had a strong association with teacher well-being. They note that value consonance was the only resource directly and indirectly related to engagement and suggest a hypothesis for additional research where "value consonance is a particularly important job resource which may increase teacher well-being as well as engagement and motivation to continuing in the teaching profession" (Skaalvik & Skaalvik, 2018, p 1269).

Teacher Stress During COVID-19

Given the multitude of changes that teachers faced as the world dealt with a deadly pandemic, many studies examined teacher stress and anxiety in the spring of 2020 and the 2020–2021 school year. Herman et al. (2021) compared survey data from 639 teachers completed in the Fall of 2019 and May of 2020. They found that during the initial months of the pandemic when online instruction was not yet required and student accountability was limited, teachers were better able to cope and as a result had lower levels of stress. They suggest that for many teachers, the lack of daily in-person instruction could have led to lower levels of reported job stress combined with higher levels of coping when student instruction was limited to reviews and make-up work only. They also found that confidence in handling student behavior was the greatest predictor of teacher health outcomes and school climate before the pandemic, while disciplinary procedures and student support consistently predicted teacher health outcomes.

Pressley et al. (2021) surveyed 329 elementary teachers in October of 2020 to identify changes in teachers' anxiety during the early parts of the 2020–2021 school year. Though 39% of teachers reported a decrease in anxiety after one month of returning to school, those who did experience an increase in anxiety identified online instruction as the greatest cause, while district technology and communicating with parents also contributed to their anxiety. As expected, they found a positive correlation between teachers' stress and anxiety from COVID-19. They note how, "these results show that various anxiety factors in rapidly changing teaching environments in pandemic situations can be linked to teachers' high-stress levels" (Pressley et al., 2021, p. 371).

In Spain, researchers found considerable higher levels of teacher stress at the beginning of 2020–2021. Of the 1633 teachers who completed the survey, 50.6% reported they were stressed, with 16.1% reporting mild stress, 15.9% reporting moderate stress, 14.1% reporting severe stress, and 4.5% reporting extremely severe stress (Ozamiz-Etxebarria et al., 2021, p. 4). They noted how teachers with school-age children at home reported higher levels of stress and had to deal with both their return to in-person instruction and their child's return to school. In England, a narrative life story interview of 24 teachers comparing their experiences eleven weeks into the lockdown with their reports six weeks earlier, identified a shift in their concerns from concern for vulnerable people to worry for students and from finding a way to practical concerns (Kim et al., 2021). Three of the six themes, uncertainty, practical concerns, and worry for pupils, provide important insight into how teaching during the pandemic impacted teachers' need for autonomy and challenged their feelings of competence.

Motivation, Demotivation, and Demoralization

The relationship between teacher stress, burnout, and motivation has been examined in different aspects of teacher education research. In 1982, Farber administered a survey to 398 New York public school teachers to examine aspects of teaching that were motivating and those that were stressful to teachers. Teachers in this study identified feeling involved with and sensitive to the needs of students as the greatest source of their satisfaction with good interpersonal relationships with colleagues and ability to spend time with friends and family and have energy for activities outside of school as additional sources of satisfaction. They identified increased paperwork demands, few opportunities for professional advancement, and meetings with administrators that were unhelpful in addressing their problems as major sources of their stress (Farber, 1982). When asked "I have felt that if I had to do it all over, I would still choose to be a teacher," only 30.4% said they frequently felt that way, while 21% said never, and 48% said never or only rarely (Farber, 1982, p. 16).

> The results of the present study, however, suggest that feelings of burnout among teachers do significantly covary with lack of commitment to the teaching profession and to a lack of satisfaction in working with students. Therefore, although we still do not know whether teachers work less hard and less effectively as a result of burnout, the present data suggest that burnout significantly lessens teachers' motivation to continue in the profession and lessens the basic satisfaction inherent in the student-teacher relationship. (Farber, 1982, p. 13)

What is needed is a more nuanced understanding of the point in which teacher stress, which to a certain extent is normal, becomes a demotivating factor.

Motivation is an important factor for enhancing learning by examining how teacher motivation influences student motivation. Teacher motivation is often studied to better understand what factors support teacher retention in an effort to stem the tide of teacher attrition. Various models of teacher motivation examine how success in teaching is mediated by whether teachers believe their ability is internally or externally controlled (Neves de Jesus & Lens, 2005). Teachers are believed to enter the profession with high levels of intrinsic motivation (Dinham & Scott, 2000; Dörnyei & Ushioda, 2021; Han & Yin, 2016; Sinclair, 2008); however, they often lack sustaining motivation needed for retention (Han & Yin, 2016), or experience demotivation (Dörnyei & Ushioda, 2021).

In their critical review of teacher motivation research, Han and Yin (2016) listed motivating factors as autonomy to choose teaching materials and curriculum resources, freedom to organize the classroom and make discipline decisions, institutional support, and positive relationships with colleagues. Higher levels of professional stress and negative influences from particular events or social environment factors were found to undermine teacher motivation. Dörnyei and Ushioda (2021) distinguish demotivation as more than the opposite of motivation and not equivalent to the absence of motivation which is known as amotivation. Instead, they define demotivation as "*...a negative process that reduces or diminishes a person's motivation in relation to a behavioural intention or ongoing action*" (Dörnyei & Ushioda, 2021, p. 140, emphasis in the original). In their previous research, they identified a decline in teacher autonomy brought on by an increase in reforms, a decrease in teacher effectiveness resulting from a lack of preparedness, the increasingly stressful nature of teaching, an unfulfilling career structure, limited opportunities for intellectual growth, and the repetitive nature of the content, as sources of demotivation (Dörnyei & Ushioda, 2011, as cited in Han & Yin, 2016).

Santoro (2018) described demoralization as "the inability to access the moral rewards offered and expected in teaching" and provided a useful distinction from burnout that often focuses on a problem in the teacher instead of a problem with teaching (p. 8). Believing that teachers are motivated from a desire to enact values and work in alignment with their moral center, Santoro (2018) argued that demoralization was a result of teachers realizing this was no longer possible and feeling as though their moral expectations were in jeopardy, thus they had no choice but to quit. She notes how

> For teachers experiencing demoralization, the moral dilemma is not what they should do to be a good teacher, but that they cannot do what they believe a good teacher should do in the face of policies, mandates, or institutional norms. The source of the problem is the dissonance between educators' moral centers and the conditions in which they teach. (Santoro, 2018, p. 45, emphasis in the original)

The concept of demoralization helps to understand how a change in the source of stress that prevents teachers from experiencing motivation resulting in demotivation, can alter a teacher's ability to stay in the profession.

Teacher well-being is impacted by teacher stress which results from an increase in exhaustion and disengagement. If teachers believe the source of their stress is outside of their control and brought on from an external factor, over time the depletion of their motivation to teach leads to demotivation. When teachers feel that what they are being asked to do violates their morals they experience demoralization and often feel as though the only solution is to leave the classroom or the profession. Teaching has always been stressful and teachers have constantly faced challenges in a profession that is feminized, underpaid, and devalued by society. However, as millions of people died from the spread of a deadly disease, the changes to the teaching profession combined with health and safety fears for themselves and loved ones, left many teachers highly stressed and demotivated. As the teaching profession faced new attacks against mask mandates, calls to ban books, and legislative limits on teachers' ability to teach certain topics, they were thrust on the path to demoralization.

METHODS

In this chapter, we pull data from the second phase of a mixed-method study examining the impact of COVID-19 on teachers. For the first phase, we conducted an exploratory mixed-methods study (1,081 survey responses in December 2020 and 22 interviews of K–12 teachers across the US in January-February of 2021) on how teachers adapted to instructional changes during the Spring of 2020 and dealt with reopening of schools during the 2020–2021 school year.

The second phase of our study aimed to explore teacher burnout and stress during the pandemic. The research questions that guided this phase were:

1. Are teachers reporting higher than normal levels of stress and burnout?
2. How are stress and burnout affecting teachers' professional and personal lives?

This time we recruited 3,982 survey participants from December to January of 2021 through teacher unions and teachers' groups on social media. Participants came from all 50 states; however, this time, we had a more diverse sample (83.4% identified as white) though still primarily female (87.7% female). We recognize that this sample of participants is slightly more White and female than the current teaching population, which may have occurred based on the population of teachers who regularly engaged with the organizations in which the survey was posted.

The survey was developed in Qualtrics and distributed nationwide. To measure depression, we used the Personal Health Questionnaire (PHQ-8), an 8-item questionnaire with scores ranging from zero to twenty-four. High scores are associated with higher levels of depression. The PHQ-8 has shown to be valid and reliable in various demographic and geographic contexts (Lua et al., 2022). Burnout was measured using the Oldenburg Burnout Inventory (OLBI), which has measures exhaustion (8 items) and disengagement (8 items) using a 4-point Likert scale. Higher scores indicating higher levels of burnout in respondents. The OLBI is validated for different professions and countries (Halbesleben & Demerouti,

2005). Perceived stress was measured using the Perceived Stress Scale (PSS), the 10-item version was used in this study which has scores ranging from 0 to 40 with higher scores indicating higher levels of perceived stress. The PSS has been validated extensively throughout the years (Baik et al., 2019). One hundred ninety-five participants completed another Qualtrics questionnaire collecting brief written explanations of their experiences with burnout and stress and indicated their willingness to sit for focus groups and/or interviews.

In June and July of 2022, we conducted nine focus groups using Zoom with a total of 37 participants and 35 individual interviews. We utilized a grounded theory approach to identify themes that emerged from the research. The initial written responses of participants were analyzed using open coding to indicate any unit of data relevant to the study. Once the focus groups and interviews were completed, we conducted open coding on the data. Then we utilized axial coding to refine categories and used selective coding to create an overall hypothesis.

Through our grounded theory analysis of the data, we identified the following three theoretical codes and one hypothesis.

Theoretical Code 1: An increase in workload combined with fears associated with COVID caused an increase in exhaustion, anxiety, and stress.

Theoretical Code 2: An increase in anxiety and stress led to an increase in disengagement.

Theoretical Code 3: Exhaustion and disengagement (traditionally used to measure burnout) combined with external factors (lack of control and fear) contributed to the process of teachers being demotivated.

Hypothesis: COVID increased teacher stress, burnout, and poor mental health, intensifying the process of demotivation and exodus from the profession.

We now share findings from the quantitative and qualitative data to provide support for the theoretical codes and hypothesis.

QUANTITATIVE FINDINGS

Addressing the question: Are teachers reporting higher than normal levels of stress and burnout?, the three major aspects of mental health in the current study were depression, perceived stress and burnout. For depression, the almost 4,000 sample population had a PHQ-8 average total of 11.35 (SD 5.99). According to the measure this falls into the "moderate" severity with a recommendation to consider counseling and psychopharmacology.

Perceived stress was measured using the perceived stress scale (PSS) yielding an average total score of 23.79 (SD 6.61). This score was well into the moderate stress level according to the scoring of the measure and approaching the cutoff for high (27) indicating a moderately high level of stress/distress within the sample of teachers who responded.

Lastly, burnout was measured using the Oldenburg Burnout Inventory (OBI). The OBI total was 47.22 (SD 6.82). The average score of the two subscales ranging from 1–4, exhaustion 3.14/4 (SD .456) and disengagement 2.76/4 (SD .484). Exploring the relationship between the two variables, a correlation showed a strong but discriminate relationship $r(3029) = .663$, $p < .001$. While no cutoffs are provided for the measure, the average scores for exhaustion (2.78, SD= .64) were elevated than a general population of working adults (Halbesleben & Demerouti, 2005) while disengagement was slightly lower than average (2.99, SD= .61).

QUALITATIVE FINDINGS

The written responses, focus groups, and interviews provided clear evidence of how the pandemic increased teacher stress, burnout, and poor mental health. Teachers became demotivated and some chose to leave the profession, while others began to explore other options in preparation to leave teaching. Others chose to stay in the profession because they were so far entrenched in the retirement and salary scale, they could not afford to leave.

Teachers described exponential increases in their workloads during the pandemic. Everyone was online from mid-March until the end of the 2019–2020 SY; however, there were a variety of modalities used in the 2020–2021 school year that added to teachers' workloads. Some schools utilized face-to-face classes full-time while following various state mandates and protocols. Others used a hybrid approach of some kind, which consisted of alternating groups of students throughout the week with some students online full-time. Some districts also utilized synchronous remote online instruction or asynchronous online instruction. Districts also cycled through all of these modalities at different points during the school year. During a focus group session, Participant 21 stated:

> [In] the 2020–2021 school year, we did have an option where students could choose online or hybrid learning, or in-person learning, and we as teachers were expected to facilitate all three. So I had some students in-person all day, some students online all day, and some students who were half and half. We were tasked with figuring it out for all three types of learners. That was a horrendous mistake.

Participants discussed feeling constantly burned out due to the way they were now required to teach during this year. So many discussed feeling exhausted and overwhelmed because they were putting in more hours planning than ever before. Participant 185 stated: "I am on all day long. Every minute of the day, doing, doing, doing. Teaching is the constant experience of trauma— my own and my students." Another increase in teacher workload was the amount of student needs that increased during this time. Teachers consistently had to work with students who were quarantined or out sick for longer amounts of time than was typical prior to the pandemic. Many participants found this constant process of catch-up exhausting as well. This made many participants feel that they were not being good teachers or providing students what they needed.

As anxiety and stress increased for teachers during the pandemic, they became increasingly disengaged with their classroom, students, and even their own families. Participant 3 stated: "I no longer get excited about delivering instruction or seeing students perform." Participant 99 added, "Every day felt like slogging through whatever I had to slog through just to mark the day off the calendar." Teachers' disengagement with the profession they once loved was clear in the comments the participants provided. One shocking comment came from a veteran educator who stated how much she loved her job prior to the pandemic. Participant 27 stated: "I'm tired and really don't care about other people's children and don't care what they are going through." Other participants described their feelings as 'combat fatigue' or moral injury in order to provide a greater context to their experiences. This disengagement also created divides between colleagues who once worked collaboratively. Participant 56 stated:

> My colleagues are clearly in various stages of mental health struggles themselves. Everyone is responding differently, but we're not there for each other because we are busy being isolated, disconnected, emotional, angry, etc. No one really has more energy for anything but their own needs.

In addition to their feelings of disengagement at work, many participants discussed the disconnect at home while they tended primarily to work during this time of survival. Participant 158 described this disconnect at home as: "I feel as though I can either be human or be a teacher, but there is not room for both." Participant 93 stated: "I just don't have the drive and ability to do anything after work anymore. All my energy— mental and physical goes into doing my job for my students." Due to the increased pressures and disengagement, many participants discussed going on medication for mental health issues or seeking out a therapist for the first time in their lives. Several participants indicated they were aware of their disengagement, but they did not know what would make these feelings improve. Exhaustion and disengagement became clear with participants who did not have autonomy or who were fearful of different aspects of teaching during the pandemic, which led to demotivation.

DISCUSSION

Through our analysis of the data, we found burnout to be an inadequate description of what many teachers are experiencing as a result of teaching during a global pandemic. Yes, teachers are exhausted and disengaged which are the two key factors used to measure burnout; however, burnout implies that the ability to fix the situation remains within the control of the individual. Teachers are constantly being told to practice self-care, set better boundaries between work and school, and get more rest as solutions for dealing with burnout. What these messages fail to recognize is when the source of the stress is not something the teachers can control, self-care becomes nothing more than a cheery slogan.

Can practicing self-care reduce their workload, provide needed support for students' mental health, and produce the autonomy needed to feel in control and motivated in the classroom? Taking care of your physical and mental health through mindfulness, sleep, nutrition, and exercise are important tools for dealing with stressful situations. Nonetheless, they are insufficient solutions for teachers whose stress levels have resulted in demotivation and demoralization. Teachers had no control over school reopening plans, district masking policies, whether schools would implement hybrid, online, or in-person instruction, or policies for dealing with the spread of COVID-19. The uncertainty of how schools would move forward forced many teachers to adapt their plans and alter their schedules on very short notice. At the same time, the initial public support for teachers during the early days of quarantine quickly shifted as a societal push to return to normal meant that teachers should be willing to return to unsafe schools and risk their personal health.

Although most schools and districts returned to in-person instruction during the 2021–2022 school year, the supposed return to normal never materialized. During the focus groups, we asked our participants to discuss the differences between teaching during 2021–2022 as compared to 2020–2021 with a focus on which year was more stressful and why. We believed the end of hybrid instruction and online teaching would have resulted in a decline in the stress reported during the 2020–2021 school year, but for the majority of our participants, the return to full time in-person instruction made the 2021–2022 school year more stressful than the previous school year. Many participants noted the challenges of helping students get back into learning mode after spending so much time learning at home as one of the major causes of stress. We heard countless stories of how "students forgot how to student" and lacked many needed social skills, likely from wearing masks and not participating in the school culture for so long. This resulted in an increase in workload for teachers having to re-norm students, cover missed content, and ensure that they were meeting the current standards. Thus, the stress that should have dissipated as schools "returned to normal" intensified for many teachers.

As if trying to survive during a global pandemic was not enough, teachers and schools became the center of conservative attacks against teaching for racial and gender justice. Labeling this work as "Critical Race Theory/CRT" and "divisive," state legislators began passing laws to ban teaching about race and racism (TRUTH BE TOLD, n.d.), sexual orientation, and gender identity (Diaz, 2022), while local communities saw a resurgence of book banning efforts by conservative parents (Friedman & Johnson, 2022). Florida sought to punish teachers who violated the new laws with suspension of their license and felony charges (Salam, 2023), while Virginia set up a hotline to report teachers who violated the new state policies against teaching CRT (Sands, 2022). The narrative quickly made it clear that teachers were to blame for wanting to enact a culturally relevant curriculum and teach the truth about racial injustice, and they could not be trusted to select their own curriculum materials without parental input and approval.

When asked about the impact book banning and anti-CRT legislation had on our participants, most were fortunate not to have direct experience, but were concerned that it was happening to educators they knew and communities nearby. A few were directly targeted as their work as Ethnic Studies teachers was seen as pushing CRT and books they used in the classroom were now being banned. These attacks on teachers who are in the midst of experiencing increasing levels of stress are likely to serve as fodder for demotivation and demoralization to occur. Participant 223 put it this way

> Educators are just over it. They're just they're walking away. Um, and I hope it doesn't come to this. But I mean, it could very well like nuff people leave the system, the system's gonna collapse, that might be a great thing and then we can rebuild it. But I know a lot of really talented educators who are just leaving because they can't. Can't handle it.

Given the widespread reports of a worsening teacher shortage at the start of the 2022–2023 school year, one must ask how much of an impact COVID-19 had on teacher attrition. Schmitt and deCourcy (2022) argued that the pandemic exacerbated the ongoing shortage of teachers emphasizing, "that the current shortage is generally not the result of an insufficient number of potentially qualified teachers. The shortage is, instead, a shortfall in the number of qualified teachers willing to work at current wages and under current working conditions" (p. 2). Noting the high levels of job-related stress reported by teachers after the onset of COVID-19, they point out how the teacher shortage caused an increase in workload which resulted in an increase in stress for those still in the classroom. Many of our participants identified the need to cover for teachers out sick and the lack of substitutes as sources of increased stress during the 2021–2022 school year.

Unfortunately, some predict the teacher shortage will get worse, causing many to worry that the current educational system is unsustainable. Querolo et al. (2022) report that 20% of teachers plan on quitting in the next two years and that there is growth of a new industry catering to those looking for new career prospects after leaving teaching behind. Others argue that claims of leaving the profession made by teachers do not necessarily result in an exodus (Nguyen et al., 2022) and that teacher shortages are localized and not wide-spread (Edwards et al., 2023). Nonetheless, even if we are moving into a post-pandemic era, the impact of COVID-19 will continue to be felt without federal, state, and local efforts to address the challenges and offer support to teachers.

IMPLICATIONS FOR THE FUTURE

The pandemic will likely have ongoing effects on the teaching profession and education in general. Our study found that teachers were poised to leave the field in the next five years for a variety of reasons. Many teachers were already feeling demotivated prior to the pandemic due to everyday stressors and a lack of autonomy in their profession. The pandemic increased these stressors, added new ones, and also increased the lack of autonomy. Because of these experiences, teachers will continue to leave the field as they create new opportunities for themselves. Many teachers discussed their 'side hustles' they began during the pandemic, while others discussed how they were going back to college to seek out degrees outside of education. This continued exodus of teachers may not be to the extent that was seen during and immediately after the primary years of the pandemic; however, this slow trickle of educators leaving the field will negatively impact schools across the United States. Given the ongoing concerns with teacher shortages prior to the pandemic in rural areas (Oyen & Schweinle, 2021) and urban areas (Garcia & Weiss, 2019), they are likely to feel the brunt of this teacher shortage. Teachers who remain in the profession may change districts in search of school districts who provide more autonomy, support, and collaboration time for their teachers. Many of these teachers will leave urban/city and rural schools in search of more desirable positions in suburban schools. While some states have created incentives for teachers to stay in the field, such as bonuses, increases to retirement, and salary increases, not all states have worked to retain teachers.

Another large effect of the pandemic on the profession is the lack of high school students who are choosing education as their field of study in college. Colleges of education have seen a large downturn of students majoring in teacher education in the last decade, which is also contributing to the teacher shortage. Students see the lack of prestige for teaching as a profession combined with low pay and a decline in teacher satisfaction which has led to a record low interest in the profession (Ingram, 2023). Furthermore, many would-be teachers are being counseled out of the field by their own teachers who have consistently weathered these attacks.

Additional research needs to be conducted into current teachers' experiences in the field. Current attacks on the curriculum, book banning, and 'divisive content' directly impact teachers' work with students. These bills work to limit teacher autonomy in the classroom and may require teachers to change their entire curriculum to satisfy a very small minority. Teacher autonomy during the pandemic and after also needs to be further investigated. While some teachers in our study indicated that they had autonomy to make decisions for their curriculum, teaching, and managing students during the pandemic, most teachers experienced the opposite. Another opportunity for further study is teachers' experiences with students in the 2021–2022 school year and after. In the aftermath of a collective trauma, students and teachers returned to school changed. Teachers have expressed witnessing student behaviors never before seen, along with a general lack of empathy, caring, and motivation.

RECOMMENDATIONS AND CONCLUSION

There are several challenges and opportunities for state legislatures, boards of education, and local school districts in order to assist teachers and to ameliorate the demotivation that many are experiencing. First, teachers' needs must be met. Administrators and teachers need to be working together to solve issues in the schools. Teachers are with students all day, so their knowledge and perspective on solving problems within the schools should be respected and utilized. Teachers also need more time to plan curriculum, grade, and to attend professional development opportunities. Those who worked a hybrid schedule during the pandemic who only had students in the classroom four days a week explained how helpful this was in planning quality lessons and collaborating with peers or PLCs. This may point to the desire for four-day school weeks in order to best serve students and to provide teachers with the planning time that they need. In the next few years, districts may want to hold off on making sweeping changes to curriculum and school structure. Too many teachers were expected to learn state-imposed or district-imposed curricular or system changes during the pandemic that were not related to pandemic needs. These changes led to more work for teachers and too much confusion for students. Teachers also need more support for students. As students continue to exhibit the trauma that they experienced during and/or prior to the pandemic, teachers need increased administrative and parental support that assists in the teachers' work with students. Local district officials can also help teachers by shielding them from parent and community attacks. Teachers' working conditions are students' learning conditions, so teachers' needs must be a priority for local district officials.

Teacher retention must be a key issue for federal, state, and local leaders moving forward. While much attention is being provided to attract new teachers to the field, working to retain current teachers will go much farther. In order to attract and retain teachers, the federal government may consider providing additional grants for teachers who remain in the profession for five years. Providing low- or no-interest student loans with shorter Public Service Loan Forgiveness time frames and much lower income caps would also serve to attract new teachers and to retain current teachers. At the state level, legislators should increase teacher salaries. Teachers know the profession is not one of the most highest-paid fields, but in many states, the credentialed career does not garner a livable wage for a family. Increasing retirement contributions would also retain educators. As many states increase individuals' contributions, increase qualifying years, and reduce monthly payment amounts, this leads teachers to leave the profession since they will not see the pensions that they were once promised. States should also improve the healthcare benefits and work to reduce costs for teachers. Local school districts should champion all of these changes for the benefit of their teachers, rather than simply accepting the paltry packages that states offer.

While all of these opportunities present challenges, we owe it to our teachers to change the profession to be one that is respected, properly compensated, and autonomous. Until these changes are made, we will continue to see demotivated teachers who want to leave the profession.

NOTES

There is no funding associated with this work. There are no conflicts of interest with this work.

Correspondence concerning this article should be addressed to Denisha Jones, Sarah Lawrence College 1 Mead Way Bronxville, NY 10708.

REFERENCES

Baik, S. H., Fox, R. S., Mills, S. D., Roesch, S. C., Sadler, G. R., Klonoff, E. A., & Malcarne, V. L. (2019). Reliability and validity of the Perceived Stress Scale-10 in Hispanic Americans with English or Spanish language preference. *Journal of Health Psychology, 24*(5), 628–639. https://doi.org/10.1177/1359105316684938

Blase, J. J. (1982). A social-psychological grounded theory of teacher stress and burnout. *Educational Administration, 18*(4), 92–113.

Burke, R. J., & Greenglass, E. R. (1996). Work stress, social support, psychological burnout and emotional and physical well-being among teachers. *Psychology, Health & Medicine, 1*, 193–205.

Chan, M., Sharkey, J. D., Lawrie, S. I., Arch, D. A. N., & Nylund-Gibson, K. (2021). Elementary school teacher well-being and supportive measures amid COVID-19: An exploratory study. *School Psychology, 36*(6), 533–545. DOI: 10.1037/spq0000441

Demerouti, E., Bakker, A. B., Nachreiner, F., & Schaufeli, W. B. (2001). The job demands–resource model of burnout. *Journal of Applied Psychology, 86*(3), 499–512. https://doi. org/10.1037//0021-9010.86.3.499

Diaz, J. (2022, March 8). *Florida's governor signs controversial law opponents dubbed "Don't Say Gay"*. National Public Radio. https://www.npr.org/2022/03/28/1089221657/dont-say-gay-florida-desantis

Dinham, S., & Scott, C. (2000). Moving into the third, outer domain of teacher satisfaction. *Journal of Educational Administration, 38*(4), 379–396. http://dx.doi.org/10.1108/09578230010373633

Dörnyei, Z., & Ushioda, E. (2021). *Teaching and researching motivation* (3rd ed.). Routledge.

Edwards, D., Kraft, M. A., Christian, A., & Candelaria, C. A. (2023). *Teacher shortages: A unifying framework for understanding and predicting vacancies. Is there a journal or anything for this one?* https://doi.org/10.26300/8T5B-2302

Evers, W. J. G., Tomic, W., & Brouwers, A. (2004). Burnout among teachers: Students' and teachers' perceptions compared. *School Psychology International, 25*, 131–148.

Farber, B. A. (1982). *Stress and burnout: Implications for teacher motivation*. Paper presented at the annual meeting of the American Educational Research Association, New York.

Fink, J. (2018, December 6). *What do teachers really think about gun violence in schools?* We Are Teachers. https://www.weareteachers.com/gun-violence-in-schools/

Friedman, J., & Johnson, N. F. (2022). *Banned in the USA: The growing movement to censor books in schools.* Pen America 100. https://pen.org/report/banned-usa-growing-movement-to-censor-books-in-schools/

Garcia, E., & Weiss, E. (2019, March 26). *The teacher shortage is real, large and growing, and worse than we thought: The first report in "the perfect storm in the teacher labor market" series.* Economic Policy Institute. https://www.epi.org/publication/the-teacher-shortage-is-real-large-and-growing-and-worse-than-we-thought-the-first-report-in-the-perfect-storm-in-the-teacher-labor-market-series/

Gewertz, C. (2022, July 12). "The world feels less stable": Educators' sense of school safety right now. *Education Week.* https://www.edweek.org/leadership/the-world-feels-less-stable-educators-sense-of-school-safety-right-now/2022/06

Grayson, J. L., & Alvarez, H. K. (2007). School climate factors relating to teacher burnout: A mediator model. *Teaching and Teacher Education, 24,* 1349–1363. DOI: 10.1016/j.tate.2007.06.005

Halbesleben, J. R. B., & Demerouti, E. (2005). The construct validity of an alternative measure of burnout: Investigating the English translation of the Oldenburg Burnout Inventory. *Work & Stress, 19*(3), 208–220, DOI: 10.1080/02678370500340728

Han, J., & Yin, H. (2016). Teacher motivation: Definition, research development and implications for teachers. *Cogent Education, 3*(1), 1–18. DOI: 10.1080/2331186X.2016.1217819

Harmsen, R., Helms-Lorenz, M., Maulana, R., & van Veen, K. (2018). The relationship between beginning teachers' stress causes, stress responses, teaching behaviour and attrition. *Teachers and Teaching: Theory and Practice, 24*(6), 626–643. https://doi.org/10.1080/13540602.2018.1465404

Herman, K. C., Sebastian, J., Reinke, W. M., & Huang, F. L. (2021). Individual and school predictors of teacher stress, coping, and wellness during the COVID-19 pandemic. *School Psychology, 36*(6), 483–493. https://doi.org/10.1037/spq0000456

Hirshberg, M. J., Davidson, R. J., & Goldberg, S. B. (2023). Educators are not alright: Mental health during COVID-19. *Educational Researcher, 52*(1), 48–52. DOI: 10.3102/00131189X221142595

Ingram, N. (2023, January 18). *Is the teaching profession in decline?* ASCD. https://www.ascd.org/blogs/is-the-teaching-profession-in-decline

Johnson, S., Cooper, C., Cartwright, S., Donald, I., Taylor, P., & Millet, C. (2005). The experience of work-related stress across occupations. *Journal of Managerial Psychology, 20,* 178–187. http://doi.org/10.1108/02683940510579803

Kim, L. E., Leary, R., & Asbury, K. (2021). Teachers' narratives during COVID-19 partial school reopenings: An exploratory study. *Educational Research, 63*(2), 244–260. DOI 10.1080/00131881.2021.1918014

Kyriacou, C. (2001). Teacher stress: Directions for future research. *Educational Review, 53*(1), 27–35. http://doi.org/10.1080.00131910120033628

Lua, I., Freitas, K. S., Teixeira, J. R. B., Reichenheim, M. E., Almeida, M. M. G., & Araújo, T. M. (2022). Measurement of depression in the Brazilian population: Validation of the Patient Health Questionnaire (PHQ-8). *Cadernos de saude publica, 38*(6), e00176421. https://doi.org/10.1590/0102-311XEN176421

Maslach, C., Jackson, S. E., & Leiter, M. P. (1996). *Maslach burnout inventory manual* (3rd ed.). CPP, Inc.

Nerlino, E. (2023). "From heroes to scapegoats": Teacher perceptions of the media and public's portrayal of teachers during COVID-19. *The Educational Forum*. DOI: 10.1080/00131725.2023.2169874

Neves de Jesus, S., & Lens, W. (2005). An integrated model for the study of teacher motivation. *Applied Psychology, 54*(1), 119–134. http://dx.doi.org/10.1111/j.1464-597.2005.00199.x

Nguyen, T. D., Bettini, E., Redding, C., & Gilmour, A. F. (2022). *Comparing turnover intentions and actual turnover in the public sector workforce: Evidence from public school teachers*. https://doi.org/10.26300/3AQ0-PV52

Oyen, K., & Schweinle, A. (2021). Teacher shortages in rural America: What factors encourage teachers to consider teaching in rural settings? *The Rural Educator, 41*(3), 12–25. https://doi.org/10.35608/ruraled.v41i3.923

Ozamiz-Etxebarria, N., Berasategi Santxo, N., Idoiaga Mondragon, N., & Dosil Santamaria, M. (2021). The psychological state of teachers during the COVID-19 crisis: The challenge of returning to face-to-face teaching. *Frontiers in Psychology,11,* 1–10. DOI: 10.3389/fpsyg.2020.620718

Parthasarathy, N., Li, F., Zhang, F., Chuang, R. J., Mathur, M., Pomeroy, M., Noyola, J., Markham, C. M., & Sharma, S. V. (2022). A cross-sectional study analyzing predictors of perceived stress among elementary school teachers during the COVID-19 pandemic. *Workplace Health and Safety, 70*(4), 180–187. DOI: 10.1177/21650799211070733

Pressley, T., Ha, C., & Learn, E. (2021). Teacher stress and anxiety during COVID-19: An empirical study. *School Psychology,* 36(5), 367–376. https://doi.org/10.1037/spq0000468

Querolo, N., Rockeman, O., & Ceron, E. (2022, Sept 2). America's broken education system: Part 1 Why teachers are quitting. *Bloomberg*. https://www.bloomberg.com/features/2022-america-teachers-great-resignation/?leadSource=uverify%20wall

Salam, E. (2023, Jan 24). Florida teachers forced to remove or cover up books to avoid felony Charges. *The Guardian*. https://www.theguardian.com/us-news/2023/jan/24/florida-manatee-county-books-certified-media-specialist

Sands, G. (2022, Nov 3). Virginia sets up a tip line for 'divisive' classroom concepts. Documents show it turned into a hotline for the state's schools. *CNN*. https://www.cnn.com/2022/11/03/politics/youngkin-tipline-parents-schools-virginia/index.html

Santoro, D. A. (2018). *Demoralized: Why teachers leave the profession they love and how they can stay*. Harvard Educational Press.

Schmitt, J., & deCourcy, K. (2022, Dec 6). *The pandemic has exacerbated a long-standing national shortage of teachers*. Economic Policy Institute. https://www.epi.org/publication/shortage-of-teachers/

Selden, T. M., Berdahl, T. A., & Fang, Z. (2020). The risk of severe COVID-19 within households of school employees and school-age children. *Health Affairs, 39*(11), 2002–2009.

Sinclair, C. (2008). Initial and changing student teacher motivation and commitment to teaching. *Asia-Pacific Journal of Teacher Education, 36*(2). 79–104. DOI: 10.1080/13598660801971658

Skaalvik, E. M., & Skaalvik, S. (2015). Job satisfaction, stress and coping strategies in the teaching profession—What do teachers say? *International Education Studies, 8*(3), 181–192. https://doi.org/10.5539/ies.v8n3p181

Skaalvik, E. M., & Skaalvik, S. (2018). Job demand and job resources as predictors of teacher motivation and well-being. *Social Psychology of Education, 21*, 1251–1275. https://doi.org/10.1007/s11218-018-9464-8

TRUTH BE TOLD. (n.d.). African American Policy Forum. https://www.aapf.org/truthbe-told

Wiley, C. (2000). A synthesis of research on the causes, effects, and reduction strategies of teacher stress. *Journal of Instructional Psychology*, *71*, 547–593.

CHAPTER 5

ELEMENTARY TEACHER MORALE AND MENTAL HEALTH FOLLOWING THE COVID-19 PANDEMIC

David T. Marshall
Auburn University

Tim Pressley
Christopher Newport University

Natalie N. Schoettler, Deja' L. Trammell
Auburn University

Natalie E. Smith
Wake Forest University

As teachers entered the 2021–2022 school year, schools tasked teachers with the challenge of closing the learning loss gap, maintaining the same standards as a typical school year, implementing COVID-19 safety protocols, and teaching to grade-level standards. The current study used the theoretical framework of teacher demoralization to explore teacher morale and mental health at the end of the 2021–2022

Instructional Survival in the Midst of the Perfect Storm:
The Experiences of K–12 Teachers During the COVID-19 Global Pandemic, pages 73–86.

Published under exclusive licence by Emerald Publishing Limited
ISBNs: 978-1-83708-502-6 HB, 978-1-83708-503-3 PB,
978-1-83708-504-0 EPDF, 978-1-83708-505-7 EPUB

school year. The sample included 459 PK–12 elementary teachers from across the United States. Hierarchical multiple regression analysis was conducted to test a set of predictors for two models – one with mental health and one with morale as a dependent variable. The results found that teacher autonomy and administrative support were significant predictors of teacher morale and mental health. Implications focus on steps school leaders can take to support teacher well-being.

Keywords: Teacher Morale; Mental Health; Elementary; COVID-19; Teachers

Teaching is a hard job that did not get any easier during the COVID-19 pandemic. Throughout the pandemic, teachers took on unprecedented challenges to provide instruction to students (Leech et al., 2022; Love & Marshall, 2022; Marshall et al., 2020; Pressley & Ha, 2022). Research also found that teachers had high-stress levels and felt overworked (Sokal et al., 2021; Walter & Fox, 2021). As teachers entered the 2021–2022 school year, schools across the United States had a variety of requirements in place for teachers to enforce to keep students safe amid the continued uncertainty of COVID-19. These safety protocols would change throughout the year leading to inconsistencies across states and schools, often with teachers having little say in policy changes. Additionally, schools were pushed to return to normalcy and address the learning loss that occurred during the pandemic (e.g., Halloran et al., 2021). This included the return of state standardized tests, new curriculum initiatives, and lofty teacher expectations. As such, it is important to understand the toll that teaching during the pandemic has had on teachers' well-being. The purpose of this study was to explore the impact of the pandemic on teacher morale and well-being by asking:

1. What is the state of elementary teacher morale and mental health at the end of the 2021–2022 school year?
2. What variables predict elementary teacher morale at the end of the 2021–2022 school year?
3. What variables predict elementary teacher mental health at the end of the 2021–2022 school year?

THEORETICAL FRAMEWORK

Demoralization occurs when teachers believe they are "violating basic moral expectations that educators should embody: do not harm students, support student learning, engage in behavior becoming of a professional" (Santoro, 2018, p. 43). Throughout the pandemic, teachers have faced new demoralization issues that have challenged their morale (Marshall et al., 2023a). Challenges included instructional requirements that did not meet student learning needs, limited parental support (Pressley, 2021a, 2021b), and limited mental health resources (Marshall et al., 2020; Roman, 2020). These aspects have led to lower teacher self-efficacy (Pressley & Ha, 2022), higher levels of burnout (Pressley, 2021a; Pressley & Ha, 2022), and higher levels of anxiety (Pressley et al., 2021).

Demoralization specifically focuses on "consistent and persistent frustrations in accessing the moral rewards of teaching" and leads teachers to "feel they no longer can do good work or teach 'right'" (Santoro, 2011, p. 3) and thus feel they must leave the classroom. As times of change influence demoralization (Santoro, 2011), new expectations and requirements from school leaders can often lead to teacher frustrations (Santoro, 2018).

Teacher Morale

Teacher morale is defined as the degree to which a teacher's needs are satisfied and the perception of how their job brought about that state of satisfaction (Rempel & Bentley, 1970). Previous research has shown a positive correlation between teacher morale and student achievement (Andrew, 1985; Houchard, 2005) where low teacher morale negatively impacts teacher productivity and results in a detachment from students (Lumsden, 1998). Recent literature has discussed factors influencing teacher morale such as motivation, effort, and job satisfaction (Huysman, 2008). During the pandemic, Kurtz and colleagues (2020) found that elementary teachers reported higher morale than secondary teachers did during the spring of 2020. Moreover, Marshall et al. (2023a) found a relationship between morale and an intention to remain in the profession, highlighting the importance of developing a better understanding of teacher morale.

Teacher Mental Health

Ample work has focused on student mental health during the COVID-19 crisis (e.g., Marshall, 2024; Naff et al., 2022). However, researchers have only recently started investigating teachers' mental health and well-being. Early findings suggest a relationship between declining teacher mental health and well-being during COVID-19 with teachers leaving the profession (Madigan & Kim, 2021). During fall of 2020, teachers' mental health and well-being drastically declined due to a variety of demands, including taking on an increased workload, managing multiple roles (i.e., covering colleagues' classes), and having a sense of uncertainty and a lack of resources at work (e.g., social support, work autonomy, and coping skills; Kim et al., 2022). In addition, the challenges of online teaching have had a negative impact on teacher well-being and mental health (Baker et al., 2021; Cormier et al., 2022). The lack of connection to students that many teachers experienced and the inability to build meaningful relationships affected teachers' mental health and posed a significant barrier to their personal and professional development (Kush et al., 2021; Rodriguez et al., 2022). For example, Kush et al. (2021) found that teachers who taught in person were significantly less likely to report feelings of depression or isolation, compared to peers teaching remotely. Other studies found teachers reporting high levels of stress, burnout, and job dissatisfaction due to the challenges of teaching online during COVID-19 (Minihan et al., 2022; Walter & Fox, 2021). Similarly, teachers who taught in a hyflex (hybrid-flexible) environment also saw an impact on their mental health (Kim et al., 2022; Pressley et al., 2021). Hyflex teaching involves teaching students who attend both in person and virtually at the same time (Liu & Rodriguez, 2019). Kim et al. (2022) found that teachers' stress and burnout reached an all-time high in November 2020 when hyflex teaching was introduced in American schools. Teachers' narratives reflected that hyflex teaching was particularly challenging, as they were never trained to teach in such a way. While instructional methods have varied throughout the pandemic, teacher mental health remains a concern.

CURRENT STUDY

This study employed an explanatory, sequential mixed methods design (Creswell & Plano-Clark, 2011) that involved two phases. The first phase involved the administration of a primarily quantitative survey of elementary school teachers in the United States to understand their experiences at the conclusion of the 2021–2022 school year. The survey also included open-ended items that solicited qualitative data; however, open-ended survey items often fail to lead to rigorous qualitative insights (LaDonna et al., 2018). As such, a second phase was necessary to help explain our initial findings. The second phase involved conducting focus groups with a subset of the Phase 1 participants to further understand teacher experiences following the COVID-19 pandemic in greater depth, with a specific focus on teacher morale and mental health. The study is considered both *sequential* and *explanatory* because the second, qualitative phase followed the initial quantitative phase and the focus groups conducted in Phase 2 were conducted to further explain and add depth to the initial findings. Both research questions were answered from data collected during both phases of the study. Institutional Review Board approval was sought and obtained prior to the start of data collection. See Figure 5.1 for a visual depiction of the study's design.

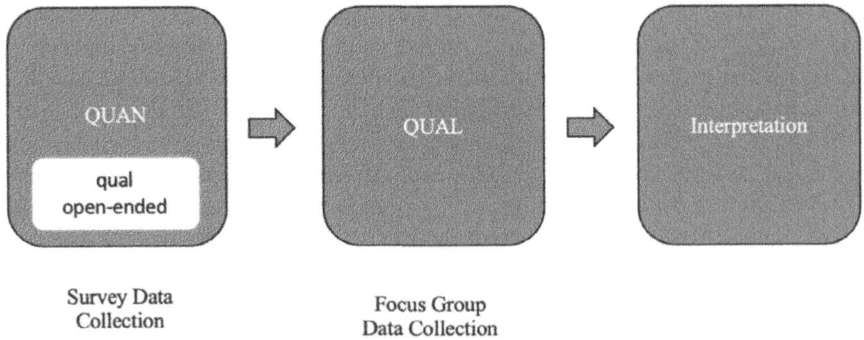

FIGURE 5.1. Explanatory Mixed Methods Design

Phase 1: Survey Component

Data Collection

We surveyed elementary school teachers between May 4–18, 2022 to gather teachers' perspectives on teacher morale and mental health. To be eligible to participate in the research, individuals had to be currently employed as elementary school teachers (grades K–5) in the United States at the time of administration. We distributed an anonymized link to the survey to personal networks and posted the link on social media platforms including Facebook, Twitter, and Reddit. Using social media platforms allowed for an extensive sample of teachers across the United States. The current sample includes 459 elementary teachers from across the United States (from 49 states); however, if a participant had missing data they were not included in the final analysis. Participants were on average 41 years of age (*M*=41.66, *SD*=10.33), had almost 15 years of teaching experience (*M*=14.77, *SD*=9.56), and were overwhelmingly White (86.8%) and female (87.8%). Two-thirds of participants (66.8%) taught in a Title 1 school, and more than six in seven (86.6%) taught in a traditional public school. Almost half of the participants (48.3%) taught in a suburban school; about a fifth taught in an urban setting (21.2%) and the rest taught in either a rural or small-town setting.

Instrumentation

The electronic survey included questions about teacher and school demographics, teacher burnout, school resources, and mental health. To measure teacher morale and teacher mental health, participants answered questions on a 0 (*very bad*) to 10-point (*very good*) scale. Questions included, "In terms of how you currently feel, rate your morale as a teacher," and "In terms of how you currently feel, rate your mental health." Additionally, the survey included scales of administration support (Seidman & Zager, 1986) and teacher autonomy (VDOE, 2021). The administrative support (α=.91) and teacher autonomy (α=.83) scales presented teachers with questions about their perspectives on a 6-point scale ranging from *strongly agree* to *strongly disagree*. Example items included "I believe that my efforts in the classroom are unappreciated by the administrators" (administrative support scale) and "I control how I use my scheduled classroom time" (teacher autonomy). Finally, the survey included an item measuring parent support. Using the same 6-point scale, we asked participants the extent to which they agreed with the following statement: "My students' parents have been supportive of my teaching." The survey included several open-ended items to elicit qualitative data to explain the quantitative findings.

Data Analysis

Two sets of models were tested to better understand teacher morale and mental health predictors. Pearson's product-moment correlations were conducted to determine the nature of the relationships between variables. We conducted a hierarchical multiple regression model to test predictor variables, controlling for race/

ethnicity, gender, years of teaching experience, and working at a Title 1 school. Finally, the researcher screened the data to check that the assumptions for multiple regression analyses were met. No issues were found with singularity, multicollinearity, the dependence of errors, normality, linearity, or homoscedasticity of residuals (Tabachnick & Fidell, 2001).

To analyze the qualitative data of the short-response question, the researchers used open coding to develop themes from teachers' short-response answers in the survey (Strauss & Corbin, 1998). The inclusion of qualitative data provided insight into teachers' perceptions of their well-being during COVID-19 (Braun et al., 2020). Data were analyzed using Microsoft Excel.

Phase 2: Focus Group Component

Data Collection

Focus groups were conducted with teachers from August 10, 2022 to September 15, 2022. Teachers who completed the Phase 1 survey were invited to share their email addresses if they were interested in participating in a follow-up focus group. A total of 40 teachers from 24 states agreed to participate in the second phase of the study. Focus groups were conducted via Zoom, lasted about an hour, were recorded, and were transcribed for analysis. Focus group participants had an average of 18.5 years of teaching experience, and like the survey sample, tended to be White (n=35, 87.5%) and female (n=34, 85.0%).

Instrumentation

A semi-structured protocol was developed based on the Phase 1 survey findings. We asked teachers about their experiences during the 2021–2022 school year, specifically student academics, behavior, and technology use. We asked about teacher mental health and morale, and what teachers needed to be successful in their jobs.

Data Analysis

The 16 focus groups that were conducted produced as many transcripts that were analyzed using ATLAS.ti version 23. A hybrid coding approach was used (Saldaña, 2015), which began with deductive codes based on our initial survey findings. We added inductive codes based on the transcripts. Additional codes were inductively added to reflect emerging themes. Two teams of researchers independently coded the transcripts, after which a code list was established. Two team members coded the remaining transcripts and an agreed-upon list of findings was established.

FINDINGS

We began analyzing our Phase 1 survey data by running bivariate correlations between the 2 dependent variables and the 3 predictors of interest – administrative

TABLE 5.1. Correlation Matrix of Dependent Variables and Predictors

	I	II	III	IV	V
Teacher Morale	1				
Teacher Mental Health	.652***	1			
Administrative Support	.460***	.400***	1		
Teacher Autonomy	.490***	.376***	.562***	1	
Parent Support	.264***	.225***	.232***	.323***	1

Note: *** p < .001; ** p < .01; * p < .05

support, teacher autonomy, and parent survey. All 5 variables positively correlated with each other at the $p < .001$ level. See Table 5.1 for a correlation matrix and Table 5.2 for regression findings for both models.

Teacher Morale

After controlling for race/ethnicity, years of teaching experience, gender, and teaching in a Title 1 school from our survey data, the teacher morale regression

TABLE 5.2. Regression Findings for Phase 1 Teacher Morale and Mental Health Models

	Teacher Morale β (SE)	**Teacher Mental Health β (SE)**
Teaching Experience	-.003 (.010)	.020* (.010)
Non-White	.333 (.285)	.075 (.293)
Female	.717 (.459)	.485 (.470)
Title I	-.073 (.196)	-.205 (.198)
Administrative Support	.082*** (.015)	.074*** (.015)
Teacher Autonomy	.782*** (.124)	.506*** (.127)
Parent Support	.180* (.078)	.185* (.080)
N	452	459
F	27.936***	17.363***
R^2	.306	.200

Note: *** p < .001; ** p < .01; *p < .05

model was significant $F(6, 436) = 32.76$, $p < .001$, and explained 31% (R^2 = .31) of the variance. Three variables remained as significant predictors for teacher morale – administrative support (b = .082, $p < .001$), teacher autonomy (b = .782, $p < .001$), and parent support (b = .180, $p = .022$). We also operationalized teacher morale similar to Senechal and colleagues (2016), coding a response of 0–3 as low morale, a response of 4–5 as medium-low morale, a response of 6–7 as medium-high morale, and a response of 8–10 as high morale. Almost half of the sample (48.2%) reported having low morale. A Chi-Square goodness-of-fit test was conducted, and findings suggest that participants reported having low morale significantly more often than any other level of morale (X^2(3 d.f.)=167.768, $p <$ .001).

Teachers also described having low morale in short-answer responses on the survey. Teachers often attributed low morale to a lack of resources and support from parents and administrators. One teacher described "constantly [being] expected to do more with less, [a] lack of subs [and a] lack of prep [time]" as reasons for this outcome. Another teacher similarly shared, "Morale in my building is terrible. Teachers are exhausted but continue to be spread thin. We have a sub shortage and I am regularly expected to sub during my prep. We are rarely praised or recognized for any of our work." In this teacher's case, their autonomy and the support they received from the administration were low. Participants shared that their low morale was leading them to reconsider remaining in the profession. One teacher shared:

> [A] lack of student motivation and engagement, extreme behavior and socialization issues, little to no support from district administration, facilities in disrepair with no solution in sight, little to no parent support or appreciation [led to] low morale of entire educational staff…every single one of these problems has caused many teachers, myself included, to seek other employment.

Similarly, many teachers in our focus groups shared that inadequate support from parents and administrators led to them experiencing low morale, which in turn led them to consider leaving the teaching profession. One teacher stated, "I would say [we need] support from the administration. We get it from each other; teachers are like families…We get that support from our coworkers but it's missing from the people who are supposed to trust us, including parents." Another teacher recalled, "When I have administrators who support me and help me with resources and help my kids feel known and loved, that makes my job so much easier. I didn't have it last year, and it was horrible. It was really hard to come back this year." While many of the teachers in our focus groups expressed feeling unsupported and unappreciated, some shared positive experiences with their administration and how their support helped them persevere. One teacher shared:

> So, a principal moved in from another school in the county and I have nothing but positive praises to sing about her. I want to shout it from the rooftops. I had a physically abusive student in the classroom last year towards the other students and my-

> self. I think any other person who was a year and a half into a career who was getting desks thrown at them every day would say "Bye. I'm going to go make $20 an hour working at Target." ...my principal and her support is why I stayed.

Our Phase 1 quantitative survey findings, open-ended survey findings, and Phase 2 focus group findings suggest that teachers with support from their students' parents and school leaders reported much better morale than those without that support.

Teacher Mental Health

Similar to our teacher morale analyses, we also began by analyzing Phase 1 survey data. After controlling for race/ethnicity, years of experience, and gender, the regression model was significant $F(6, 436) = 18.92, p < .001$, and it explained 21% ($R^2 = .21$) of the variance. Again, administrative support ($b = .074, p < .001$), teacher autonomy ($b = .506, p < .001$), and parent support ($b = .185, p = .021$) significantly predicted teacher mental health. Teaching experience was also a significant predictor ($b = .020, p = .044$). Teachers who had more classroom experience also reported having better mental health. A follow-up item asked participants if they had seen a mental health counselor during the pandemic, and 27.4% responded affirmatively.

Teachers also shared reports of low mental health in short answers. Teachers shared that increased workloads and reduced administrative support were contributors to poor mental health. One teacher shared, "My mental health has declined mainly due to the school district: (1) making decisions without input from the teachers about what would work/wouldn't work for our grade level, and (2) decisions that add extra unnecessary work for teachers with no regard for our mental health." Another teacher shared, "My mental health and morale are directly tied to my [school's] leadership trying to pretend that the pandemic didn't happen and doesn't impact kids or families." A lack of autonomy and perceived administrator support led several teachers to have low mental health during the 2021–2022 school year.

Teachers shared the same sentiments in our focus groups, reiterating a lack of support from their administration and parents, as well as a lack of resources to combat the grave learning loss their students were displaying post-COVID-19 contributed to their mental health. One teacher shared how they felt pressured by their administration to "grade with grace" and pass their students despite not producing grade-level work. She elaborated, "I'm like, they can't write a thesis statement or essay. I have to teach them that next year when they are sophomores, and they can't write a freshman-level paper. But that phrase ["grade with grace"], in particular, became something very challenging...It hasn't been great for sure." Another teacher added, "[administrators] still wanted to dictate our pay based on the performance of students. It was a lot...I am already feeling drained and burned out." In addition to a general lack of support for teachers, some highlighted how particularly new teachers and their mental health have been impacted by COVID-19. One veteran teacher stated, "So as an older teacher, I think teacher support at our school is lacking. It's alright. Maybe I don't see it all. But it seems as a whole new teacher you get burnt out so quickly. It's an old stat that half of the teachers are done after 5 years. I heard that when I was with the credential program 20+ years ago."

DISCUSSION

As of this writing (August, 2023), schools have mostly returned to pre-pandemic norms in terms of procedures. However, teacher morale and teacher mental health have suffered during the crisis. The current study found that administrative support, teacher autonomy, and parent support all positively predicted teacher morale and mental health. Teachers receiving more support from parents and school leaders reported higher morale and better mental health. This ties in with previous findings, suggesting that supported teachers have greater morale (e.g., Lambersky, 2016) and mental health (e.g., Iachini et al., 2016). Teachers who had been in the classroom longer also reported improved mental health. This is consistent with research published in *JAMA*, which suggests that older adults fared better regarding their mental health than younger adults during the COVID-19 pandemic (Vahia et al., 2020). It would make sense that teachers would not be exceptions to these findings. These results are important as states and schools continue to see an exodus of teachers leaving the profession. School leaders can use the results from the current study as a starting point to support teacher well-being moving forward.

There are some limitations associated with this work that are worth noting. First, the Phase 1 survey participants were drawn from a voluntary sample, mostly from social media. It is possible that teachers who frequent education-related social media sites differ in important ways from those who do not, and those who saw the invitation to participate in this research and decided to participate may differ from those who elected not to do so. Since Phase 2 participants were a subset of the Phase 1 sample, the same limitations apply. Additionally, it is possible that teachers who elected to participate in a focus group also differed systematically from those who completed the survey but opted not to participate in the second phase of this work.

Second, a strength of this work is the triangulation of three types of data from two sources (survey quantitative, survey open-ended qualitative, focus group qualitative). Given that participants responded similarly in the closed-response items comprising scales, in the open-ended item generically asking teachers about the challenges they faced, as well as in the focus groups we conducted strengthens the validity of our findings. However, the teacher morale model we tested explained only about 30% of the variance and our mental health model explained approximately 20% of the variance. Both models suggest that other factors are contributing to teacher morale and mental health that are worth exploring. Future work should attempt to understand other factors that impact teachers in these ways, especially those within a school leader's locus of control.

Implications

As schools return to normalcy it remains crucial for school leaders to prioritize the well-being of teachers. School administrators can initiate communication with teachers to understand their needs and explore ways to support teachers' mental health (Pendola et al., 2023). School leaders may also consider implementing mental health programs in the classroom and providing telehealth resources for accessing professional counselors or allowing mental health days throughout the school year. In addition, school leaders may also support teachers within the school environment by providing resources, flexibility, and understanding. Throughout the pandemic, teachers have expressed feelings of being overworked, experiencing limited flexibility in their instructional approaches, and facing increased expectations as schools return to normalcy (Love & Marshall, 2022; Pressley, 2021a; Walter & Fox, 2021). School leaders must offer flexibility and establish realistic expectations for teachers, acknowledging that students may be lagging and trusting teachers to make informed decisions to support student learning (Chan et al., 2021; Walter & Fox, 2021). Furthermore, it is important to protect dedicated planning time for teachers, allowing them opportunities to plan the lessons, communicate with other stakeholders, and get a break during the day (Marshall et al., 2023b; Pendola et al., 2023).

Finally, school leaders must take proactive measures to ensure teachers are fairly compensated for their work (Mackenzie, 2007). Throughout the pandemic, teachers dedicated extensive time to their teaching (Kaden, 2020; Pressley, 2021a) without receiving adequate compensation. School leaders and policymakers must prioritize appropriate compensation for teachers' efforts in educating the future generation, especially if they wish to retain them in the classroom beyond the pandemic.

REFERENCES

Andrew, L. D. (1985). *Administrator's handbook for improving faculty morale*. Phi Delta Kappa.

Baker, C. N., Peele, H., Daniels, M., Saybe, M., Whalen, K., Overstreet, S., & The New Orleans, T.-I. S. L. C. (2021). The experience of COVID-19 and its impact on teachers' mental health, coping, and teaching. *School Psychology Review, 50*(4), 491–504. https://doi.org/10.1080/2372966X.2020.1855473

Braun, V., Clarke, V., Boulton, E., Davey, L., & McEvoy, C. (2020). The online survey as a qualitative research tool. *International Journal of Social Research Methodology*, 1–14. https://doi.org/10.1080/13645579.2020.1805550

Chan, M. K., Sharkey, J. D., Lawrie, S. I., Arch, D. A. N., & Nylund-Gibson, K. (2021). Elementary school teacher well-being and supportive measures amid COVID-19: An exploratory study. *School Psychology*. http://doi.org/10.1037/spq0000441

Cormier, C. J., McGrew, J., Ruble, L., & Fischer, M. (2022). Socially distanced teaching: The mental health impact of the COVID-19 pandemic on special education teachers. *Journal of Community Psychology, 50*(3), 1768–1772. https://doi.org/10.1002/jcop.22736

Creswell, J. W., & Plano-Clark, V. L. (2011). *Designing and conducting mixed methods research* (2nd ed.). Sage.

Halloran, C., Jack, R., Okun, J. C., & Oster, E. (2021). *Pandemic schooling mode and student test scores: Evidence from US states* (No. w29497). National Bureau of Economic Research. http://www.nber.org/papers/w29497

Houchard, M. A. (2005). *Principal leadership, teacher morale, and student achievement in seven schools in Mitchell County, North Carolina*. East Tennessee State University.

Huysman, J. T. (2008). Rural teacher satisfaction: An analysis of beliefs and attitudes of rural teachers' job satisfaction. *Rural Educator, 29*(2), 31–38.

Iachini, A. L., Pitner, R. O., Morgan, F., & Rhodes, K. (2016). Exploring the principal perspective: Implications for expanded school improvement and school mental health. *Children & Schools, 38*(1), 40–48. https://doi.org/10.1093/cs/cdv038

Kaden, U. (2020). COVID-19 school closure-related changes to the professional life of a K–12 teacher. *Educational Sciences, 10*(165), 1–13. https://doi.org/10.3390/educsci10060165

Kim, L. E., Oxley, L., & Asbury, K. (2022). "My brain feels like a browser with 100 tabs open": A longitudinal study of teachers' mental health and well-being during the COVID-19 pandemic. *The British Journal of Educational Psychology, 92*(1), 299–318. https://doi.org/10.1111/bjep.12450

Kurtz, H., Lloyd, S., Harwin, A., Chen, V., & Furuya, Y. (2020). *Crisis of confidence: Results of national surveys on educator morale during a pandemic*. EdWeek Research Center. https://www.edweek.org/research-center/research-center-reports/crisis-of-confidence-results-of-national-surveys-on-educator-morale-during-a-pandemic

Kush, J. M., Badillo-Goicoechea, E., Musci, R. J., & Stuart, E. A. (2021). Teacher mental health during the COVID-19 pandemic: Informing policies to support teacher well-being and effective teaching practices. *arXiv*. https://doi.org/10.48550/arXiv.2109.01547

LaDonna, K. A., Taylor, T., & Lingard, L. (2018). Why open-ended survey questions are unlikely to support rigorous qualitative insights. *Academic Medicine, 93*(3), 347–349. https://doi.org/10.1097/ACD.0000000000002088

Lambersky, J. (2016). Understanding the human side of school leadership: Principals' impact on teachers' morale, self-efficacy, stress, and commitment. *Leadership and Policy in Schools, 15*(4), 379–405. https://doi.org/10.1080/15700763.2016.1181188

Leech, N. L., Gullett, S., Cummings, M. H., & Haug, C. A. (2022). The challenges of remote K–12 education during the COVID-19 pandemic: Differences by grade level. *Online Learning, 26*(1), 245–267. https://doi.org/10.24059/olj.v26i1.2609

Liu, C. A., & Rodriguez, R. C. (2019). Evaluation of the impact of the hyflex learning model. *International Journal of Innovation and Learning, 25*(4), 393–411. https://doi.org/10.1504/IJIL.2019.099986

Love, S. M., & Marshall, D. T. (2022). Teacher experiences during COVID-19. In Marshall, D. M. (Ed.), *COVID-19 and the classroom: How schools navigated the great disruption* (pp. 21–66). Lexington Books.

Lumsden, L. (1998). Teacher Morale. ERIC Digest, Number 120.

Mackenzie, N. (2007). Teacher morale: More complex than we think?. *The Australian Educational Researcher*, *34*(1), 89–104.

Madigan, D. J., & Kim, L. E. (2021). Towards an understanding of teacher attrition: A meta-analysis of burnout, job satisfaction, and teachers' intentions to quit. *Teaching and Teacher Education*, *105*. https://doi.org/10.1016/j.tate.2021.103425

Marshall, D. T. (2024). COVID-19 and school closures: A narrative review of pediatric mental health impacts. *Journal of School Choice, 18*(1), 67–76. https://doi.org/10.1080/15582159.2023.2201734

Marshall, D. T., & Pressley, T. (2024). *Lessons of the pandemic: Disruption, innovation, and what schools need to move forward.* The Guilford Press.

Marshall, D. T., Shannon, D. M., & Love, S. M. (2020). How teachers experienced the COVID-19 transition to remote instruction. *Phi Delta Kappan*, *102*(3), 46–50. https://doi.org/10.1177/0031721720970702

Marshall, D. T., Shannon, D. M., Love, S. M., & Neugebauer, N. M. (2023a). Factors related to teacher resilience during COVID-19. *International Journal of Education Policy & Leadership, 19*(1), 1–18. https://doi.org/10.22230/ijepl.2023v19n1a1257

Marshall, D. T. Love S. M., Neugebauer, N. M., & Smith, N. E. (2023b). How additional professional time benefitted teachers during COVID-19. In S. M. McCarther & D. M. Davis (Eds.), *Breakthrough: From pandemic panic to promising practice* (pp. 61–72). Information Age Publishing.

Minihan, E., Adamis, D., Dunleavy, M., Martin, A., Gavin, B., & McNicholas, F. (2022). COVID-19 related occupational stress in teachers in Ireland. *International Journal of Educational Research Open*, *3*.https://doi.org/10.1016/j.ijedro.2021.100114

Naff, D., Williams, S., Furman-Darby, J., & Yeong, M. (2022). The mental health impacts of COVID-19 on PK–12 students: A systematic review of emerging literature. *AERA Open, 8*(1), 1–40. https://doi.org/10.1177/23328584221084722

Pendola, A., Marshall, D. T., Pressley, T., & Trammell, D. L. (2023). Why teachers leave: It isn't what you think. *Phi Delta Kappan, 105*(1), 51–55. https://doi.org/10.1177/00317217231197477

Pressley, T. (2021a). Elementary hybrid and virtual teacher stress during COVID-19. *Journal of Research in Education*, *30*(3), 97–116.

Pressley, T. (2021b). Factors contributing to teacher burnout during COVID-19. *Educational Researcher*, *50*(5), 325–327. https://doi.org/10.3102/0013189X211004138

Pressley, T., & Ha, C. (2022). Teacher exhaustion during COVID-19: Exploring the role of administrators, self-efficacy, and anxiety. *The Teacher Educator Journal*, *57*(1), 61–78. https://doi.org/10.1080/08878730.2021.1995094

Pressley, T., Ha, C., & Learn, E. (2021). Teacher stress and anxiety during COVID-19: An empirical study. *School Psychology*, *36*(5), 367–376. https://doi.org/10.1037/spq0000468

Rempel, A. M., & Bentley, R. R. (1970). Teacher morale: Relationship with selected factors. *Journal of Teacher Education, 21*(4), 534–539. https://doi.org/10.1177/002248717002100414

Rodriguez, V., Rojas, N. M., Rabadi-Raol, A., Souto-Manning, M. V., & Brotman, L. M. (2022). Silent expectations: An exploration of women pre-Kindergarten teachers' mental health and wellness during COVID-19 and beyond. *Early Childhood Research Quarterly*, *60*, 80–95. https://doi.org/10.1016/j.ecresq.2021.12.006

Roman, T. (2020). Supporting the mental health of preservice teachers in COVID-19 through trauma-informed educational practices and adaptive formative assessment tools. *Journal of Technology and Teacher Education, 28*(2), 473–481. https://www.learntechlib.org/primary/p/216363

Saldaña, J. (2015). *The coding manual for qualitative researchers* (3rd ed.). Sage.

Santoro, D. A. (2011). Good teaching in difficult times: Demoralization in the pursuit of good work. *American Journal of Education, 118*(1), 1–23. https://doi.org/10.1086/662010

Santoro, D. A. (2018). *Demoralized: Why teachers leave the profession they love and how they can stay*. Harvard Education Press

Seidman, S. A., & Zager, J. (1986). The teacher burnout scale. *Educational Research Quarterly, 11*(1), 26–33.

Senechal, J., Sober, T., Hope, S., Johnson, T., Buckhalter, F., Castelow, T., Gilfillan, D., Jackson, K., Nabors, A., Neuman, P., Robinson, R., Sargeant, R., Stanford, S., & Varljen, D. (2016). *Understanding teacher morale.* Metropolitan Educational Research Consortium. https://scholarscompas.vcu.edu/merc_pubs/56

Sokal, L., Trudel, L. E., & Babb, J. (2021). I've had it! Factors associated with burnout and low organizational commitment in Canadian teachers during the second wave of the COVID-19 pandemic. *International Journal of Educational Research Open, 2*(2), 1–9. https://doi.org/10.1016/j.ijedro.2020.100023

Strauss, A., & Corbin, J. (1998). *Basics of qualitative research* (2nd ed.). Sage.

Tabachnick, B. G., & Fidell, L. S. (2001). *Using multivariate statistics* (4th ed.). Alyn & Bacon.

Vahia, I. V., Jeste, D. V., & Reynolds, C. F. (2020). Older adults and the mental health effects of COVID-19. *JAMA, 324*(22), 2253–2254. https://doi.org/10.1001/jama.2020.21753

Virginia Department of Education. (2021). *Review copy 2021 Virginia school survey: Classroom instructors.* https://doe.virginia.gov/support/201-va-school-survey-classroom-instructors

Walter, H. L., & Fox, H. B. (2021). Understanding teacher well-being during the COVID-19 pandemic over time: A qualitative longitudinal study. *Journal of Organizational Psychology, 27*(5), 36–50.

CHAPTER 6

SOCIAL SUPPORT AND COVID-19

How U.S. K–12 Teachers Were Impacted by Gratitude and Mentoring During the COVID-19 Pandemic

Kristen C. Mosley, Christopher J. McCarthy and Aradhita Gupta
University of Texas at Austin

Functioning as frontline workers, teachers have experienced heightened stress during the COVID-19 pandemic, which presents consequences for their well-being and job sustainability. Prior research demonstrates teacher wellbeing can be facilitated by both vertical support (school leadership) and horizontal support (colleagues), but the current U.S. educational landscape includes new stressors threatening the bounds of old support systems. The current study extends prior research on teacher support by conducting a modified grounded theory to explore the mechanisms underlying the ways in which teachers experienced social support during the COVID-19 pandemic and how this resource supports them in a high-stress career. Forty teachers from a stratified random sample of 300 public school teachers in a large

Instructional Survival in the Midst of the Perfect Storm:
The Experiences of K–12 Teachers During the COVID-19 Global Pandemic, pages 87–106.

Published under exclusive licence by Emerald Publishing Limited
ISBNs: 978-1-83708-502-6 HB, 978-1-83708-503-3 PB,
978-1-83708-504-0 EPDF, 978-1-83708-505-7 EPUB

southwestern district were recruited, resulting in 23 participants of varying vulnerability to stress based on a prior phase of the study. Two researchers analyzed transcriptions from six, one-hour focus groups, with an audit trail, peer debriefing, and other triangulation techniques employed. Three thematic outcomes illustrated how social support—specifically mentoring and gratitude—was helpful for teachers at the individual level (affective support), the classroom level (instructional support), and the building level (community support). The unique combinations of these varying levels of support ultimately provided sustenance for teachers who were working in an ever-changing and challenging environment during COVID-19. Such findings have implications for school and district leaders, as they reveal the importance of building multi-tiered systems of support in which teachers have opportunities to positively interact with their professional community.

Keywords: Teacher Stress, Social Support, Modified Grounded Theory

Teachers have experienced heightened stress during the COVID-19 pandemic, with roughly half of the workforce resigning since the pandemic's onset (Diliberti et al., 2021). The pandemic has presented teachers with additional stressors (e.g., lesson conversion, health concerns, increased negative emotions, social distancing; Chang et al., 2022; MacIntyre et al., 2020), all of which likely increased attrition. Yet, not all teachers experienced pandemic-related stress in the same way nor did their stress present uniform impacts on their occupational health. The current study aims to understand how social support experiences during the COVID-19 pandemic assisted teachers working during this turbulent time.

The current investigation was part of a larger study which used a quantitative measure, the Classroom Appraisal of Resources and Demands (CARD; Lambert et al., 2009), to track teachers' risk-for-stress during the 2020–2021 school year. The term risk-for-stress is used in accordance with transactional theory (Lazarus & Folkman, 1984), in that a teacher's overall appraisal that demands in their classroom exceed resources, often, but not always, results in a stress response (cognitive, emotional, and physiological symptoms of stress). McCarthy et al. (2016) found reliable associations between teachers classified as at-risk for stress and reduced occupational health across 18 studies, and more recent research has found associations between risk-for-stress and occupational health outcomes in pre- and peri-pandemic educational contexts (McCarthy et al., 2022; Mosley, 2022). This study aimed to develop a grounded theory of how teachers of varying risk-for-stress levels experienced social support (operationalized as the reception and provision of mentoring and gratitude) during the pandemic.

LITERATURE REVIEW

The literature review will first introduce teacher stress from the perspective of the transactional theory of stress and coping. Next, literature concerning social support will be reviewed with particular attention paid to social support within the K–12 teaching environment. This section concludes with a discussion of the current study in light of the selected literature presented.

Teacher Stress

Teacher stress is a universal problem that has consequences for not only teachers but also their students and colleagues (Skaalvik & Skaalvik, 2017). The demands on teachers are numerous. Research has identified a variety of stressors that teachers face including student misbehavior and demotivation, minimal autonomy support, administration demands, and racial incongruence in their workplace (Betoret & Artiga, 2010; Chang et al., 2022; Mosley et al., 2023). While these job demands ebb and flow across any given academic year, their persistence in the field of education has posed many barriers to teachers maintaining optimal occupational health across varying time points across their career (Mosley et al., 2022; Mosley & McCarthy, 2023).

According to Lazarus and Folkman (1984), stress results from the relationship between a person and their environment, which they appraise as threatening their well-being and exceeding their available resources. The current study defines teacher stress via Lazarus and Folkman's transactional model, understanding risk-for-stress as the result of a unique transaction between a teacher and their working environment. The teacher first appraises what demands are personally relevant and taxing and then determines what available resources they do(n't) have to meet those demands. Thus, the (im)balance of perceived demands and resources determines the teachers' risk-for-stress (Lazarus & Folkman, 1984).

As previously described, the current study uses the term 'risk-for-stress' to account for the extent to which a teacher is at-risk of experiencing stress as a result of their workplace appraisals of demands and resources. A teacher is at high risk-for-stress if they perceive workplace demands as greater than available resources, and a teacher is at low risk-for-stress if they perceive workplace demands as less than available resources. Importantly, risk-for-stress is meant to signify that an imbalance of resources and demands may exist, but such an imbalance may or may not result in a stress response that is physiological, cognitive, or emotional in nature. In the context of this study, a teacher may be at-risk for stress but this risk may not materialize into a stress response.

The COVID-19 pandemic presented new and unique demands on teachers, which have threatened their wellbeing and job sustainability. The onset of social distancing as a public health practice spurred isolation in many shades – teachers navigated remote teaching, complex and inconsistent school safety protocols, limited opportunities to interface with colleagues, and decreased in-classroom support (Chang et al., 2022). However, prior research demonstrates teacher retention can be facilitated by both vertical support, such as responsive school leadership (Súarez & Wright, 2019), and horizontal support, such as positive social interaction with peers, students, and families (Geiger & Pivovaroya, 2018). Additionally, Lazarus and Folkman (1984) have noted how social relationships may moderate to what extent individuals are at-risk for appraising their environments as demanding.

Teacher Social Support

House and colleagues (1988) defined social support as "the positive, potentially health promoting or stress-buffering aspects of relationships such as instrumental aid, emotional caring or concern, and information" (p. 302). Social support's benefit to health has been attributed to either main effects (directly affecting the relationship between stress and health) or buffering effects (moderating the relationship between stress and health); the buffering effects of social support is the focus of the current study. Of note, the main effect of social support has been found to occur in a myriad of contexts (both with and without stress as a key variable), whereas evidence for the buffering effect of social support has solely been identified in situations in which stress is a key variable (Cohen & McKay, 2020). A diverse range of studies has found evidence to support the multifaceted benefits of social support, yet the ways in which such a resource is provided within U.S. K–12 educational contexts vary greatly. The current study operationalized social support as the reception and provision of one common practice in education—mentoring—as well as the reception and provision of a more universal practice—gratitude.

Cutrona and Russell (1990) analyzed the social support literature to classify five commonly occurring support types: emotional support (e.g., providing comfort and caring), social integration support (e.g., being a member of a group with shared interests), esteem support (e.g., bolstering competence and perception of self-esteem), tangible aid (e.g., offering resources and services), and informational support (e.g., giving advice). These different types of social support have been linked to specific stressors for which they may be most effective (Cohen & McKay, 2020). For example, tangible social support such as money was most helpful in buffering stressors involving resource deficits. Alternatively, self-esteem support was seen as most helpful for distress arising from feelings of failure or inadequacy, and emotional support was seen as most helpful in the loss of significant relationships.

Teachers can experience the full range of these social supports from either internal or external sources (Fiorilli et al., 2019). Internal support stems from within the workplace (e.g., colleagues, administration, supervisors), whereas external support is derived from the teacher's life outside of work (e.g., friends, family and significant others). Prior research has found associations between internal support and increased feelings of belonging and well-being (Travers, 2017), as well as between external support and increased job satisfaction and performance (Skaalvik & Skaalvik, 2009). As social support may present a scalable and effective tool to promote occupational health among teachers, the current study aimed to understand how internal sources of social support resource teachers in times of high demands. Thus, in order to explore which types of internal social support were most salient for teachers and how they functioned as resources during the COVID-19 pandemic, teachers in the current study were asked to focus on social support they received from individuals directly related to their work. Specifically, teachers were asked about a common practice in their line of work, mentorship (Mosley & McCarthy, 2023), as well as the extent to which they either gave or received gratitude in their work.

Social support for teachers has been most commonly studied in association with burnout. Receiving minimal social support has been found to coincide with an increased likelihood for burnout (Ju et al., 2015), whereas experiencing supportive workplace relationships has been identified as protective against burnout (Russel et al., 1987). However, findings on the extent to which workplace relationships buffer against burnout have been inconsistent. For example, Ju et al. (2015) found that the presence of supportive colleagues and supervisors was linked to a lower vulnerability for burnout, yet Burke and Greenglass (1993) did not find any relationship between social support and burnout in their study of 833 teachers. Kyriacou (1981) argued that because social support outcomes can vary by the giver and receiver, several support options should be provided to teachers so that they can appropriately match their personal coping styles and needs to the support they seek. For the current study, teachers were asked to reflect on their experiences with two specific types of social support: giving and receiving gratitude and mentorship.

The Current Study

The current study explores how social support experiences impacted teachers during a time of heightened stress—the COVID-19 pandemic. Patterns across the 23 participating teacher responses were analyzed to construct a grounded theory of how two forms of social support—mentorship and gratitude—ultimately supported their persistence in the field during the pandemic. In better understanding how teachers are impacted by social support during a time of increased stress, the goal was to develop a model of teachers' social support experiences during COVID-19. The study is guided by the research question: How were teachers impacted by social support experiences during the COVID-19 pandemic?

METHODS

A modified grounded theory approach was used to develop a theory of how social support experiences during the pandemic impacted teachers' sustainability in the field (Corbin & Strauss, 1990). The use of grounded theory affords researchers an opportunity to move beyond thematic analysis and explore how a process unfolds within a specific context. The context of the current study was a large southwestern U.S. K–12 public school district during the COVID-19 pandemic.

Participants

The study sample was derived from a stratified random sample of 300 public school teachers in a large southwestern district who had completed a quantitative measure of stress risk (Classroom Appraisal of Resources and Demands; Lambert et al., 2009) during March 2021. Forty teachers were contacted to participate, which resulted in 23 participants, 11 of whom were identified as high risk-for-stress and 12 of whom were identified as low risk-for-stress. The balanced sample of teachers with high and low risk-for-stress enabled an investigation of varying perspectives, experiences with stress, and social support experiences, which felt particularly important given the unique demands and range of experiences presented by the COVID-19 pandemic.

The 23 participating teachers had taught for an average of 11 years, primarily identified as White women, and ranged in age from 22–56 (average age was 42 years old). All participants were full-time teachers who worked in a variety of roles (see Table 6.1 for all demographics). Participating teachers attended focus groups via Zoom in May 2021, which took place both before and after regular school hours. Focus groups consisted of 2–5 teachers and included eight open-ended questions and several follow-up probes about teachers' experiences with gratitude and mentoring during the pandemic (see Appendix). Participating teachers were compensated $45 each for their time.

Data Analysis

Data analysis was conducted inductively and grounded in the research question: How were teachers impacted by social support experiences during the COVID-19 pandemic? For the purposes of this study, social support was conceptualized as teachers' experiences with giving and receiving mentoring and gratitude within their school context. The decision to include these specific social support experiences was driven by an interest in hearing about social support experiences across a spectrum within the field of education—from a well-studied area of research (mentoring) to a burgeoning area of research (gratitude). All focus groups were conducted prior to analysis, which necessitated intentional selective and then theoretical sampling of previously collected data to ensure the processes were interrelated and researcher bias was guarded against as much as possible. Rodgers and colleagues (1993) assert, "the credibility of the reported findings rests not only on the procedures by which the data are generated and analyzed, but on the self-awareness of the researcher throughout the research process" (p. 223). As such, an audit trail was maintained across the six months of analysis, which provided a space for writing theoretical memos and iterating the theory across several cycles of coding (Corbin & Strauss, 1990).

The six transcripts and corresponding audio files were coded and analyzed via Strauss and Corbin's (1990) detailed grounded theory procedure of open, axial, and selective coding, all of which included the use of constant comparisons across

TABLE 6.1. Participant Demographics

Pseudonym	Race/ Ethnicity	Age	School Level	Years Taught	Content Area	Gender	Risk for Stress
Abby	White	49	Elem.	26	All Subjects	Female	Resourced
Barbara	White	43	High	16	CTE	Female	Resourced
Cassie	White	45	High	3	CTE	Female	Resourced
Diana	White	56	Elem.	24	ESL	Female	Resourced
Emily	Asian	48	High	21	Music	Female	Demanded
Francis	White	29	Elem.	2	All Subjects	Female	Demanded
Grace	Hispanic	31	Elem.	7	SPED	Female	Demanded
Henry	White	37	High	11	Art	Male	Demanded
Irene	White	22	Elem.	1	All Subjects	Female	Demanded
Jamie	White	34	Elem.	7	ESL	Female	Resourced
Kevin	Hispanic	35	Middle	10	Music	Male	Resourced
Leo	Asian	23	High	1	Art	Male	Resourced
Megan	White	58	Elem.	5	SPED	Female	Resourced
Norah	White	41	Elem.	17	Music	Female	Demanded
Olivia	White	44	Elem.	20	Theatre	Female	Demanded
Penny	White	34	Elem.	8	SPED	Female	Demanded
Quinn	White	49	Elem.	5	SPED	Female	Demanded
Robert	White	43	Middle	13	Athletics	Male	Demanded
Sarah	White	44	Middle	12	Science	Female	Demanded
Tessa	White	56	Elem.	8	SPED	Female	Demanded
Ursula	Hispanic	48	Elem.	14	ESL	Female	Resourced
Violet	White	54	Elem.	26	All Subjects	Female	Resourced
Wendy	White	26	Middle	4	English & History	Female	Resourced

Note. White=White, Non-Hispanic; Hispanic= White, Hispanic; Asian= Asian American; CTE= Career and Technical Education; SPED= Special Education; ESL= English as a Second Language

data. First, the open coding process explored what teachers shared about their experiences and led to the development of initial categories that parsed teachers' similar and dissimilar experiences. Second, during axial coding, conceptual linkages were developed and tested by reviewing how, under what conditions, and when, for example, categories were emerging and teachers were sharing about specific experiences. This step of the process led to six iterations of the codebook, after which saturation of categories was achieved. At peak, there were 13 categories that emerged, which were later captured more parsimoniously via 11 categories. Finally, during selective coding, the linkages across the 11 categories

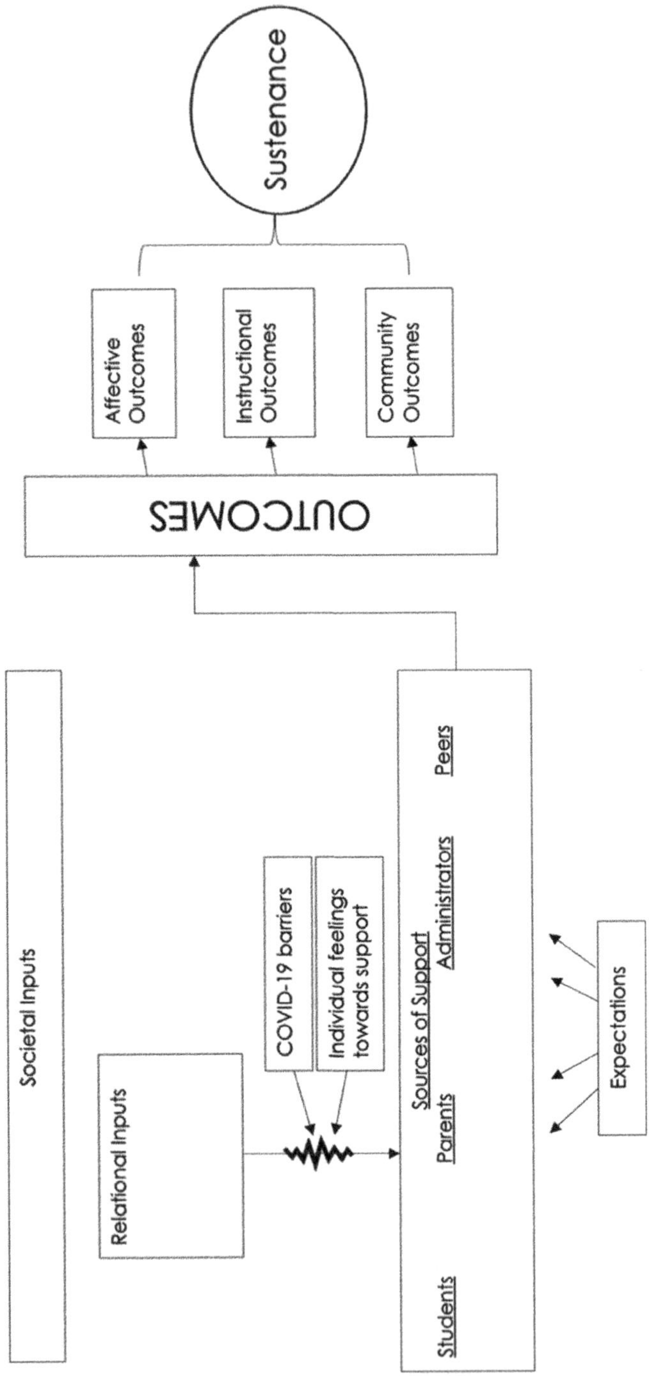

FIGURE 6.1. A Model of Social Support for Teachers During COVID-19

were examined to ultimately determine the core idea underlying how teachers were impacted by social support during the COVID-19 pandemic. Selecting coding involved four iterations of the process model (see Figure 6.1 for final model). To add trustworthiness to the study and its findings, all analyses were triangulated via collaborative workshops with other qualitative researchers in a large U.S. university.

Positionality

The lead author has a doctorate in educational psychology with prior experience as a K–12 teacher and administrator in an urban public elementary school. She first became curious about teacher turnover while working in an under-resourced school setting and experiencing teacher turnover both during and after each subsequent school year. She therefore entered this study with personal experiences of the impact of social support on her own prior work. Having received impactful mentorship and gratitude from various stakeholders in the educational sphere, she was interested in learning more about how teachers were faring working in public education during the COVID-19 pandemic and to what extent social support was, or was not, still an impactful aspect of their work. Given that the current U.S. public education teacher population is predominantly composed of White women, it is important to also disclose that she identifies as a White woman. The second author is an international student from India, currently pursuing a master's degree in the field of counseling psychology. Her work with teachers in rural districts of India has focused on their access to and utilization of Western conceptualizations of psychological concepts and highlighted the need for context-specific knowledge and traditions. Her field work has been focused on the integration of community support into the educational environment. The third author is a White male faculty member in Educational Psychology, with decades of research experience studying U.S. teacher stress and coping. His experience as a researcher has illuminated how teachers' lives can become unmanageable due to stress, but also the many ways in which they can mobilize resources and foster interpersonal connections as resources for coping.

FINDINGS

Figure 6.1 illustrates the model that was borne out of the current study's exploration. The model reads from left to right, beginning with social inputs and ending with the core idea: that social support provided sustenance for U.S. K–12 public education teachers during the COVID-19 pandemic. The core idea of sustenance therefore provides a parsimonious picture of how teachers' experiences of social support impacted them during the pandemic turbulence. The following sections follow the flow of the figure, from left to right, first discussing societal and relational inputs and mediators, then describing teachers' experiences with the four sources of social support, and finally discussing the three thematic outcomes and the core idea that captures it all: sustenance.

Societal Inputs

Societal inputs reflect the outermost source of influence on how teachers were impacted by social support during the COVID-19 pandemic. Whereas the bulk of teachers' experiences with social support were more insular in nature—they tended to all occur within the microcosm of their school district—there was a larger source of impact that they identified. The more global impact of society seemed to capture the ways in which social and cultural aspects of their work during the pandemic influenced how they received or needed social support.

Both positive and negative inputs were mentioned with regard to the influence of society. For example, when teachers were identified as a priority group to receive the vaccine immediately after it received FDA approval, this messaged to teachers that the greater society, or western U.S. culture, valued them. This positive societal input felt like an acknowledgement of the way that teachers were risking their health to continue their jobs during the pandemic. However, regarding the negative inputs from society, teachers also felt as though society viewed them as little more than babysitters: "I feel like it's a lack of feeling valued and maybe it's because of my perception where I feel like I'm not really a teacher. In their eyes, I'm a babysitter." Teachers recalled feeling like families only sent their children to school so that they could get their own work done but then didn't hold their children accountable for the same level of respect and care for their schooling experiences as they did in pre-pandemic times. Additionally, teachers identified that their perpetually low salaries felt like a reflection of low worth and little respect for the profession:

> I definitely feel like we are not appreciated just like a profession in general. I think the words are there. People are like, "Oh yes, we need our teachers. We support our teachers," [...] but I think that the salary definitely makes it hard sometimes [...] I don't think I could live comfortably if I didn't have a roommate or have somebody to split the bills with.

While this issue has been an identified issue for teachers before, during, and after the pandemic, the additional pressure of working an in-person job and exposing one's self to all of the pandemic-related demands and risks made this negative input feel particularly palpable.

Relational Inputs and Mediators

The impact of social support depended upon the relationships that each teacher had with the support giver. Teachers therefore identified three requisite relational inputs that enabled them to receive support in a helpful way: reciprocity, sincerity, and regularity. For a teacher to be impacted by someone giving them social support during COVID-19, they needed to feel as though they were in partnership with the support giver (reciprocity), support was not provided in a calculated way (sincerity), and the frequency of contact with the support giver was consistent (regularity).

In addition to these three inputs, two other variables were identified that mediated how a teacher received social support: (1) barriers and (2) the individual teacher's feelings towards social support. These variables introduced noise into the connection between the social support relationship and how the support was perceived—as reflected by the jagged line in the model. Barriers negatively impacted how teachers received social support, and the individual teacher's feelings positively impacted their social support experiences.

First, participating teachers identified barriers that negatively impacted teachers' experiences of social support. For example, teachers identified several physical and emotional barriers that were erected as a result of COVID-19 safety protocols. With the new forms of teaching modalities (e.g., hybrid teaching and virtual teaching), teachers felt disconnected from others in the building—students, peers, and administrators—and experienced noticeably reduced opportunities for interactions with others. For example, one teacher noted, "I think there has been a huge disconnect between teachers and administration. I think COVID just exacerbates the situation." Another teacher shared, "We're not connected. I feel like a lot of teachers have struggled this year [...] if they have interactions with people, it's usually negative about something they did wrong instead of finding ways to bring people up and uplift them." The combination of feeling disconnected from the larger community and experiencing minimal opportunities to interact face-to-face with others negatively impacted how teachers perceived social support.

Conversely, the second variable—the individual teacher's feelings towards social support—positively impacted teachers' experiences. A teacher's personal feelings towards receiving support was especially pertinent when receiving social support from peers: "With [peers], it's more specific and they're your support system, your lifeline when you have any questions." Teachers were therefore more receptive to receiving support from this group. Teachers also discussed how they perceived social support as "invaluable" and necessary for the profession, which propelled their general openness to receiving support from others. Thus, both relational inputs (reciprocity, sincerity, and regularity) and mediating variables (barriers to and a teacher's feelings about social support) played a role in what sources of support teachers had access to, what expectations they held about receiving support, and how they were ultimately impacted by their social support experiences during COVID-19.

The four groups of support providers that teachers also discussed, which are detailed in the following section, are illustrative of how these relational inputs and mediating variables led to differential support opportunities. That is, whether a teacher had access to or sought support from one or more of these particular groups of people depended upon these relational inputs (reciprocity, sincerity, and regularity) and mediating variables (barriers to and a teacher's feelings about social support). For example, one teacher demonstrated the impact of receiving support from a colleague that lifted her spirits during a time in which she felt she had minimal validation that her efforts mattered:

> A lot of times this year, I feel like I'm not doing enough for my kids. There's no way I could do enough for my mix of virtual and in-person kids. I just feel like I can't give them everything I need to give. I feel like that [encouraging] text [from my colleague] just really told me, what you're doing, it's good and it matters.

Alternatively, a different teacher who experienced barriers in access to administrative support identified student support as vital: "I think the only gratitude I've experienced this year was from students. I feel like that's much more important than admin gratitude or whatever. I felt completely admin-less this year, unless it was something negative." In these ways, teachers were identifying different sources and sharing different experiences of social support based upon the relational inputs and mediators described in this section.

Sources of Support

Teachers identified four main sources of support as impactful during COVID-19: students, parents, administrators, and peers. Interestingly, teacher perceptions of and expectations for support from each group varied.

When discussing student support, teachers shared how this type of support fostered connection. Teachers discussed how receiving support from current and former students sustained them during difficult days. In this way, student-driven sources of support were viewed as more impactful than any other sources of support. However, despite the high value placed on receiving student support, the expectations held for support from this group were consistently low. Teachers mentioned how simply hearing "Thank you" from students felt like support, particularly if they were hearing this gesture from a former student:

> Sometimes when I get emails from students that I taught last year that are seniors or have graduated that are emailing me to actually just take time out of their lives to personally thank me or let me know something. When Ruth Bader Ginsburg passed away, I had two students that were off at college email me like, "Ms. [teacher], did you see this?" That really makes me feel like I'm having a connection, which is for me the most important.

Regarding parent sources of support, these tended to be more indirect sources of support, and again the expectations teachers held for receiving parent support were low. For example, merely the presence of a parent response to any form of teacher communication felt like support for teachers. Such responses were interpreted by teachers as confirmation that a home-school connection was present: "The email this morning from that parent, it made me feel good that first of all, they want their child to pass and are responding to emails that I send because honestly, that doesn't happen all the time, unfortunately." The presence of a home-school connection, spanning from simple communication responses to more involved volunteering with the school's parent teacher association (PTA), therefore fostered feelings of social support among teachers.

For administrator support, several types of administrative roles were discussed as sources of support. Teachers identified assistant principals, principals, instructional coaches, and school counselors as sources of support for their work during the COVID-19 pandemic. Administrator support was therefore predominantly focused at the school-level, as opposed to receiving support from district-level employees. In contrast to the low expectations that teachers held for student and parent support, the unspoken bar for administrator support was quite high. For example, teachers spoke of their frustration with receiving empty support from this group and feeling as though any verbalized support from administration always came with an additional request. For example:

> Our administrators will often sing a praise in paragraph one, and paragraph two is like, "Oh, and by the way, all [grade-level] teachers must now start lunch duty, so work that out." You're like, "Ah, so you're buttering me up."

Unlike student-driven support, which was unequivocally determined to be positively impactful for teachers, administrator support tended to garner mixed reactions. As a result, teachers expected a lot from administrator support, and they desired support beyond the verbal affirmation of their work or the occasional bringing of edible treats. Instead, teachers communicated that the strongest form of administrator support was receiving their trust and respect. Teachers especially desired to be given appropriate amounts of autonomy, as this messaged to them that they were seen by their administration as a trusted partner in the work.

The final source of support discussed by participating teachers was peer support. When discussing support from peers, teachers spoke of the power of "side-by-side" support. Not only did they feel that their peers were available to help them with their specific needs, but teachers also viewed peers as catalysts for receiving support from other groups. For example, teachers spoke to how peer support helped initiate greater support from students and the larger school community. In this way, teachers supported one another in "feeling seen" in their work and feeling as though they were a part of a larger supportive environment.

Teachers also reflected on the power of intergenerational support that peers provided during the COVID-19 pandemic. For example, one veteran teacher with over 20 years of experience needed to rely heavily upon a novice teacher who had less teaching experience but greater competency in navigating the new virtual and hybrid teaching modalities. Whereas this veteran teacher had never before sought help from a novice teacher, the pandemic-spurred technology requirements initiated new opportunities for intergenerational peer support. Overall, there was a tenderness in participating teachers' tone when discussing support given to and received by their peers. The impact of colleagues' support during such a difficult time in education was palpable for participating teachers. Additionally, unlike the clear ways in which expectations for social support from all other groups manifested, teachers appeared to view peer social support in the most neutral or welcoming way. Teachers' expectations for supporting one another felt discernible in this way and seemed to keep teachers open to the opportunity that their peers may be their greatest source of strength during such a turbulent time.

Support Outcomes

Three overarching outcomes were captured in participants' support experiences during the COVID-19 pandemic: affective, instructional, and community outcomes. Each of these outcomes impacted a teacher's work during the pandemic in unique ways. The three thematic outcomes illustrate how support was helpful for teachers at the individual level (affective), the classroom level (instructional), and the building level (community).

Regarding affective outcomes from receiving support, teachers shared several somatically oriented effects. For example, teachers shared that receiving support "made me relax my shoulders", "[felt] like a recharge of the battery", and "made me feel worthy". Another teacher shared the apt takeaway that, "In a field driven by thinking of others, feeling thought of makes waves." In this way, teachers experienced a broad range of personally impactful and affective outcomes as a result of receiving social support during the COVID-19 pandemic. These affective outcomes therefore served as sources of resilience, persistence, and motivation to continue in their work. Teachers also voiced that support helped them with necessary mindset shifts in the midst of the chaos of their working environment and ultimately helped them with boundary drawing in order to sustain their work.

The second group of outcomes was characterized by the instructional benefits that resulted from social support, which varied based upon the support provider. For example, when a teacher was able to connect with a parent about a specific student need, the teacher felt reassured that they were making an impact in their classroom. Teachers also noted feeling validated in their instructional choices when they received support from administrators. Additionally, support from peers was noted to feel organic and provided just-in-time support in terms of instructional needs related to COVID-19 teaching adaptations:

> Somebody would learn about a program and then they would teach all of us, but it wasn't like a staff development on it. It was like, "Hey, who wants to learn about [instructional software]," or whatever all these [technology requirements] were. I think it made me better because I had time for my family because I wasn't having to learn all these things all on my own. People could help you…I don't know, it just helped me not have to reinvent the wheel. It does make you feel closer, especially in a year like this when you're all going through this crazy time together.

The final group of social support outcomes were related to community outcomes. These outcomes occurred at the broadest level of a teacher's work, impacting not just their individual lives and classrooms, but also the larger community in which they operate. For example, teachers identified feeling greatly impacted by support that was received from individuals beyond their immediate grade-level or subject-area team, which supported them in feeling grounded in a larger community and greater purpose. Teachers also shared how the broader community often felt disapproving of or disrespectful to their work during the pandemic. Community outcomes therefore bolstered teachers' resilience against the larger negativity of this time, because while teachers knew they were functioning as front-line workers, the media did not always portray such. Similar to the experience of healthcare workers during COVID-19, teachers felt like a lot was placed on their shoulders, and the opportunity to foster relationships in their school building and nurture their empathy for one another was critical. One teacher noted that feeling more connected in their school community was impactful for them as it "made me feel like I'm not adrift in the ocean." Community outcomes were therefore anchoring for teachers and provided connection during a time in which COVID-19 protocols greatly limited the usual interactions associated with their work.

Core Idea—Sustenance

The presence of support from the various groups of support providers—students, parents, administrators, and peers—as well as the ways in which teachers were impacted by the support at an affective, instructional, and community level, ultimately served as sustenance for teachers working in an ever-changing and challenging environment during COVID-19. Receiving support while teaching during the pandemic therefore sustained teachers in their work; support didn't necessarily enable them to thrive or cheer in jubilee at the end of each school day, but it did help them to continue to put one foot in front of the other and face each new day and challenge.

DISCUSSION AND CONCLUSIONS

Findings revealed a modified grounded theory of how social support served as sustenance for teachers and buoyed them in the turbulent pandemic waters. Research conducted before the COVID-19 pandemic showed the promise of practices that facilitate social support in education, such as beginning teacher mentoring (Mosley & McCarthy, 2023), but the disruptions that occurred due to social distancing during the pandemic posed questions for how previously identified support practices may persist in the face of new working environments. This study presents evidence that social support for teachers can be given and received in the face of ever-changing and uncertain workplace demands and that such support enables teachers to sustain their work.

Social support was particularly salient for teachers during this difficult time, as they felt they were putting their own lives at risk each day and receiving little concern from others for their wellbeing. Teachers shared about unexpectedly receiving negative societal messages about their commitment to work during the pandemic. These messages communicated that the broader society held little regard for the ways in which teachers were exposing themselves to the deadly virus in order to conduct their work. These findings aligned with recent research that has shown that teachers felt their health to be taken for granted during the COVID-19 pandemic, with inconsistent and/or unclear COVID-19 protocols carried out (Chang et al., 2022). However, the current study demonstrated how social support provided teachers with sustenance in their work during a difficult time, which demonstrates the power of close personal ties in the workplace. In practice, these findings imply that making time for teachers to engage in positive interactions with students, students' parents, peers, and administrators is pertinent; these interactions signal to teachers that they matter, their work is necessary, and they are not alone in their endeavors.

Prior research has identified social support as tending to be greater in smaller (versus larger) communities, which may account for how teachers perceived societal messages about their work (House et al., 1988). That is, whereas teachers spoke highly of receiving support from closer sources in which they were more intimately connected, such as with colleagues and students, fewer instances of positive social support were perceived from more ancillary sources, such as those from administrators and society. The impact of administrators and the school culture they foster has long been understood to impact teachers' experiences (Skaalvik & Skaalvik, 2009), and the current study further underpins the understanding that a positive leader-teacher relationship is vital to a teacher's success. The implications of the negative interactions between some teachers and administrators in the current study reveals that this is a relationship that should be fostered as diligently as other support groups, particularly when teachers are facing stark workplace changes like they experienced during the pandemic.

Regarding the outcomes of social support that participating teachers shared, the three overarching outcomes align with the types of support that Cutrona and Russell (1990) posited. Specifically, the affective, instructional, and community outcomes revealed in the current study map onto Cutrona and Russell's descriptions of the emotional, informational, and social integration types of support, respectively. The current study's outcomes are also in conversation with Kyriacou's (1981) descriptions of the three outcomes of coping through social support: relieving tension through social interaction, receiving advice on direct-action techniques to reduce stressors in the classroom, and perspective building on the nature of problems. Thus, the current study's findings theoretically add to well-cited social support theories that are both work-agnostic (Cutrona & Russell, 1990) and work-specific (Kyriacou, 1981). The resultant grounded theory of how teachers experienced social support during the COVID-19 pandemic presents new evidence to support these existing theories as well as a sturdy foundation on which additional research can be conducted beyond the pandemic years.

The breadth of support types shared by participating teachers demonstrates the wide-reaching nature of their work (Sandilos et al., 2018). Teachers wear many hats during any given workday, yet their role was further expanded as they adjusted to COVID-19 changes and barriers in their work. The difficulties of the added roles likely warranted additional social support, which not all participating teachers experienced. It is worrisome to note that many of the participating teachers—among others in the field—are likely at greater risk for experiencing stress and burnout as a result of an insidious mix of high expectations, numerous changes, and low support (Ju et al., 2015). Moving forward, school leaders should prioritize teacher wellbeing when navigating broad changes or new obstacles, and the current study's findings illustrate how the presence of social support—especially in the form of gratitude and mentoring—is a viable and scalable way to ensure teachers are able to sustain their jobs in the face of new challenges.

REFERENCES

Betoret, F. D., & Artiga, A. G. (2010). Barriers perceived by teachers at work, coping strategies, self-efficacy and burnout. *The Spanish Journal of Psychology, 13*(2), 637–654. http://dx.doi.org/10.1017/S1138741600002316

Burke, R. J., & Greenglass, E. (1993). Work stress, role conflict, social support, and psychological burnout among teachers. *Psychological Reports, 73*(2), 371–380. http://dx.doi.org/10.2466/pr0.1993.73.2.371

Chang, M. L., Gaines, R. E., & Mosley, K. C. (2022). Effects of autonomy support and emotion regulation on teacher burnout in the era of the COVID-19 pandemic. *Frontiers in Psychology, 13*, 846290. http://dx.doi.org/10.3389/fpsyg.2022.846290

Cohen, S., & McKay, G. (2020). Social support, stress and the buffering hypothesis: A theoretical analysis. In *Handbook of psychology and health* (vol. IV, pp. 253–267). Routledge. http://dx.doi.org/10.4324/9781003044307-10

Corbin, J. M., & Strauss, A. (1990). Grounded theory research: Procedures, canons, and evaluative criteria. *Qualitative Sociology, 13*(1), 3–21. http://dx.doi.org/10.1007/BF00988593

Cutrona, C. E., & Russell, D. W. (1990). Type of social support and specific stress: Toward a theory of optimal matching. In B. R. Sarason, I. G. Sarason, & G. R. Pierce (Eds.), *Social support: An interactional view* (pp. 319–366). John Wiley & Sons.

Diliberti, M., Schwartz, H. L., & Grant, D. M. (2021). *Stress topped the reasons why public school teachers quit, even before COVID-19*. RAND. https://www.rand.org/content/dam/rand/pubs/research_reports/RRA1100/RRA1121-2/RAND_RRA1121-2.pdf

Fiorilli, C., Benevene, P., De Stasio, S., Buonomo, I., Romano, L., Pepe, A., & Addimando, L. (2019). Teachers' burnout: The role of trait emotional intelligence and social support. *Frontiers in Psychology, 10*, 2743. http://dx.doi.org/10.3389/fpsyg.2019.02743

Geiger, T., & Pivovarova, M. (2018). The effects of working conditions on teacher retention. *Teachers and Teaching, 602*, 1–22. doi: 10.1080/13540602.2018.1457524

House, J. S., Umberson, D., & Landis, K. R. (1988). Structures and processes of social support. *Annual Review of Sociology, 14*(1), 293–318. http://dx.doi.org/10.1146/annurev.so.14.080188.001453

Ju, C., Lan, J., Li, Y., Feng, W., & You, X. (2015). The mediating role of workplace social support on the relationship between trait emotional intelligence and teacher burnout. *Teaching and Teacher Education*, *51*, 58–67. http://dx.doi.org/10.1016/j.tate.2015.06.001

Kyriacou, C. (1981). Social support and occupational stress among schoolteachers. *Educational Studies, 7*(1), 55–60. http://dx.doi.org/10.1080/0305569810070108

Lambert, R. G., McCarthy, C., O'Donnell, M., & Wang, C. (2009). Measuring elementary teacher stress and coping in the classroom: Validity evidence for the classroom appraisal of resources and demands. *Psychology in the Schools*, *46*(10), 973–988. http://dx.doi.org/10.1002/pits.20438

Lazarus, R. S., & Folkman, S. (1984). *Stress, appraisal, and coping*. Springer Publishing Company.

MacIntyre, P. D., Gregersen, T., & Mercer, S. (2020). Language teachers' coping strategies during the COVID-19 conversion to online teaching: Correlations with stress, wellbeing and negative emotions. *System*, *94*, 102352. http://dx.doi.org/10.1016/j.system.2020.102352

McCarthy, C. J., Lambert, R. G., Lineback, S., Fitchett, P., & Baddouh, P. G. (2016). Assessing teacher appraisals and stress in the classroom: Review of the classroom appraisal of resources and demands. *Educational Psychology Review, 28*, 577–603. http://dx.doi.org/10.1007/s10648-015-9322-6

McCarthy, C. J., Mosley, K. C., & Dillard, J. B. (2022). Teacher stress and classroom management. In *Handbook of classroom management* (pp. 189–210). Routledge. http://dx.doi.org/10.4324/9781003275312-14

Mérida-López, S., Extremera, N., & Rey, L. (2017). Contributions of work-related stress and emotional intelligence to teacher engagement: Additive and interactive effects. *International Journal of Environmental Research and Public Health*, *14*(10), 1156. http://dx.doi.org/10.3390/ijerph14101156

Mosley, K. C. (2022). *Measuring teacher stress: validity and reliability evidence for the classroom appraisal of resources and demands-revised* (CARD-R) (Doctoral dissertation). https://repositories.lib.utexas.edu/server/api/core/bitstreams/63e1e7c3-9b29-4c5e-87a3-91f6180157bf/content

Mosley, K. C., & McCarthy, C. J. (2023). Beginning teacher mentoring: Associations between mentoring experiences and stress among first year teachers. *The Teacher Educator*, 1–19. http://dx.doi.org/10.1080/08878730.2023.2175402

Mosley, K. C., McCarthy, C. J., Lambert, R. G., Fitchett, P. G., & Dillard, J. B. (2023). Elementary teacher occupational health outcomes across schools with varying resources and demographics. *Psychology in the Schools*, *60*(4), 943–964. DOI: 10.1002/pits.22814

Norwich, B., & Daniels, H. (1997). Teacher support teams for special educational needs in primary schools: Evaluating a teacher-focused support scheme. *Educational Studies*, *23*(1), 5–24. http://dx.doi.org/10.1080/0305569970230101

Rodgers, B. L., & Cowles, K. V. (1993). The qualitative research audit trail: A complex collection of documentation. *Research in Nursing & Health*, *16*(3), 219–226. http://dx.doi.org/10.1002/nur.4770160309

Sandilos, L. E., Goble, P., Rimm-Kaufman, S. E., & Pianta, R. C. (2018). Does professional development reduce the influence of teacher stress on teacher–child interactions in pre-kindergarten classrooms? *Early Childhood Research Quarterly*, *42*, 280–290. http://dx.doi.org/10.1016/j.ecresq.2017.10.009

Skaalvik, E. M., & Skaalvik, S. (2009). Does school context matter? Relations with teacher burnout and job satisfaction. *Teaching and Teacher Education*, *25*(3), 518–524. http://dx.doi.org/10.1016/j.tate.2008.12.006

Skaalvik, E. M., & Skaalvik, S. (2017). Teacher stress and teacher self-efficacy: Relations and consequences. In *Educator Stress* (pp. 101–125). Springer, Cham. http://dx.doi.org/10.1007/978-3-319-53053-6_5

Suárez, M. I., & Wright, K. B. (2019). Investigating school climate and school leadership factors that impact secondary STEM teacher retention. *Journal for STEM Education Research*, *2*(1), 55–74. http://dx.doi.org/10.1007/s41979-019-00012-z

Travers, C. (2017). Current knowledge on the nature, prevalence, sources and potential impact of teacher stress. *Educator Stress*, 23–54. http://dx.doi.org/10.1007/978-3-319-53053-6_2

APPENDIX: FOCUS GROUP QUESTIONS

1. In your view how can receiving gratitude be helpful to teachers?
2. What, if any, forms of gratitude do you receive from students and their families?
    a. How frequently do you receive gratitude from them?
    b. What are contexts in which you receive gratitude from them?
    c. What impact does this have on you?
3. What, if any, forms of gratitude do you receive from colleagues and administrators?
    a. How frequently do you receive gratitude from them?
    b. What are contexts in which you receive gratitude from them?
    c. What impact does this have on you?
4. What makes gratitude meaningful to you?
5. Do you feel you receive adequate gratitude for the work you do as a teacher?
6. In your experience does receiving gratitude impact your belief in your ability to teach your students successfully?
7. In your experience does receiving gratitude impact your stress levels?
8. Does receiving gratitude have any other impacts on you that we have not discussed today?
9. Do you have any experience with mentoring? If so, what has your experience with a mentor been like?
    a. What was this mentorship like? (formal, informal, multiple, etc.)
10. How do you define or know when you are receiving mentorship in your work?
    a. How do you think mentorship is different from professional development, coaching, or working with your supervisor?
11. In what specific ways has receiving mentorship helped your work?

a. How has your mentor helped {if needed} teaching grade/subject matter, selecting/adapting curriculum, classroom management, using tech, assessing students & interpreting data, interacting with parents, reflection/development
b. Or, for example, has receiving mentorship helped you socially, emotionally, navigate demands, stay motivated/encouraged, etc.?

12. Overall, to what extent did your mentoring experience improve your teaching?
    a. Are there areas in which mentoring is lacking/needed?
    b. Are there ways that you think mentorship could be more helpful?

CHAPTER 7

TEACHER SELF-EFFICACY DURING COVID-19

A Qualitative Study on Experienced High School Teachers

Sarah M. Conley
George Mason University

With the entire structure of education forced to change to online learning during COVID-19, insights from Bandura's (1997) Social Cognitive Theory, specifically teacher self-efficacy, can provide a framework to view how teachers adapted during this time. This qualitative study focused on teacher's experiences within the four sources that have been observed to impact self-efficacy, including mastery experiences, vicarious experiences, social persuasion, and physiological state (Usher & Pajares, 2006). Seven teachers with at least ten or more years of experience in a public high school were interviewed for this research. This study observed that each teacher was impacted, to varying degrees, in each of the four sources of self-efficacy between March 2020 and June 2022. The most impacted sources of self-efficacy among all participants were with mastery experiences, social persuasion, and personal physiological state. This study's findings suggest that the amount of support from schools and leadership played a significant role in how well teachers were

Instructional Survival in the Midst of the Perfect Storm:
The Experiences of K–12 Teachers During the COVID-19 Global Pandemic, pages 107–126.

Published under exclusive licence by Emerald Publishing Limited
ISBNs: 978-1-83708-502-6 HB, 978-1-83708-503-3 PB,
978-1-83708-504-0 EPDF, 978-1-83708-505-7 EPUB

able to regain their self-efficacy beliefs to where they were pre-COVID. In addition, results found that teachers who had an adaptable growth mindset toward teaching were more likely to easily rebound from self-efficacy loss. Based on these findings, school districts should evaluate what kinds of support they provide to teachers, both pre- and post-COVID. Focusing on what teachers need most, considerations should potentially address emotional adaptability and wellness opportunities to help teachers not only recover from the lingering effects of COVID-19, but also the everyday changes they face in the classroom.

INTRODUCTION

In March of 2020, education around the world completely changed as schools needed to react to the global health crisis, close their doors, and move to online learning. In the state of Virginia, all schools were ordered to close on March 23, 2020 for the rest of the 2019–2020 school year by Governor Northam in Executive Order # 61 (VDOE: School Closure FAQ., n.d.). At that time, Virginia's only formal guidance on teaching was to keep equity, accessibility, and intention in mind if schools chose to move to online learning (VDOE :: School Closure FAQ., n.d.). While some schools and communities were able to pivot quickly to live virtual classes, other schools had a more challenging time reaching that point, due to internet connectivity issues and a lack of student devices (United Nations Educational, Scientific and Cultural Organization, 2020). School closures spurred a sequence of immediate concerns including learning loss, low-income students not receiving meals, and students being home alone or caring for siblings (United Nations Educational, Scientific and Cultural Organization, 2020). At the start of the 2020–2021 school year, most schools in Virginia began with a 100% online model. By June of 2021, out of a total of 2,045 schools, 868 schools were operating in a hybrid format and 1,097 were conducting in-person instruction (VDOE :: State Snapshot: Virginia School Operational Status., n.d.). At the start of the 2021–2022 school year, all divisions in the state of Virginia were required to offer in-person learning, (VDOE :: State Snapshot: Virginia School Operational Status., n.d.). Moreover, long-term concerns about teachers and how they were able to adapt to the changes are still being identified two years later. This study seeks to observe and explore the phenomenon of COVID-19's impact on teachers' self-efficacy beliefs as educators. A specific focus was on experienced high school teachers, who had at least ten or more years of teaching experience when the pandemic began.

SELF-EFFICACY DEFINED

When a person is facing an obstacle or challenge that they have never experienced, their first thoughts are often whether they will be able to work through it. Depending on the situation, some people might feel confident and ready to take on the challenge, but others might feel the opposite. Bandura defined this construct of whether a person feels and believes that they can successfully complete a task as self-efficacy; a component of social cognitive theory (1997). Self-efficacy, explored further by Usher and Pajares (2006), can be influenced by four major sources including mastery experiences, vicarious experiences, social persuasion, and physiological state. The first source of influence on a person's self-efficacy is mastery experiences, which is whether a person has had previous success at a task prior to facing a new challenge (Usher & Pajares, 2006). Second is vicarious experiences, or how a person perceives they can complete a task based solely on how others like them can do it (Usher & Pajares, 2006). Next, social persuasion refers to the messages received from others about one's ability to be successful at a task (Usher & Pajares, 2006). The last influential source in Usher and Pajares' (2006) research is a person's physiological state. This component focuses on the idea that a person who normally would feel confident in achieving a task might not feel the same if they are experiencing elevated levels of stress or anxiety. Self-efficacy suggests that a person's temperament, experiences they have gone through, and experiences they are currently going through, will impact whether they have a high or low self-efficacy belief about if they can accomplish new and different tasks (Bandura, 1997).

Teacher Self-Efficacy

The concept of self-efficacy can also be related to how individuals perceive themselves in their careers. Applying this theory to education, teachers and their personal views of self-efficacy can have an impact on their students, instruction quality, and overall mindset on their careers. Researchers Dicke et al. (2014) identify teacher self-efficacy as the confidence and belief a teacher has about their ability to be a successful educator. Further, the number of years of experience and individual successes and failures in the classroom can impact their self-efficacy beliefs. Research done by Klassen and Chiu (2010) assessed three domains of teacher self-efficacy, including student engagement, instructional strategies, and classroom management. Moreover, they discovered that a teacher's self-efficacy increases as they have more years of experience, but that soon begins to decrease as they enter their veteran years of teaching (Klassen & Chiu, 2010). Teachers will experience highs and lows in their sense of teaching self-efficacy beliefs throughout their careers, depending on the support they receive as a teacher and the experiences they have in the classroom. With the variety of influences, this suggests that teacher self-efficacy is dynamic and will be impacted by factors at different points throughout a person's teaching career.

PROBLEM STATEMENT

Knowing the dynamic nature of teacher self-efficacy beliefs, continued and specified research on COVID-19's impact on educators could provide new insights on teacher self-efficacy beliefs. Pre-existing teacher self-efficacy research by Klassen and Chiu (2010) suggests that experienced teachers typically identify a high level of self-efficacy. As a result, it is important to observe if teachers at the suggested high point of teacher self-efficacy were negatively impacted from COVID-19. Therefore, the guiding research questions of this study are: What were teachers' experiences adjusting to changes in education during the COVID-19 pandemic? How did the experiences of veteran teachers during this time impact their teacher self-efficacy beliefs and outlook on their career? Additionally, building on the emerging findings of the study, a third question was added. What external factors helped support teachers' self-efficacy during these two years?

REVIEW OF THE LITERATURE

Technology Roadblocks

A few years before the pandemic, researchers Corry and Stella (2018) conducted a literature review on technology's impact on teacher self-efficacy, which suggested that a lack of mastery experiences specifically with technology can cause decreased teacher self-efficacy. Looking at current research, many teachers identified that the biggest challenge for them was lacking proficient knowledge of the online teaching tools (Cardullo et al., 2021). This supports findings from other studies that observed teachers with proper training or prior experience displayed both higher self-efficacy and higher student success overall (Baroudi & Shaya, 2022; Buric et al., 2021; Dolighan & Owen, 2021; Ladendorf et al., 2021). In fact, researchers Tas et al. (2021) observed that teachers with prior experience teaching online courses identified higher self-efficacy during COVID-19 than educators with several years of only in-person teaching experiences. Connecting this to Usher and Pajares' (2006) self-efficacy research, teachers' mastery experiences with technology played a role in how well they maintained their self-efficacy beliefs when moving to an online format.

Observing technology's influence on teachers' physiological and mental state, Fernández-Batanero et al. (2021) conducted a literature review that found increased levels of teacher stress and anxiety were related to educational technology. Moreover, several studies conducted on teachers' stress levels with technology found increased psychological fatigue, stress, and anxiety when they were faced with teaching online (Aktan & Toraman, 2022; Pressley et al., 2021; Toto & Limone, 2021). However, a study conducted in China by Ma et al. (2021) found that, while most teachers experienced a struggle initially, some were able to improve if they had personal adaptive qualities and prior knowledge of how to teach online.

Instructional Content: Delivery and Effectiveness

Current COVID-19 research is finding that teachers felt they were unable to provide meaningful and effective instruction when teaching online, even if they were confident in using online teaching resources (Ladendorf et al., 2021). In the Turkish study done by Tas et al. (2021), 90% of teachers surveyed felt that online teaching was not as efficient as face-to-face instruction. A survey done by Pressley and Ha (2021) identified lower instructional self-efficacy scores for teachers who taught 100% online, compared to the higher scores from the teachers who were teaching in-person. However, teachers' confidence in their instructional quality did vary depending on the content they taught, with some content being able to better transition to an online format than others (Ladendorf et al., 2021; Menabò et al., 2022; Tas et al., 2021).

Students: Absent and Disconnected

Reviewing past research on self-efficacy, Hajovsky et al. (2019) observed that teachers with better connections and relationships with their students tend to have higher self- efficacy beliefs. In a current COVID-19 study, Tas et al. found that most teachers had less than 75% of their students attending on a regular basis when teaching moved to an online format (2021). They also found that 80% of their sample identified they were less motivated when teaching because of the lack of student engagement (Tas et al., 2021). Research by Yang et al. (2021) found that teachers struggled to find ways to connect to their students since their only interaction was through a computer. In fact, several studies found that teachers' inability to form relationships with their students resulted in a type of "disorientation" and feeling that they lost their purpose (Narayanan & Ordynans, 2022; Soncini et al., 2021). Observing a wider group, a survey including in-person teachers, hybrid teachers, and 100% virtual teachers were asked about their confidence and ability to engage students. Among the three groups, the lowest scoring on the engagement self-efficacy measurement was the group of teachers who were teaching 100% virtually (Pressley & Ha, 2021).

Years of Teaching Experience

Among current research, there are mixed results identifying how self-efficacy beliefs of teachers with several years of teaching experience changed during COVID-19. Some research identifies that the number of years of face-to-face classroom teaching experience had no significant impact on how well a teacher adjusted to online teaching (Pressley, 2021; Pressley & Ha, 2021; Tas et al., 2021). However, research done by Yang et al. (2021) identified teachers who had more years of teaching experience suffered less from emotional fatigue brought on by a lack of student connections, which would suggest that the more years of experience was an asset. Another example, with research done by Pellerone (2021) in Italy, found that the strength of teacher self-efficacy before COVID-19 helped teachers overcome more of the emotional challenges brought on by it. Research done by Cataudella et al., (2021) identified that teachers who had more experience at the start of the pandemic had a more notable change in self-efficacy during this time than people with fewer years of experience. In line with these findings, Rabaglietti et al. (2021) concluded that an increase in teacher's perceived stress levels when they transitioned to a new form of teaching through distance learning caused a decrease in a teacher's self-efficacy beliefs for even the most experienced teachers.

METHODS

Design

One of the primary goals of the study was to learn about how teachers experienced the events of COVID-19 and how teachers' sense of effectiveness and abilities in their classroom changed. The design for this research was a qualitative interview study consisting of individual semi-structured interviews. A sample of seven teachers were interviewed in the Summer of 2022, just over two years from when schools initially shut down. With research by Klassen and Chiu (2010) showing that teachers typically have a high self-efficacy at the mid-point of their teaching career, this study chose to define the mid-point of teacher's careers as having ten years or more of experience as of the 2019–2020 school year. Due to the researcher's personal background and experience in education during the time of COVID-19, the researcher role is considered a participant observer, who was not known by the participants prior to the study. Institutional Review Board approval was requested and approved. Before the interviews began, all participants signed informed consent documentation that reassured teachers of confidentiality and their voluntary participation. All data was documented under pseudonyms and any identifiable details were removed, altered, and modified to create anonymity prior to coding.

Participants

The specific population being researched was high school teachers who were at or close to the mid-point of their career when COVID-19 began impacting the education system. Criterion sampling was used to identify teachers from a public high school in the state of Virginia, at least 10 years of teaching experience as of the beginning of the 2019–2020 school year and have continued to teach in the same teaching role since the 2019 school year. The sample was open to contain any variety of genders, racial and cultural backgrounds, school districts, and content areas that they teach. Research flyers were sent to teachers who are members of the Virginia Education Association (VEA) through direct email and social media channels. The VEA is a teachers' union for the state of Virginia that consists of over 40,000 teachers in VA public schools. Snowball sampling also occurred when teachers who heard about the study through the VEA shared the research flyer with other coworkers. To formally express interest in participating in the study, teachers completed an interest survey that was included on the research flyers.

There were eighteen volunteers in total who completed the interest survey, resulting in seven teachers selected to be interviewed. Of those not interviewed, seven teachers submitted the interest survey but did not fit the correct criteria. Ad-

TABLE 7.1. Participants Selected for the Study

Participant	#1 Jack	#2 Jen	#3 Laura	#4 Megan	#5 Marissa	#6 Barbara	#7 Rob
Years of Experience	27	36	13	18	18	23	22
Subject Taught	Theater	Theater & English	History	German	English	Earth Science	History
School District Identifier	1	2	3	1	2	4	2
VDOE Region Information	#4: Northern Virginia	# 3: Northern Neck	# 5: Valley	# 4: Northern Virginia	# 3: Northern Neck	# 3: Northern Neck	# 3: Northern Neck

ditionally, four teachers who completed the survey met the criteria but did not respond to the researcher's email follow-up requesting a formal interview. It should be noted, two extra interviews were conducted with teachers who misinterpreted the requirements when asked or left out information on the interest survey. Those two interviews were not analyzed as part of this study since the teachers did not fit the inclusion criteria. Table 7.1 provides details about each of the seven participants who were selected for the sample, including each teacher's pseudonym and years of experience at the time of the interview (interviews were conducted in the Summer of 2022).

Data Collection

To collect meaningful data about each teacher's self-efficacy beliefs during COVID-19, each participant participated in one semi-structured interview that lasted approximately 1 hour, with the option for follow-up interviews if requested. Each interview focused on teacher's experiences during COVID-19 as they relate to Usher and Pajares's (2006) four sources known to influence teacher self-efficacy beliefs, including mastery experiences, vicarious experiences, social persuasion, and physiological state, which was based on Bandura's 1997 self-efficacy research. When interviewing the participants, several phenomenological interview techniques were used to help the teachers remember specific details and events as they occurred over the last two years (McMillan, 2016). The interview was sectioned into four chunks of time to best support teacher memories and encourage reflection based on the changes that were occurring. The sections of time were, March 2020- August 2020, August 2020- December 2020, January 2021–June 2021, and August 2021- June 2022. At the start of each section, the researcher described briefly what was happening with COVID-19 in the state of Virginia at that time, including the state decisions being made and what the expectations were for schools. Teachers were then asked descriptive/narrative context questions about what their specific schools and school districts were doing during that time, to help further contextualize. They were asked descriptive structural questions to describe sequences of events as they occurred, since many different changes were happening in the initial months of the COVID-19 shut-down. This prompted the participants to recall more specifically the events that unfolded and provided insight as to how they saw it happen. Before moving on to the next section of time, imaginative variation questions were asked to encourage the teacher to reflect on how the events would have been different with different situations or supports. Using these phenomenological prompt structures, the teachers were able to provide meaningful details and recollections of what they went through.

After the teacher recalled and contextualized events, participants were asked a series of questions relating to the four main sources of teacher self-efficacy (Usher & Pajares, 2006). They were asked questions about how their successes and failures during each period impacted their ability to adapt content. They were asked about how their peers worked through the events and what impact those peer-influenced vicarious experiences had on their own perspective. Teachers were prompted to explain what verbal/social responses they were receiving from students, parents, administrators, etc. and how those social interactions impacted their beliefs as a teacher during each chunk of time. There were a series of questions asking what teachers were experiencing physiologically and if they felt that those feelings impacted their ability to cope with the changes. Additional questions were asked of teachers to define their confidence as a teacher pre-COVID compared to now, and where they see their career moving forward. Interviews were conducted virtually to ensure the participant felt safe and comfortable during the ongoing health crisis.

Data Analysis

The interviews were transcribed verbatim, removed of identifiable information, and coded using the software program MAXQDA 2022 (VERBI Software, 2021). Information was coded initially using emic and in vivo coding to gather preliminary information based on the participants unique word choices and emotions. Then, the transcriptions were reviewed to search for etic codes, with the goal to begin connecting common trends across multiple participants. With these cross-interview observations, thematic coding began, which was identified and sorted into the a priori codes of the four sources known to influence self-efficacy (e.g., mastery experiences, vicarious experiences, social persuasion, and physiological state). Major codes were the four sources of self-efficacy and sub-codes included specific topics that teachers mentioned relating to the major code. This sorting was used to observe any trends in self-efficacy and to identify where there were shared experiences of the participants during these past two years. Additional inductive codes were created based on additional insights teachers were having that did not fit within the a priori coding system.

RESULTS

After coding the interviews, a detailed review began with a focus to identify any trends relating to the main sources that impact teacher self-efficacy. Each interview was explored to see what teachers' experiences were when adapting to changes during the COVID-19 pandemic and how veteran teachers felt throughout those two years. Moreover, after reviewing findings, a third research question was added to address additional factors that helped support teachers' self-efficacy during this time.

Mastery Experiences

Reviewing results relating to teachers' mastery experiences, many teachers identified they already had some experiences that influenced how they adapted during that time. For example, prior to COVID-19, Jen had earned a master's degree in Curriculum design and Technology in the Classroom. In fact, she directly attributed this degree to her ease of adapting online and said she was fortunate to have that academic preparation. Additionally, all seven interviewed teachers identified as having already been incorporating some types of technology into their classrooms, at least in a very basic level, pre-pandemic. Several said that they were using Google Classroom to provide digital versions of notes and collect essays/projects. This prior use was helpful, but when schools purchased more complex Learning Management Systems (online platforms where teachers could build assignments, quizzes, tests), some struggled with the more advanced type of software and converting their materials. Barbara identified that her school district had become a 1:1 school about two years earlier, providing each student with their own computer to use for schoolwork, and purchased a Learning Management System called Schoology. With both Schoology and the regular use of computers already implemented, Barbara's district had very few adjustments to make when the pandemic shut schools down.

However, it was not only prior technology use that teachers found helpful. Some teachers identified that their everyday experiences in the classroom over the years were helpful during COVID-19. For example, Rob identified that he has always been the go-to teacher to be given special education classes. As a result, he explained that he is used to constantly teaching large class sizes, having different accommodations to provide to individual students, all while managing different types of behavioral challenges. Faced with these types of situations daily, he commented that he had a lot of experience being adaptable. He learned early on in his career that he needed to constantly reflect and evaluate what was working or not and be ready to adapt to anything.

Looking further into these teachers' mastery experiences during the initial months of the pandemic, teachers identified that successfully adapting their curriculum was a roller-coaster at times. Teachers felt purpose and passion when activities were successful and self-doubt when they were not well-received. A successful example was when Rob found a way to adapt his history projects to still be engaging online. He explained that the project they were doing would normally ask students to come to class dressed as one of the historical characters for extra credit. Being online, he instead had students get dressed up at home and turn on their cameras to show off their costumes. For another project, he had them go on a scavenger hunt in their houses, saying "… find these spices in your house. Because this was part of the Silk Road." With these projects, Rob quickly discovered that teaching students from home could be, in some ways, more exciting since they were using items at home to engage with the content and make even stronger connections. Another example of adapting successfully was when Jack, a theater teacher, found a way to put on performances using Zoom. He said they "literally edited together videos that we made talking on the camera and scenes and the cutaways." Although Jack commented that the method and quality of the production might not be what he was used to, he knew that he had to find a way that students could still perform together during this time.

However, not all teachers had successful experiences when adapting their curriculum. An example can be seen with Laura, the 13-year History teacher, "I put all this effort to make it [engaging content] available to virtual kids and then virtual kids wouldn't touch it. … And it just- each time decreased my effort to want to give them the same experience." Unlike her peers, she often left classes feeling that her students were completely disengaged and uninterested in her attempts. These ongoing negative experiences started having an impact on her belief in her ability to be successful teaching online. Moreover, even though all the teachers in the sample came into COVID-19 with basic levels of technology experience and prior teaching mastery experiences, that preparedness did not support all teacher's self-efficacy beliefs in the same way.

Vicarious Experiences

Even before COVID-19, teachers often placed judgements on themselves when they saw how other teachers completed tasks compared to themselves. So, with some teachers being more naturally technology literate than others, this self-judgment continued. Jack commented, "I think a lot of people went through a self-deprecating phase of 'I am not good enough. I can't do it.' My colleagues are doing it… this new world of digital expectation, this digital presence." An observation Megan had at her school was, "it [teacher motivation and enthusiasm] was one way or the other. Either it was like, 'None of these kids care. So, I'm not going to do anything.' And they did very, very little. Or like, 'I have to do my job. So, I'm going to create these huge lessons to make the kids try and be engaged." Megan said she had to be mindful when she was around her peers that were giving up, "… everything was negative, everything was wrong. And it's just… it was almost toxic. Like, I just can't be around this…" Similarly, other teachers in this study made comments about how challenging it was when some of their peers were only focused on the negative all the time.

Most teachers in this study identified that they sought out peers who were willing to work together to overcome obstacles with online teaching. Working with content-related teachers, Marissa said they would consistently plan units together; "We'd say, 'Okay, someone's going to take the test, someone's going to take the warmup, someone's going to take…' and then we would rotate it for the next unit so that you weren't always doing the same thing." Some teachers, who were the only teachers of that content in their building, found a way to overcome the challenge of not having anyone to work with by using technology. For example, Megan used the online video platforms made available to teachers to meet virtually with other foreign language teachers in her school district. For her, technology opened a door to a type of collaboration that she never experienced before. Similarly, Rob was able to rely on his other AP teacher peers for planning support, even though they were not the exact same content as him. Reflecting on these past two years, he said, "If it weren't for the other two AP teachers that I have a good relationship with, you know, I may have considered moving on, but they're… a key piece. That's very important to me." Overall, teachers observed a very clear divide among their peers during this time, between those who wanted to do the best they could and worked together as a team, and others choosing to give up completely.

Social Persuasion

Relating to the impact of social persuasion, it was noted in the findings that when teachers spoke about students being absent or disengaged, it was often closely followed with teachers commenting on their belief in their ability to provide instruction. This insight suggests that student engagement (or lack of engagement) had a significant role in how participants saw themselves as a teacher. Jack explained, "… the kids wouldn't be there with me… Because they weren't physically with me, or their cameras weren't on or they weren't there or- and there was no one around… It became very isolating." Similarly, Laura reached a point where she stopped trying to reach the students, saying "I don't want to say I gave up on the virtual kids, but I stopped trying to coordinate those virtual classes. I really stopped putting effort into office hours because … you know, you sat there for an hour looking at a blank screen waiting for kids to show up." Having these feelings as well, Rob decided to stop and reflect on why he was feeling the emotions he felt. He elaborated, saying, "… it was psychologically very hard for me. I didn't realize actually how important the performing aspect of teaching was to me. I always thought, yeah, I enjoy being in the classroom. But then when you get it, it just kind of yanked away... It was hard." Looking at each interview, all teachers in the sample group expressed frustration, sadness, or other types of emotions that were directly related to how little students were engaging.

Another critical area of social influence was support from their school leadership, which impacted how confidently teachers took on challenges and recovered from setbacks. Table 7.2 provides a consolidated overview of the reported types

TABLE 7.2. Teacher- Reported Support Received During COVID-19

Teacher	Subject	District	Technology Resources: Hardware and/or Software	Administration Support	County/ District Support
Jack	Theater	1	Yes	Yes	Some
Jen	Theater & English	2	Some	Yes	Yes
Laura	History	3	Yes*	No	No
Megan	German	1	Yes	Some	No
Marissa	English	2	Yes	Yes	Some
Barbara	Earth Science	4	Yes*	Yes	Yes
Rob	History	2	Yes	Some	Yes

*School later took away/stopped paying for some of the software they had purchased in 2020-2021.

of support each teacher identified as receiving from their school, administration, and county overall. The table shows that teachers who were from the same county had slightly different perceptions of the support they received, providing insight into how the teachers' individual experiences impacted how they felt. It is important to note that Table 7.2 was created from the interview responses and their own recollection of events. This is not a comprehensive table.

Looking at specific examples of support, Barbara, Jack, and Rob commented that each of their respective schools were practically throwing new technology at them to use, such as webcams, microphones, TVs, and extra computer screens. Whereas Megan's school planned a whole week of asynchronous learning (no live classes) before they transitioned to concurrent teaching, in order give them time to set up their rooms and practice with the tools. Additionally, some teachers commented on how school leadership showed support through both actions and words. Jen talked briefly about when she saw a problem with one of the new policies being rolled out, she expressed her concern to the principal and was told that she should "… Do what you feel is best." Experiencing changes in her own school, Barbara had a similar experience of support and said that she and her peers felt they were finally given the time and space by their administration to get their work done.

Comparatively, Laura went to her administration for support after several months of not finding success with online teaching, feeling burnt out, stressed, and overwhelmed. The response she got was, "she [the principal] told me she thought I should seek counseling." Laura later in the interview commented, "… we just feel like nobody heard us." However, she was not the only teacher who felt a lack of support from her school leadership. When talking about coming back in the building to teach, Megan said, "I didn't trust their [school leadership's] decision making. I didn't trust, they were gonna keep me safe if I did go back in."

While Megan could not fully know what the environment would look like if she chose to return to the building, she felt a lack of trust with her county that they would not have her health and best interests in mind. Although these examples are from a small sample size, it provides a snapshot of the variety of experiences these teachers had. While some teachers in the sample thrived being provided the tools, time, and respect to do what they had to do, others felt unsure, overwhelmed, and lost without support from their leaders.

Physiological/ Mental State

Exploring the emotional state of teachers, each participant in this study had been teaching for at least 10 or more years prior to COVID-19. Knowing this, participants were not only experiencing stress and sadness from the changes and lack of student engagement, but they had to also rethink everything they knew in their career. It is significant to observe in Figure 7.1 the negative emotions teachers expressed that were impacting their mental health.

Almost all teachers mentioned feelings of burnout, sadness, and fear, with several openly discussing specific mental health struggles. Talking about the transition to teaching virtually, Rob commented, "A lot of teachers were absolutely kind of traumatized and devastated by teaching in this [virtual] way." With all the experience these teachers had, the fact that they could no longer do what worked for them was what caused the most frustration. Marissa tried to make light of her sadness by trying to hype herself up. She said, "'Okay… you are Jimmy Fallon. And you're putting on a show. And hopefully they're going to tune in and continue to come back." With all these negative emotions bringing down teachers' mental and emotional states, there was a clear negative impact on teachers' physiological state, which decreased their personal confidence and belief in their ability to be the teacher they once knew themselves to be.

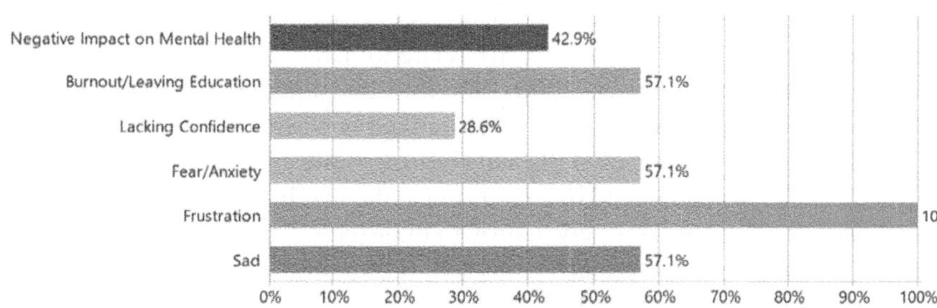

FIGURE 7.1. Percentage of Teachers who Identified Experiencing Negative Emotions. *Note*. This chart identifies the percentage of the seven teachers in the study whose responses were coded with these specific emotion codes throughout the interviews. For example, a code that shows 100% means that all seven teachers interviewed in this study identified that type of emotion at least once in their interview.

Nonetheless, many teachers made efforts to cope and recover from the emotional strain. Several found ways to manage stress through various methods, including faith, positive affirmations, physical tasks, and volunteering. As an example, when Rob was reflecting on what helped him get through the events of the past two years, he said it was a combination of peer support and his faith in God. Similarly, when talking about how she handled the levels of frustration she had, Jen said, "... every morning, I would draw a dove on my wrist and I wrote 'Grace,' like, you know, where the olive leaf would be. I wrote 'Grace' there. And every time I felt like it- I looked at it. And it just made me calm down." By drawing a visual cue on herself to look at when she was overwhelmed, she created her own emotional anchoring point. As another example, Laura, the teacher who had the highest number of coded segments relating to stress and anxiety, explained how she coped. She said, "As a teacher, that's part of why we have the job we do is because you want to feel like you have a purpose in your life. And when I didn't, I think that's part of what really was getting me down. So I found it somewhere else. I could look and be like I saved 10 animals." Throughout the interview, Laura talked often about how her passion for teaching was rooted in the connections and growth she saw in her students. So, being unable to engage with and support students, she was able to find comfort by caring for animals. It is insightful to observe the different types of coping methods teachers used to manage the mental and emotional toll of COVID-19 and how they were able to work through any negative emotions.

Personal Mindset & Perspective

Results from these interviews show that each teacher struggled with their mastery experiences, vicarious experiences, social persuasions, and personal physiological state to varying degrees, impacting their self-efficacy beliefs. Further, there is no obvious trend with age, experience level, school, or content area; however, there are patterns when comparing their personal mindset. Reflecting on Carol Dweck's research, she suggests that a person's success at completing new or challenging tasks does not necessarily relate to natural intelligence or skill, it comes from a person's mindset (2006). She says that a person can take on either a fixed or a growth mindset (Dweck, 2006). Fixed is when a person believes that they are allotted only one set of skills and abilities in life and that there is no room for growth, so those people tend to stop trying at the first hint of failure or not face the challenge at all. Comparatively, a growth mindset is one where people believe that there is always room for growth and that, if they work hard enough, they can achieve anything (Dweck, 2006).

Considering Dweck's perspective on mindset when reviewing the findings, some teachers approached the challenges of COVID-19 with a growth mindset whereas some developed a fixed mindset. Teachers made growth mindset comments about how they feel that they have been through so much at this point in their career, they know they can get through anything else that comes their way.

Jen commented that she has now been able to "step back and say, hey, you know, it was just the thing. I'll get through it. We'll get through it." Marissa addressed her own mindset by saying, "I just feel like, what I have learned with myself, over the course of the years is that I can roll with the punches. I can make anything work. And if it doesn't work, I'll make it work for me and what's best for my students." Jack stated that "I have had to invent and reinvent myself more times in the last three years than in my entire career.... I feel like there's nothing that I haven't tried to do or experienced... Every day I've had to learn new inventive ways to do this job." While Jack and Megan viewed challenges and obstacles in the classroom as an opportunity to grow and thrive, others like Jen and Marissa used self-reflective growth techniques as a reminder that they will get through these challenges as they always have done. Moreover, one of the most direct examples of teachers demonstrating a growth mindset through these years was when both Barbara and Rob identified that their perspective has always been, "Semper Gumby." Rob explained that "Semper Gumby" is a play on the Marine Corps *Semper Fi*, but referring to the flexible cartoon character, Gumby. Both Rob and Barbara said they learned early on in education that they had to be "Semper Gumby" "Always Flexible" and always ready to adjust.

In contrast, some teachers developed a fixed mindset during COVID-19 when they experienced negative social persuasions and failures. For example, Laura made several comments during her interview about how she personally does not like change and when COVID-19 changed everything she knew about teaching, she struggled. She talked in the interview about a lesson that she successfully taught every year pre-pandemic and when students were back in the classroom, the students did not engage with the lesson at all. The negative response resulted in Laura giving up the lesson completely. After already experiencing many failures during the two years teaching online, when these failures continued back when students were in person, it devastated her. Her continued failure and lack of support when she needed it caused her to develop a fixed mindset about her abilities as a teacher.

CONCLUSIONS

This study explored the specific experiences of teachers going through changes in teaching during the COVID-19 pandemic. The findings suggest that teachers struggled the most with the loss of student connection and engagement when they had to teach virtually, which had varying degrees of impact on their physiological and mental states. Looking at current findings, each teacher in this study mentioned negative emotions they felt when students were no longer engaging and interacting with them while teaching online. These feelings of loss relate to other COVID-19 studies, by Narayanan and Ordynans (2022) and Soncini et al. (2021), where they found teachers expressed a type of "disorientation" and disconnect from teaching when they no longer had students with them.

The second research question sought to identify any changes with teacher self-efficacy beliefs among veteran-level teachers. Interviews from the sample group found that each teacher struggled to varying degrees within the four areas that have been identified to impact teacher self-efficacy: mastery experiences, vicarious experiences, social persuasion, and physiological state (Usher & Pajares, 2006). However, teachers who personally embraced a growth mindset when faced with challenges, were more likely to adapt to the changes and regain their self-efficacy beliefs. This finding was also observed in a previously mentioned COVID-19 study by Ma et al., where they found that teachers with personal adaptable qualities were more likely to improve during COVID-19 (2021).

With each teacher in the study self-identifying that they were confident in their abilities as a teacher prior to the pandemic, the findings showed that they regained their self-efficacy beliefs quickly if they also had an adaptable and resilient mindset. If teachers did not have a sense of adaptability, they had a harder time overcoming setbacks and it took them longer to recover that previous confidence. However, at the end of all the interviews, each teacher did regain at least some of their teacher self-efficacy beliefs and feelings toward their career. Some teachers felt they had recovered completely, stating that after all they had been through, they were at the prime of their career. Whereas some teachers said they still had a lot they needed to do and learn to get back to where they were before as an educator.

The final research question, exploring the external factors that helped support teachers' self-efficacy, was added after an initial review of the findings. Although each teacher received varying levels of support, the most significant support came from positive vicarious experiences of peer support and support given by their school leadership. This conclusion is supported from other COVID-19 related research which found that leadership decisions and school climate were often directly related to teacher mental health changes (Herman et al., 2021). Teachers who were provided reliable online tools, resources, and training support, were better able to adapt their teaching methods resulting in positive mastery experiences. Comparatively, teachers who did not have the resources or support to be successful were more likely to have failed mastery experiences. This observation about proper training connects to findings from current COVID-19 studies that found teachers who had access to, and prior use of online teaching tools were less overwhelmed than their non-technological peers (Baroudi & Shaya, 2022; Buric et al., 2021; Dolighan & Owen, 2021; Ladendorf et al., 2021). Therefore, it is suggested that positive experiences of external social persuasion and supportive vicarious peer experiences were connected to teachers' ability to regain their self-efficacy beliefs.

Limitations

Due to the interviews occurring just over two years after COVID-19 shut down schools, there could be a limitation of how much teachers remember about the initial months during the pandemic. To ensure credibility with the limitation of time, the interview was structured into four time periods, with each being introduced with brief contextual reminders. Another validity concern with the research was the potential for participant bias to influence the results. To combat this, participants were asked a wide range of questions during the interview that encouraged teachers to reflect on both the good and the bad experiences in the past two years. Participants were also asked several self-reflective questions to combat any fixed thinking. Finally, knowing that the researcher experienced the events of COVID-19 while working in a non-teaching role in the public school system, there could be concern with researcher bias. To combat issues of trustworthiness, member checking, peer debriefing, external audit, and researcher reflections were utilized.

IMPLICATIONS FOR THE FUTURE

While this current study provided several insights on how experienced teachers adjusted during COVID-19, there are many directions where this research can continue. Future COVID-19-related research could be conducted on how teachers' self-efficacy changed among teachers with five or fewer years of experience. Comparative research could also be done on how public-school teachers' self-efficacy changed compared to private-school teachers. Further, future research should explore what schools can do to better support teachers who are still trying to regain their self-efficacy beliefs. A study conducted in the Netherlands by Brassey et al. (2020) sought to provide emotional flexibility training to workers to improve their adaptability to changing and emotional environments in the workplace. Their study suggested that emotional flexibility is a skill that can be developed through mindfulness training and strategies that help workers focus on what is important to them and not focusing on negative behaviors in the workplace (Brassey et al., 2020). This type of emotional flexibility training could be a valuable resource to provide teachers with support when rebuilding their self-efficacy beliefs and combat a fixed mindset. Seeing how many teachers identified that they needed support adapting to the changes, this type of training could benefit teachers moving forward when they are faced with any changes in their school climate or emotional challenges they face daily in the classroom.

SUMMARY

With so many teachers currently leaving the profession, it is important to take a closer look at what teachers went through during these past few years to hopefully prevent teachers from leaving education due to burnout, a consequence of low self-efficacy (Federičová, 2021; Toropova et al., 2021). This study suggests that experience in the classroom is often not enough to protect teachers from emotional and mental stressors in their workplace. The teachers who ended the interviews saying they were at the prime of their career were the same teachers who said they received support when it was needed. Even though it appears that the worst of COVID-19 changes are in the past, schools still must take the time to evaluate the needs of their teachers and observe the sources that impact their self-efficacy, including mastery experiences, vicarious experiences, social persuasion, and physiological state. By reviewing and continuing to consider teacher's self-efficacy, school districts will be able to provide teachers with the support they need to adapt and grow as educators. If students going through school hope to get a quality education, they need to be taught by confident, skilled, and supported educators.

AUTHOR NOTE

Sarah M. Conley https://orcid.org/0009-0007-3335-8972

There is no funding associated with this work. There are no conflicts of interest associated with this work.

Research conducted for master's thesis at George Mason University.

Correspondence concerning this research should be addressed to Sarah M. Conley. Email: sconley4@gmu.edu, smc8389@gmail.com

REFERENCES

Aktan, O., & Toraman, Ç. (2022). The relationship between technostress levels and job satisfaction of teachers within the COVID-19 period. *Education and Information Technologies, 27*(7), 10429–10453. https://doi.org/10.1007/s10639-022-11027-2

Bandura, A. (1997). *Self-efficacy: The exercise of control.* W H Freeman/Times Books/ Henry Holt & Co.

Baroudi, S., & Shaya, N. (2022). Exploring predictors of teachers' self-efficacy for online teaching in the Arab world amid COVID-19. *Education and Information Technologies, 27*(6), 8093–8110. https://doi-org.mutex.gmu.edu/10.1007/s10639-022-10946-4

Brassey, J., van Witteloostuijn, A., Huszka, C., Silberzahn, T., & van Dam, N. (2020). Emotional flexibility and general self-efficacy: A pilot training intervention study with knowledge workers. *PLoS ONE, 15*(10). https://doi.org/10.1371/journal.pone.0237821

Buric, I., Parmac Kovacic, M., & Huic, A. (2021). Transformational leadership and instructional quality during the COVID-19 pandemic: A moderated mediation analysis. *Drustvena Istrazivanja, 30*(2), 181–202. https://doi.org/10.5559/di.30.2.01

Cardullo, V., Wang, C., Burton, M., & Dong, J. (2021). K–12 teachers' remote teaching self-efficacy during the pandemic. *Journal of Research in Innovative Teaching & Learning, 14*(1), 32–45. https://doi.org/10.1108/JRIT-10-2020-0055

Cataudella, S., Carta, S. M., Mascia, M. L., Masala, C., Petretto, D. R., Agus, M., & Penna, M. P. (2021). Teaching in times of the COVID-19 pandemic: A pilot study on teachers' self-esteem and self-efficacy in an Italian sample. *International Journal of Environmental Research and Public Health, 18*(15), 8211. https://doi.org/10.3390/ijerph18158211

Corry, M., & Stella, J. (2018). Teacher self-efficacy in online education: A review of the literature. *Research in Learning Technology, 26*. https://doi.org/10.25304/rlt.v26.204

Dicke, T., Parker, P. D., Marsh, H. W., Kunter, M., Schmeck, A., & Leutner, D. (2014). Self-efficacy in classroom management, classroom disturbances, and emotional exhaustion: A moderated mediation analysis of teacher candidates. *Journal of Educational Psychology, 106*(2), 569–583. https://doi.org/10.1037/a0035504

Dolighan, T., & Owen, M. (2021). Teacher efficacy for online teaching during the COVID-19 pandemic. *Brock Education Journal, 30*(1), 95–95. https://doi.org/10.26522/brocked.v30i1.851

Dweck, C. S. (2006). *Mindset: The new psychology of success*. Random House.

Federičová, M. (2021). Teacher turnover: What can we learn from Europe? *European Journal of Education, 56*(1), 102–116. https://doi.org/10.1111/ejed.12429

Fernández-Batanero, J.-M., Román-Graván, P., Reyes-Rebollo, M.-M., & Montenegro-Rueda, M. (2021). Impact of educational technology on teacher stress and anxiety: A literature review. *International Journal of Environmental Research and Public Health, 18*(2), 548. https://doi.org/10.3390/ijerph18020548

Hajovsky, D. B., Oyen, K. A., Chesnut, S. R., & Curtin, S. J. (2019). Teacher–student relationship quality and math achievement: The mediating role of teacher self-efficacy. *Psychology in the Schools, 57*(1), 111–134. https://doi.org/10.1002/pits.22322

Herman, K. C., Sebastian, J., Reinke, W. M., & Huang, F. L. (2021). Individual and school predictors of teacher stress, coping, and wellness during the COVID-19 pandemic. *School Psychology, 36*(6), 483–493. https://doi.org/10.1037/spq0000456

Klassen, R. M., & Chiu, M. M. (2010). Effects on teachers' self-efficacy and job satisfaction: Teacher gender, years of experience, and job stress. *Journal of Educational Psychology, 102*(3), 741–756. https://doi.org/10.1037/a0019237

Ladendorf, K., Muehsler, H., Xie, Y., & Hinderliter, H. (2021). Teacher perspectives of self-efficacy and remote learning due to the emergency school closings of 2020. *Educational Media International, 58*(2), 124–144. https://doi.org/10.1080/09523987.2021.1930481

Ma, K., Chutiyami, M., Zhang, Y., & Nicoll, S. (2021). Online teaching self-efficacy during COVID-19: Changes, its associated factors and moderators. *Education and Information Technologies, 26*, 6675–6697. https://doi.org/10.1007/s10639-021-10486-3

McMillan, J. H. (2016). *Fundamentals of educational research* (7th ed.). Pearson.

Menabò, L., Skrzypiec, G., Sansavini, A., Brighi, A., & Guarini, A. (2022). Distance education among Italian teachers: Differences and experiences. *Education and Information Technologies, 27*(7), 9263–9292. https://doi.org/10.1007/s10639-022-11008-5

Narayanan, M., & Ordynans, J. G. (2022). Meaning making and self-efficacy: Teacher reflections through COVID-19. *The Teacher Educator, 57*(1), 26–44. https://doi.org/10.1080/08878730.2021.1990455

Pellerone, M. (2021). Self-perceived instructional competence, self-efficacy and burnout during the COVID-19 pandemic: A study of a group of Italian school teachers. *European Journal of Investigation in Health Psychology and Education, 11*(2), 496–512. https://doi.org/10.3390/ejihpe11020035

Pressley, T. (2021). Returning to teaching during COVID-19: An empirical study on elementary teachers' self-efficacy. *Psychology in the Schools, 58*(8), 1611–1623. https://doi.org/10.1002/pits.22528

Pressley, T., & Ha, C. (2021). Teaching during a pandemic: United States teachers' self-efficacy during COVID-19. *Teaching and Teacher Education*, *106*, 103465. https://doi.org/10.1016/j.tate.2021.103465

Pressley, T., Ha, C., & Learn, E. (2021). Teacher stress and anxiety during COVID-19: An empirical study. *School Psychology (Washington, D.C.)*, *36*(5), 367–376. https://doi.org/10.1037/spq0000468

Rabaglietti, E., Lattke, L. S., Tesauri, B., Settanni, M., & De Lorenzo, A. (2021). A balancing act during COVID-19: Teachers' self-efficacy, perception of stress in the distance learning experience. *Frontiers in Psychology*, *12*, 644108. https://doi.org/10.3389/fpsyg.2021.644108

Soncini, A., Politi, E., & Matteucci, M. C. (2021). Teachers navigating distance learning during COVID-19 without feeling emotionally exhausted: The protective role of self-efficacy. *School Psychology*, *36*(6), 494–503. https://doi.org/10.1037/spq0000469

Tas, Y., Eminoglu, S., Atila, G., Yildiz, Y., & Bozkurt, U. (2021). Teachers' self-efficacy beliefs and opinions about distance education during the COVID-19 pandemic. *Turkish Online Journal of Distance Education (TOJDE)*, *22*(4), 229–251. https://doi.org/10.17718/tojde.1002868

Toropova, A., Myrberg, E., & Johansson, S. (2021). Teacher job satisfaction: the importance of school working conditions and teacher characteristics. *Educational Review*, *73*(1), 71–97. https://doi.org/10.1080/00131911.2019.1705247

Toto, G. A., & Limone, P. (2021). Motivation, stress and impact of online teaching on Italian teachers during COVID-19. *Computers*, *10*(6), 75. https://doi.org/10.3390/computers10060075

United Nations Educational, Scientific and Cultural Organization. (2020). *Half of world's student population not attending school: UNESCO launches global coalition to accelerate deployment of remote learning solutions.* https://en.unesco.org/news/half-worlds-student-population-not-attending-school-unesco-launches-global-coalition-accelerate

Usher, E. L., & Pajares, F. (2006). Sources of academic and self-regulatory efficacy beliefs of entering middle school students. *Contemporary Educational Psychology*, 31(2), 125–141. https://doi.org/10.1016/j.cedpsych.2005.03.00

VDOE :: School closure FAQ. (n.d.). Retrieved February 14, 2022, from https://www.doe.virginia.gov/support/health_medical/office/COVID-19-faq.shtml

VDOE :: State snapshot: Virginia school operational status. (n.d.). Retrieved February 15, 2022, from https://www.doe.virginia.gov/support/health_medical/office/reopen-status.shtml

VERBI Software. (2021). MAXQDA 2022 [computer software]. VERBI Software. Available from maxqda.com.

Yang, C., Manchanda, S., & Greenstein, J. (2021). Educators' online teaching self-efficacy and compassion fatigue during the COVID-19 pandemic: The dual roles of "connect." *School Psychology*, *36*(6), 504–515. https://doi.org/10.1037/spq0000475

CHAPTER 8

IMPACT OF COVID-19 ON STUDENTS WITH SPECIAL NEEDS AND PARENT INVOLVEMENT

Jo Nell "Jody" Wood,
Saint Louis University

Amanda Wood
Liberty High School

COVID-19 pandemic impacted students around the world. It shut down schools without the necessary preparation for teachers to pivot to online teaching and left students and parents struggling to figure out how to continue their education without the school facility. Further, maintaining daily routines was challenging for all students, especially for those with special needs. These students who needed routine and additional supports found themselves without routines and for those who needed additional supports in terms of adaptive behaviors, they were at a loss. This period of schools being shuttered left students with a void in their normal learning opportunities.

Instructional Survival in the Midst of the Perfect Storm:
The Experiences of K–12 Teachers During the COVID-19 Global Pandemic, pages 127–144.

Published under exclusive licence by Emerald Publishing Limited
ISBNs: 978-1-83708-502-6 HB, 978-1-83708-503-3 PB,
978-1-83708-504-0 EPDF, 978-1-83708-505-7 EPUB

This sequential mixed-methods case study conducted in one Midwestern high school with special education teachers utilized a mixed-methods type approach to determine the teachers' perceptions and concerns regarding the impact COVID-19 had on their students and the lasting results they now face. The quantitative data focused on how the school provided needed services and whether this time of shutdown created any positives. In the qualitative analysis, three themes emerged. These themes focused on loss of academic skills and lack of student accountability, lack of services such as the Internet, and lack of attendance, attention, and social-emotional stability. Not only did the teachers feel their students had lost ground academically, but they also found that their students had forgotten how to "do school".

Keywords: COVID-19, School Shutdown, Return To Learn, Students With Disabilities, Family Engagement

INTRODUCTION

As COVID-19 interfered with schooling, teachers found themselves concerned with how the remote learning and even the results of the missing time in school would impact students with special needs. Additionally, questions abounded in terms of how well schools provided learning opportunities to students during the pandemic. This sequential mixed-methods study was conducted to gather teachers' perceptions of how the pandemic and resulting loss of in- person education impacted students with special needs and how it might have also affected parent involvement. The study was conducted using a sequential mixed-methods approach within one high school in a Midwestern state.

Investigation Focus and Questions to Guide the Study

The problem focus was whether students with special needs exhibited gaps in their learning and how losing months of in-person learning affected their ability to function well academically, socially, and emotionally in the school setting upon their return to school. Further, the present study sought to investigate how this gap in school learning may have changed parental involvement. The research questions that guided the investigation included:

1. How well did the school provide services to students with special needs during the COVID 19 global pandemic?
2. What changes have teachers seen in students with special needs following COVID-19 as they returned to School?
3. How has the switch to technology impacted parent involvement?

Review of Current Literature

Over the first few months of 2020, the schooling sector shifted to distance education as governments moved to bring the virus, COVID-19, under control. Education

> sectors rapidly developed online environments. In this milieu, teachers made swift changes to accommodate their students' diverse range of learning needs. (Charteris et al., 2021, p. 1)

This rapid move to distance education surprised most schools because policies were not in place or designed for teachers to work remotely nor were students or families prepared for this type of school. Further, teachers were not prepared with the pedagogical structures, plans, or expectations for students and communication systems were not in place for providing quality communication with parents, students, and staff (Hood, 2020). As Saavedar (2020) found, as many as 1.6 billion children were out of school in 161 countries which was nearly 80% of the world's enrolled students. During this closure, school administration was attempting to figure out how to best handle educating students who were not present in classrooms. For schools, it became readily apparent that connectedness to school and students' sense of belonging was a significant concern.

According to Murphy and McFerran (2017), students with special needs tend to have low levels of social connectedness and with COVID-19's school closure, they may have been marginalized even more. Charteris, et al. (2021) determined "The COVID-19 pandemic may have served to exacerbate existing stressors faced by students with special educational needs" (p. 4). This research found that peer relationships were affected as reported by teachers, and students were affected by peer isolation. To further explore the effect of COVID-19's impact on students with special needs, Averett (2021) insisted "while COVID-19 affected the education of nearly all school children worldwide, pandemic-related school closures did not affect all children in equal ways" (p. 1). She found one of the major problems experienced was that many families struggled with remote learning because schools did not provide adequate accommodations and services remotely. Even though IDEA provides services and accommodations for a free appropriate public education in the least restrictive environment, when schools closed, providing the necessary services and accommodations became a challenge for many schools. During this time, the US Department of Education understood that "teachers, schools, and districts struggled to understand the implications of IDEA and Section 504 for their ability to offer remote instruction" (Averett, 2021, p. 2).

Beyond the issue of providing appropriate technology and support, other issues which appeared as concerns included the disruption of schedules for students with special needs, the isolation from peers, depression, mental health, psychological and emotional challenges, as well as communication issues between the schools and the home. The issue of social distancing influenced students with special needs because it disrupted their routines. Additionally, they were affected by the fact they were away from a familiar environment at school.

As Kong et al. (2020) outlined "Disruptions in their schedule conflicted with the stability of routines and when coupled with any communication difficulties, can lead to anxiety, frustration, and negative behaviors" (p. 1012). These researchers insisted that for children with special needs, there may be difficulty in expressing their emotions even if it is because of fear, anxiety, or frustration with what is unknown to them. Obviously, this situation did occur with students during the shutdown during the COVID pandemic.

Hoofman and Secord (2021) reported that the transition to an online education during the coronavirus pandemic may bring about adverse educational changes and adverse health consequences for children. These effects may differ by age, maturity, and socioeconomic class. Further, many researchers examined how this "new learning environment affected learners' mental, physical, and social health so they can be better prepared for future pandemics" (pp. 1071–1075). Their research found that high schoolers have lost schooling opportunities during the pandemic because their independence was hampered by the shelter-in-place recommendations, and they missed so many high school activities which cannot be recaptured which resulted in higher rates of depression and anxiety. They cited one study by Laing et al. (2020) where 14.4% of teenagers reported post-traumatic stress disorder and 40.4% reported having depression and anxiety. They found the gap for those already at a disadvantage because of socioeconomic class, language, and special needs were severely affected by the COVID-19 pandemic and determined that those impacted by school closures had the hardest time compensating. The concerns around depression and anxiety during COVID-19 experienced by students remained an issue. The impact of isolation for students with disabilities was even more pronounced because students with disabilities are a population that is already at a greater risk medically and socially (Berger et al, 2020).

According to May's 2022 study (Goldhaber et al.) that explored the impact of remote and hybrid instruction during the COVID-19 global pandemic, achievement growth among students whose schools went remote lagged those students whose schools remained open. Although remote instruction may not be the (sole) cause for differences in achievement growth, educators acknowledge that student achievement is more difficult to maintain when students unexpectedly lose access to on-campus, in-person, full-day instruction for significant periods of time.

Research has explored the disaster experience of individuals with disabilities (Rooney & White, 2007; Smith & Notaro, 2009). A January study by the Government Accountability Office found that more than 300 presidentially-declared major disasters have occurred since 2017 across the United States, with devastating effects on K–12 schools including trauma and mental health issues among students and staff, lost instructional time, and financial strain (Marsh, 2022). What has been missing in the literature is research that evaluates the experiences and perceptions of the effect of the shutdown on students, as provided by educators working in special education settings. This case study utilized a mixed-methods approach using a survey of all seven special education teachers in one Midwestern high school with a 60% response rate, followed by convenience sampling interviews with teachers to further investigate how COVID 19 impacted the delivery of services to students with special needs and what possible positives/negatives have resulted due to the closure of the schools during COVID 19. Thus, the present study represented one effort to engage the teacher's perceptions and voices following the return to school concerning the effects of the shutdown on students with special needs.

METHODOLOGY

The researchers used a sequential mixed-methods study approach to gather data in one Midwestern high school in a suburban area. An increased number of researchers have utilized a mixed-methodological research approach because of the benefits of having both quantitative trends and qualitative insights (Sahin & Öztük, 2019). Quantitative research uses a process to identify themes or trends in an area of interest, and then to collect numerical data to explain, predict, or test various hypotheses (Turner et al., 2013). To find themes or trends, the researcher uses an investigation that collected responses to demonstrate a tendency of responses and whether these responses vary in a given set of individuals (Guetterman & Creswell et al., 2019). This sequential design was based on time order. The quantitative data was collected through a survey first and then interview questions were designed to gather additional and more in-depth qualitative data following the analysis of the quantitative data in an effort to further explain the quantitative data gathered. Member checking was completed using the transcripts and returning them to the interviewees for their review and corrections if needed. The researchers provided inter-rater reliability by first reading and determining themes and then comparing the themes each found to have emerged. Transcripts were read individually then read together to ensure reliability. The quantitative data was triangulated with the qualitative data and the literature to determine the findings.

Participants

The current findings are a result of a sequential mixed-methods study by researchers interested in determining what teachers reported as effects they were seeing in their students with special needs following the return-to-learn in one high school in one Midwestern State. We used a mixed methods approach to do the investigation. A total of seven teachers of special education worked in the high school and five participated in the survey followed by interviews of four of those teachers as saturation was reached at four interviews. The participants were all special education teachers in one high school. Gender, race, and age were not variables in this study. Since this was a case study approach in one suburban high school in one Midwestern state no demographic data was gathered to protect the identities of the participants.

Survey

Based on a review of the relevant literature, a survey was created that included both quantitative and open-ended qualitative questions. The survey consisted of thirty questions. Twenty-two questions were multiple choice questions focused on how well the school had provided support to students and parents of students with special needs as well as how well technology had provided easy access for student and parent participation. The Likert style multiple-choice options included: Always, Most of the time, About half the time, Sometimes, and Never. Multiple-choice questions about levels of support had options of highest level of support, high support, adequate support, some support, or little support. The additional eight questions were qualitative in nature and requested explanations of the choices from the quantitative questions such as how well education was being provided in the least restrictive environment and the degree to which parents participated in online support of their students. These questions were designed to gather initial information regarding trends perceived about how well the school provided learning opportunities during the pandemic and how COVID-19's school closure impacted students with special needs when they returned to school as well as their parents' engagement.

Respondents were then invited to participate in a qualitative interview to gather additional insights and information regarding their perceptions of how students have been impacted and whether parents were engaged in an effort to clarify data collected from the survey. This was designed to gather richer and deeper data to support the findings from the quantitative data. The quantitative and qualitative questions in this study provided a descriptive methodology to understand the effects that COVID-19 had on the school's provision of educational opportunities while it was shuttered, and on students with special needs' resulting behaviors following their return to school. One question was included to gather teacher's perceptions of parent engagement during and following the pandemic's school closure. Descriptive methodology does not tend to look for correlations between variables; rather the research provides insight into the experiences, issues, and perceptions of those issues in a particular environment (Leedy & Ormrod, 2016). The quantitative questions were used to research the prevalence of perceived COVID effects of school closure on students with special needs. The qualitative methods provided corresponding viewpoints identifying personal views, experiences, and perspectives (Hesse-Biber, 2010). The survey was distributed to all the special education teachers in this high school for them to complete. Since this study was conducted in one high school, no demographic information was collected to protect the participants' identities. Once the quantitative and qualitative data from the survey was analyzed, questions needing further explanation or further information were designed for the follow-up interviews.

Interviews

The interview questions were determined based on the survey data and the need for additional deeper and richer data to support the quantitative findings. The interview consisted of six questions. Prior to beginning the interview, a script explaining the purpose of the study, the interviewee's voluntary participation, and the protections being used to protect their identity was read to all interview participants. Further, all participants were asked if they had any questions to be answered prior to beginning the interview. Each interviewee was asked the exact same questions which consisted of:

1. Since the pandemic, can you please explain your perceptions about whether students lost academic progress and how would you describe their loss?
2. Please describe any differences you have noticed in students with disabilities in terms of behaviors, attendance, or social-emotional needs since returning to school following the pandemic.
3. Based on what you have described in terms of academic, behavior, attendance, or social-emotional loss, what changes or training would you want to see the school do to better prepare students and teachers in the event of an extended school closing in the future?
4. Assuming the pandemic helped educators understand shortcomings in special education delivery during a pandemic or school closure, what might some of those shortcomings be?
5. Based on the shortcomings you shared, what do you believe needs to be done to prepare in case a pandemic or extended school closing should ever occur again?
6. Please describe how or what the school district has done to create a curriculum that can be implemented in the event of any disaster or pandemic in the future.

The interviewees were coded alphabetically (a, b, c, etc.) to protect their identity and data from these interviews are reported using the codes. The interviews were recorded in speech to text to further protect interviewee's identities. After all interviews were administered, the transcribed interviews were provided to the participants by the researcher for member checking. This was done to allow participants to provide accuracy of the transcriptions or to make any desired changes or additions to their transcripts. When participant's feedback on transcription accuracy was completed, the researcher needed to reread the transcripts several times, which was the initial process of exploring data (Creswell, 2013).

Data Analysis

It is important to clarify in qualitative research data analysis that it "is not a linear, step-by-step process" (Merriam & Tisdell, 2016, p. 191). When analyzing the data, the goal was to reduce "the data into themes through a process of coding and condensing codes" (Creswell, 2013, p. 180). Codes were grouped through "coding" to begin formulating the categories or themes (Merriam & Tisdell, 2016, p. 206). It encompassed detailed pieces of data grouped into data themes that go together (Merriam & Tisdell, 2016). The data was sorted into groups by color coding so recurring themes could be identified. The themes were then compared to the themes identified during the review of literature. The team members each read the responses individually and highlighted the themes. The team then came together to compare and discuss the themes which had emerged. The team did a second reading to ensure they had identified the important themes from the participant responses. This was done until the researchers came to a sense of saturation; meaning nothing new came forth.

Saturation of Data

When the researchers began to see or hear the same things repeatedly and no new information surfaced during data collection, then saturation of data was reached. Since it was not possible to know in advance when saturation might occur, the researcher needed to engage in analysis while collecting the data (Merriam & Tisdell, 2016). For this study to reach saturation, probes during the interview were used whenever it was necessary in an effort to obtain rich and thick descriptions of participants' perceptions and experiences.

Triangulation

Triangulation "is a powerful strategy used to increase the credibility or internal validity" of a study (Merriam & Tisdell, 2016, p. 245). Methodological triangulation is the most frequently used method in qualitative research and is employed when the researcher combines different methods to address the research question(s) (Carter et al., 2014). For this study, methodological triangulation was utilized through participant's interview responses, quantitative data from the survey, and support from the literature review regarding the topic under investigation.

FINDINGS

Findings are presented as related to the research questions which included:

1. How well did the school provide services to students with special needs during COVID 19?
2. What changes have teachers seen in students with special needs following COVID-19 as they returned to School?
3. How has using technology impacted parent involvement?

Findings for Question 1: How Well Did the School Provide Services to Students With Special Needs During COVID-19?

One of the survey questions asked about the level of support provided by the school to students and faculty during the shutdown. Responses demonstrated that the school focused on academic support at a higher level than any other support provided. It further demonstrated that additional support and future preparation were not highly supported. In terms of academic support, most respondents felt the school provided a high level of academic support, but the social and emotional support for students was viewed as either adequate or some by most respondents and those responding felt that parent support was only adequate. In the area of additional support, it was viewed as adequate for the most part, but participants responded that future preparation was at a high level, indicating the school is considering how to best handle this type of situation in the future. These responses aligned to the research findings of Charteris, et al. (2021) who found "The COVID-19 pandemic may have served to "exacerbate existing stressors faced by students with special educational needs" (p. 4). Additionally, the research of Hoofman and Secord (2021) which reported "adverse educational changes . . .[create] adverse health consequences for children" (1071–1075). These findings corroborated the findings of Kong et al. (2020) which insisted "disruptions in their schedule conflict with the stability of routines" (p. 1012) and the Marsh (2022) findings that disasters have resulted in devastating effects on K–12 schools which underscores the importance of making adaptations as outlined in the findings from the current research. According to Charteris et al. (2021) there was rapid movement to distance education to accommodate learning for students during the time of the disruption.

Another question inquired about whether the school district has now created a curriculum that can be implemented in the event of any disaster or pandemic in the future. The results indicated the district has not done any specific adaptation for curriculum to be delivered in the event of a future crisis. The survey data indicated the school has not made it clear whether the curriculum has been redesigned to align to assessment or activities in the event of another disaster or pandemic. This indicates that if they face any future disasters or pandemic, they may not be more prepared than they were for the COVID-19 school closure.

The respondents' responses indicated that it appeared unclear to them in terms of alignment or best practices. About half of the survey responses indicated they were ensuring alignment to assessments, while the same number felt not only was there alignment to assessments but suggestions for activities were being added to help ensure engagement of the students. Additionally, some of the answers indicated that respondents felt there were clear effective interactive activities being added to the curriculum.

A question on the survey and asked during the interviews provided data that it was concerning whether the pandemic has helped teachers recognize shortcomings in special education services. The responses indicated some discussions about shortcomings had been held and that teachers were focused on making adjustments; however, some felt that very little was happening in terms of making the adjustments needed and that no one was following up on ensuring that changes were happening. This question was triangulated against the research of Kong et al. (2020), Hoofman and Secord (2021), and May (2020.

Participants were asked which areas of disabilities they believed were most impacted by the school shutdown during the pandemic. It was apparent the special education teachers felt the students most affected by the shutdown were those with intellectual disabilities. The next most impacted students were those with ADHD. Students with ASD were the third highest group impacted.

When asked about whether they really gained a picture of the shortcomings and special education delivery during the pandemic and what they saw as the most pressing issues, their responses included responses such as Interview M's (1–3, 2023) who said, "Mental health issues" and "the delivery of daily routine". And their comments were "not all of them have access to the same things, so delivery was hard because there just weren't things that every single person had access to". That was further supported by her stating, "We really tried hard to make it work, but when you're used to having OT with the person who sits right next to you it's really hard to virtually teach somebody how to do buttons or it's really hard to virtually try to teach someone shoe tying or pencil grasping or things like that, like that part was really hard". Another issue was presented by Interviewee C (1-6, 2023) when he said, "Internet access is one shortcoming because it shouldn't go down because too many people are on it". Interviewee J (1-4, 2023) focused on other services but also had concerns. These were expressed when she said "not holding our kids accountable and it's hard to provide specialized services to students when you're not in person, but you have kids who need a test read to them or that have extended time or need notes provided to them, well they're not in front of you so if they're taking a test this kid might need a modified test and have it read to them or this kid just needs a break but when you're online you just to read it to the whole class but then the students don't always need that so they don't want hear to read to them; therefore, if we're classes online yeah it was difficult to read a test because they don't want to listen". Interviewee M (1-3, 2023) followed up and said "I think there are some populations that we service as a department that have lost some academic progress. They were those lower achieving students who thrive with the repetition and the repeated instruction and familiar routine. I think there definitely was, but part of my population that I serviced didn't seem to have skills lost, but I know they had a heavy support system at home that was there to remediate those skills and I know that's not the case for everybody, but I definitely think there was some loss there for especially those lower achieving students who are just really used to that structured setting and maybe don't have the socioeconomic means to have parents at home to help them." But Interviewee C (1-6, 2023) felt, "Academic progress loss should probably be depending on the student I would say, maybe 25%, but if there is that's probably just those students who need to be in an environment where they're face to face with the instructor versus those needing some adaptive assistance."

Findings Related to Question Two: What Changes Have Teachers Seen in Students With Special Needs Following COVID-19 as They Returned to School?

As Kong et al. (2020) indicated, children with special needs may have difficulty in expressing their emotions even if it is because of fear, anxiety, or frustration with what is unknown to them. Participants explained their concerns during the pandemic while working with students included "getting students involved and apparent mental health issues", that "virtual electives were very hard for part of the population limiting their participation", that "virtual learning was a challenge for those students who need the physical and daily routines they are used to", and that "students benefit the most from in-person learning" which they saw as a missing piece (Interviewees M,C,J, 2023). When asked about their greatest concerns seen since students returned to school, teachers reported it was the "loss of academic skills". They further stated, "lack of student accountability, or services such as the Internet at home" and "lack of attendance, attention, and social-emotional stability". Interviewee J (1-4, 2023) felt specifically, "They just don't do their work and they don't care. Yeah, that's despite the behaviors, attendance is very poor. I have students that just don't come to school and it's very sporadic and then parents say how do I get my kid up and attend school. Social-emotional is the one that I see the most. We have a lot of students that can't even get out of the car in the morning to come to school and they're all my freshmen. I'm telling you, I guess when they were in 7th grade what happened or 6th grade, I guess these are 6th graders, but I have a lot more social-emotional issues. I have kids in here crying. I have kids in here that aren't freshmen and aren't doing well that did fine in middle school. I have an increase of all the kids that need counseling, need time to come in here and chill, yeah that makes sense". Interviewee M (1-3, 2023) insisted "I think there are some populations that we service as a department that have lost some academic progress. They were those lower achieving students who thrive with the repetition and the repeated instruction and familiar routine. I think there definitely was, but part of my population that I serviced didn't seem to have skills lost, but I know they had a heavy support system at home that was there to remediate those skills and I know that's not the case for everybody, but I definitely think there was some loss there for especially those lower achieving students who are just really used to that structured setting and maybe don't have the socioeconomic means to have parents at home to help them". This focus on academic progress was emphasized by Interviewee C (1-6, 2023) when he said, "Academic progress loss should probably be depending on the student I would say, maybe 25%, but if there is that's probably just those students who need to be in an environment where they're face to face with the instructor versus those needing some adaptive assistance." He continued by stating, "The biggest difference I noticed is their distraction. I know electronics was a deal prior to, but it's even on another level now. Just because we used electronics for the pandemic, the time they had it's almost at this point within the school environment if there's not something electronic in front of them it's almost like it has no relevance". Interviewee M (1-3, 2023) expressed the same feelings by stating, "They became much more dependent on having a device in their hands and so when they came back that's another behavior, I've seen is the device has not gone away because they've become so connected to the device that it has just become an extension of them and they're really hesitant to get rid of it. I even have some of my kids who do have social-emotional needs who now say their phone is their calming strategy and that was not something I heard pre pandemic". Interviewee M (1-3,2023) focused more on attendance. She said "I see a lot more parents who are willing to call out for attendance because they just call it social-emotional needs or they're having an off day. that could just be purely a coincidence, but it didn't happen near as much pre COVID. Social-emotional needs I have some kids who have kind of spiraled into a hot mess since they've been back from being at home which was not good. They maintained their academics that part was fine, but the isolation from being around other people was really hard for them, yeah attendance has been bad for quite a few". She continued by saying, "This is where I've seen the biggest impact especially for my students that I service. The whole behavior thing they kind of forgot how to school for a little bit". These responses were in line with the research of Murphy and McFerran (2017) which insisted that students with special needs have low levels of social connectedness and with COVID-19's school closure, it marginalized them even further beyond their normal limitations.

Findings Related to Question Three: How Has Using Technology Impacted Parent Involvement?

A survey question, which was open ended, inquired about the types of communication provided for parent communication. Teachers' responses included various approaches. Methods of communicating with students included Google classroom, canvas, and virtual conferences. Some of the methods used to offer parent engagement during the pandemic included Google meetings, texts, newsletters, emails, phone calls, and virtual conferences.

When asked about the effect of moving to online meetings with parents and their level of engagement, teacher responses indicated it has assisted parents in multiple ways. They felt parents tended to be more engaged in meetings and often felt parents were present while students were online. To further investigate how the teachers believe the online work had assisted parent involvement, one-on-one interviews were held with selected teachers. These interviews were conducted until saturation was reached. This was done to get deeper, richer data to support the quantitative data findings. The responses aligned to how meeting online has helped parents and included the statements it "has helped facilitate more parent involvement for parents who were previously unable to make it to meetings", "it lacks the human contact element but it creates flexibility"," parents are able to have great flexibility to their participation for meetings", "They do not have to leave work", "They are on time and I have seen greater participation due to the lack of transportation to arrange", "has allowed them to manage their time more", "More parents are willing to attend a virtual meeting" (Interviewees M,C, J, I, 2023).

When asked if they believed that during the pandemic, students with special needs were provided education in the least restrictive environment, participants reported they "continued to meet with all of their classes online", they "offered support as needed", they provided "options to participate in virtual meetings at the same time as same age peers", they limited distractions of the school environment when online", and because students were at home they felt "they were in a quiet setting on the virtual call with the teacher". These responses were seen in the research literature from the U.S. Department of Education (2020) and as seen in Averett (2021), where there were quotes as outlining that "teachers, schools, and districts struggled to understand the implications of IDEA and Section 504 for their ability to offer remote instruction" (p.2).

THEMES

Following the coding of themes, three major themes were found. The first theme was the loss of academic skills. The second theme was the lack of services such as the Internet and social-emotional services. The third theme was focused on lack of attendance, attention, and social-emotional stability.

Theme 1:

When asked about their greatest concerns since students returned to school, they reported it was the "loss of academic skills". Interviewee M stated, "I think there are some populations that we service as a department that have lost some academic progress. They were those lower achieving students who thrive with the repetition and the repeated instruction and familiar routine. I think there definitely was, but part of my population that I serviced didn't seem to have skills lost, but I know they had a heavy support system at home that was there to remediate those skills and I know that's not the case for everybody, but I definitely think there was some loss there for especially those lower achieving students who are just really used to that structured setting and maybe don't have the socioeconomic means to have parents at home to help them" (M, 1-3-23). Interviewee C while agreeing with the academic loss also stated a concern with adaptive assistance by stating "Academic progress loss should probably be depending on the student I would say, maybe 25%, but if there is that's probably just those students who need to be in an environment where they're face to face with the instructor versus those needing some adaptive assistance "(C, 1-6-23).

Theme 2:

This theme focused on the lack of services such as the Internet at home and other educational supports. As Chartris et al., (2021) found, the rapid move to distance education was problematic due to lack of policies and teachers were not accustomed to working remotely, but students and families were less prepared for this type of school. Interviewee M responded, "We really tried hard to make it work but when you're used to having OT with the person who sits right next to you it's really hard to virtually teach somebody how to do buttons or it's really hard to virtually try to teach somebody shoe tying or pencil grasp or things like that, like that part was really hard" (M, 1-3-23). She continued by stating "Mental health issues" and "the delivery of daily routine". And their comments were "not all of them have access to the same things so delivery was hard because there just weren't things every single person had access to "(interviewee M, 1-3-2023). Interviewee C insisted "Internet access is one shortcoming because it shouldn't go down because too many people are on it" (C, 1-6-23). Interviewee J focused on the issue of "not holding our kids accountable and it's hard to provide specialized services to students when you're not in person, but you have kids that need a test read to them or that have extended time or need notes provided to them, well they're not in front of you so if they're taking a test this kid might need a modified test and have to read to them or this kid just needs a break but when you're online you just read it to the whole class but then the students don't always need that so they don't want hear it read to them therefore if we're classes online yeah it was difficult to read a test because they don't want to listen" (J, 1-4-23).

Theme 3:

This theme focused on the issue of lack of attendance, attention, and social-emotional stability. As Laing et al. (2020) (cited in Hoofman & Secord, 2021) found, 40.4% of students reported having depression and anxiety. With this in mind, the response of Interviewee J aligned when this person said "they just don't do their work and they don't care. Yeah, that's despite the behaviors, attendance is very poor. I have students that just don't come to school and it's very sporadic and then parents say how do I get my kid up and attend school. Social-emotional is the one that I see the most. We have a lot of students that can't even get out of the car in the morning to come to school and it's all my freshmen. I'm telling you, I guess when they were in 7th grade what happened or 6th grade, I guess these are 6th graders, but I have a lot more social-emotional issues. I have kids in here crying. I have kids in here that aren't freshmen and aren't doing well that did fine in middle school. I have an increase of all the kids that need counseling, needing time to come in here and chill, yeah that makes sense (J, 1-4,23). This directly was supported by the research done by Laing et al. Interviewee C insisted, "The biggest difference I noticed is their distraction. I know electronics was a deal prior to, but it's even on another level now. Just because we used electronics for the pandemic, the time they had is almost at this point within the school environment if there's not something electronic in front of them it's almost like it has no relevance" (C, 1-6-23). But interviewee M felt "They became much more dependent on having a device in their hands and so when they came back that's another behavior, I've seen is the device has not gone away because they've become so connected to the device that it has just become an extension of them and they're really hesitant to get rid of it. I even have some of my kids who do have social-emotional needs who now say their phone is their calming strategy and that was not something I heard pre-pandemic" (M, 1-3-23). Interviewee T contended "Attendance—I see a lot more parents who are willing to call out for attendance because they just call it social-emotional needs or they're having an off day. that could just be purely a coincidence, but it didn't happen near as much pre COVID. Social-emotional needs— I have some kids who have kind of spiraled into a hot mess since they've been back from being at home which was not good. They maintained their academics that part was fine, but the isolation from being around other people was really hard for them, yeah attendance has been bad for quite a few" (M, 1-3-23). She believed "This is where I've seen the biggest impact especially for my students that I service. the whole behavior thing they kind of forgot how to school for a little bit" (M, 1-3-23).

DISCUSSION

While teachers were attempting to remediate the loss of time and learning, they were faced with student social-emotional issues which have been intensified by the loss of time within the school setting. These findings aligned to the findings of Murphy and McFerran (2017) concerning school connectedness and belonging. Additionally, these issues were discussed by Hoofman and Secord (2021) concerning how the pandemic brought about adverse educational changes including the area of mental health and social health. During the pandemic, far too many students became accustomed to "not having their work count toward a grade" which has resulted in the decline in student attention in class and the motivation to complete assignments. Students have become so accustomed to using some type of device at this point, they refuse to put it away and focus on the task at hand. Instead, students contend the phone has become a calming device and it is necessary to always have it in hand. The teachers expressed the need to begin to make changes and restructure teaching processes to help students return to paying attention in class and completing the assignments to close the gap caused by being out of school during COVID-19. At this point, based on responses from participants, this school has not begun to address the social-emotional concerns seen by the teachers. Many schools in the area have begun providing professional development on how to assist students with social-emotional needs so based on these findings, it would appear that this approach to developing teachers' ability to address social-emotional needs is an important next step to take in supporting students and moving to the level needed for success.

IMPLICATIONS

Based on the findings from this study, evidence indicated a need for schools to ensure that teachers are trained in how to deliver social-emotional support for students and families. Perhaps districts should consider purchasing a social-emotional curriculum to put in place to provide the needed guidance for teachers to implement this curriculum. Schools should ensure that parents are provided effective communication about student needs. There appears to be a need for future research in terms of how schools have updated curriculum to ensure they are prepared for any future disaster or pandemic. Based on the findings from this study, it is obvious that schools must prepare for better technology if a future pandemic or disaster should occur. With the changing climate issues, it would appear more likely that a disaster could happen causing schools to close and thus, they must be better prepared and not caught without plans and processes in place which should include online curriculum as well as teacher preparation. Further, more research is needed to investigate the long-haul effects of the pandemic. The question of how the academic loss and the loss of social-emotional growth is yet to be determined but should be considered in terms of preparing teachers to deal with student social-emotional issues. Future research on the changes in plans and policies of school districts for possible future shutdowns should be investigated to determine if schools have made plans for possible future disasters and if possible, to do a policy analysis to determine the best policies and plans to be implemented. Future research should be conducted to determine the best and most appropriate way to train teachers on addressing social-emotional needs of students and what curriculum(s) provides the best support. With the findings from this research, a follow up study could interview teachers at schools using the most appropriate social-emotional training and curriculum to gather their perceptions of the effects on students.

SUMMARY

While teachers have begun to recognize those areas where schools have not risen to the level of service needed by the students who experienced the gap in their academics and social-emotional development, schools and districts will need to investigate how to provide services that have been missing during the pandemic. If schools and districts are to graduate students who can become independent citizens, changes must begin. To remedy the issues created and left behind by the COVID-19 pandemic and the shuttering of schools, it will take a joint effort among teachers, administrators, and parents as well as the community to ensure that students regain what was lost.

AUTHORS NOTE

Both authors contributed equally.

There is no funding associated with this work. There are no conflicts of interest associated with this work.

Correspondence should be directed to: Jo Nell Wood, Saint Louis University, 3500 Lindell, Fitzgerald Hall, Suite 177, St. Louis, MO 63103, USA. Email: jo.wood@slu.edu

REFERENCES

Averett, K. (2021). Remote learning, COVID-19, and children with disabilities. *AERA Open, 7*(1), 1–12.

Bergerl, Z., Evans, N., Phelan, A., & Silverman, R. (2020). COVID-19 Control measures must be equitable and inclusive. *British Medical Journal, 1*, 368–369. https://doi.org/10.1136/bmj.m1141

Carter, N., Bryant-Lukosius, D., DiCenso, A., Blythe, J., & Neville, A. J. (2014). The use of triangulation in qualitative research. *Oncology Nursing Forum, 41*(5), 545–547. https://doi.org/10.1188/14.ONF.545-547

Charteris, P, Anderson, J., & Boyle, C. (2021). Fostering school connectedness online for students with special education needs: Inclusive education in Australia during the COVID-19 pandemic. *European Journal of Special Needs Education, 31*(2), 142–156.

Creswell, J. W. (2013). *Research design: Qualitative, quantitative, and mixed methods approaches* (4th ed.). SAGE Publications.

Goldhaber, D., & Theobald, R. (2022). Teacher attrition and mobility in the pandemic. *Educational Evaluation and Policy Analysis, 0*(0). https://doi.org/10.3102/01623737221139285

Guetterman, T. C., Creswell, J. W., Deutsch, C., & Gallo, J. J. (2019). Process evaluation of a retreat for scholars in the first cohort: The NIH mixed methods research training program for the health sciences. *Journal of Mixed Methods Research, 13*(1), 52–68.

Hesse-Biber, S. (2010). Qualitative approaches to mixed methods practice. *Qualitative Inquiry, 16*(6), 455–468.

Hood, N. (2020). Learning from lockdown: What the experiences of teachers, students and parents can tell us about what happened and where to next for New Zealand's school system. *The Education Hub*, 1–31. https://theeducationhub.org.nz/wp-content/uploads/2020/08/Learning-from-lockdown.pdf. .

Hoofman, J., & Secord, E. (2021). The effect of COVID-19 on education. *Pediatric Clinics of North America, 68*(5), 1071–1079. https://doi.org/10.1016/j.pcl.2021.05.009.

Individuals with Disabilities Education Improvement Act of 2004, 20 U.S.C. § 1400 et seq. (2004).

Kong, W. H., Li, Y., Peng, M. W., Kong, D. G., Yang, X. B., Wang, L., & Liu, M. Q. (2020). SARS-CoV-2 detection in patients with influenza-like illness. *Nature Microbiology, 5*(5), 675–678.

Laing, L, Ren, J., Cao R., et al. (2020) The effects of COVID-19 on youth mental health. *Psychiatry Q, 91,* 841–852.

Leedy, P. D., & Ormrod, J. E. (2016). Practical research: Planning and design. 11. In J. W. Johnston (Series Ed.), *Planning and Design*. Pearson Publishing.

Marsh, R. (2022). *Extreme weather has devastated schools around the country. Now their students are suffering.* CNN. n.d. https://www.cnn.com/2022/10/17/us/extreme-weather-schools-hurricane-ian-climate/index.html

Merriam, S. B., & Tisdell, E. J. (2016). *Qualitative Research. A guide to design and implementation* (4th ed.). Jossey-Bass.

Murphy, M., & McFerran, K. (2017). Exploring the literature on music participation and social connectedness for young people with intellectual disability: A critical interpretive synthesis. *Journal of Intellectual Disabilities, 21*(4), 297–314. https://doi.org/10.1177/1744629516650128

Rooney, C., & White, G. W. (2007). Consumer perspective: Narrative analysis of a disaster preparedness and emergency response survey from persons with mobility impairments. *Journal of Disability Policy Studies, 17*(4), 206–215.

Saavedar, J. (2020). *Educational challenges and opportunities of the coronavirus (COVID-19) pandemic. Education for global development: A blog about the power of investing in people.* http://blogs.workbank.org/education/educational-challenges-and-opportunities-COVID-19-pandemic.

Sahin, M. D., & Öztürk, G. (2019). Mixed method research: Theoretical foundations, designs, and Its use in educational research. *International Journal of Contemporary Educational Research, 6*(2), 301–310.

Smith, D. L., & Notaro, S. J. (2009). Personal emergency preparedness for people with disabilities from the 2006–2007 Behavioral Risk Factor Surveillance System. *Disability and Health Journal, 2*(2), 86–94.

Turner, T. L., Balmer, D. F., & Coverdale, J. H. (2013). Methodologies and study designs relevant to medical education research. *International Review of Psychiatry, 25*(3), 301–310.

U.S. Department of Education. (2020). *Addressing the risk of COVID-19 in preschool, elementary and secondary schools while serving children with disabilities.* Office for Civil Rights, Office of Special Education and Rehabilitative Services. http:/www.2.ed.gov/about/offices/list/ocr/frontpage/faq/rr/policyguidance/Sypple%20Fact%20Sheet%203.21.20%%20FINAL.pdf

CHAPTER 9

THE ENTANGLED

Post-COVID-19 Cognitive, Psychological and Motivational States

Pınar Ayyildiz
Ankara Lokman Hekim University, Türkiye

Adem Yilmaz
Kastamonu University, Türkiye.

The COVID-19 pandemic has hindered the provision of educational services for a considerably long time. Even today, students, teachers, educators, and other stakeholders continue to struggle with the permanent traces of the pandemic. The present research intends to delve into the opinions of students and teachers at the high school and at the tertiary level while investigating some key variables. A combination (variation) design, one of the mixed research methods, was deployed in this regard. Utilizing random sampling, 428 high school students, 189 teachers of different branches, 673 university students and 105 faculty members were employed in the research. The Montreal Cognitive Assessment (MoCA), Zung Self-Rating Depression Scale (SDS), Generalized Anxiety Disorder Screener (GAD-7), Motivation Scale (MS) and Semi-Structured Interview Questions were utilized as the data collection instruments. The data obtained within the scope of the research were ana-

Instructional Survival in the Midst of the Perfect Storm:
The Experiences of K–12 Teachers During the COVID-19 Global Pandemic, pages 145–168.

Published under exclusive licence by Emerald Publishing Limited
ISBNs: 978-1-83708-502-6 HB, 978-1-83708-503-3 PB,
978-1-83708-504-0 EPDF, 978-1-83708-505-7 EPUB

lyzed using SPSS 25, AMOS 24, and The PROCESS macro for the SPSS (Hayes, 2018) program. In addition to the models developed by Hayes (2018), path analyses produced by the researchers of the current study were also referred to. At the end, it was determined that the cognitive test results of high school students were low, and their motivation results were affected by the variables of depression and anxiety. These variations appear to be creating significant differences in variables such as gender, receiving psychological support, providing mentor support, adaptation to the post-pandemic process, digital competence and infrastructure competence.

Keywords: Post-Pandemic, Cognitive, Psychological, Depression, Anxiety, Motivation.

INTRODUCTION

Since the outbreak of the COVID-19 pandemic, individuals have been experiencing cognitive, psychological (Bareket-Bojmel et al., 2021), motivational and other severe issues of varying nature (Akdeniz & Gültekin Ahçı, 2023). Long-term fatigue, has arguably led to numerous permanent and characteristic problems (Horigian et al., 2021; Mondelli & Pariante, 2021). The individuals ill with COVID-19 have started to show persistent and unknown symptoms such as mental confusion, muscle pain, weakness, learning difficulties, cognitive impairment, depression, anxiety, myalgia, fatigue, insomnia, and mood disorders (De Pedraza et al., 2020; Torjesen, 2021). In addition to these challenges, low energy, and "brain fog", is frequently encountered through concentration problems, disorientation, inability to focus, and difficulty in finding the right words whilst being engaged in communication (Jennings et al., 2022). With that being said, long-term psychological, cognitive or negative mental health conditions have resulted (Diamond & Ling, 2019; Stokes et al., 2021). Thus, it is clear that the effects of the COVID-19 pandemic have negatively affected different spheres of the lives of humans (Rumas et al., 2021). Amongst the spheres in question, education has a unique place considering its societal connections along with its links to the development of persons at a rather micro level and with its links to development at a relatively more macro level. Education is a service that must be accomplished in a continuous and consistent fashion (Groarke et al., 2021) particularly bearing in mind the aforementioned links to a number of areas. Nevertheless, it seems that the COVID-19 global pandemic has hindered both the provision of the relevant services and the total fulfilment of any related tasks for a considerably long time. The current day reveals that plentiful measures have been lifted for the COVID-19 pandemic, vaccination has become a part of everyday routines, and countries worldwide have begun to adjust themselves to the "life after the pandemic" (Ayyıldız & Yılmaz, 2021). Albeit it is worthy of reiterating that the pandemic does not only have impacts related to health. The struggle with the permanent traces left by the pandemic on students, teachers, educators, on higher education organizations and other institutions remains highly visible (Genç & Aslan, 2021).

There exist many studies in the literature regarding the permanent effects on individuals during and post-COVID-19. When these studies are scrutinized, the subject areas emerge as follows: cognitive flexibility (Akdeniz & Gültekin Ahçı, 2023), social support and adaptation (Bareket-Bojmel et al., 2021; Grey et al., 2020), loneliness and introversion (Chang et al., 2019), anxiety and dissatisfaction (De Pedraza et al., 2020; Demirtaş, 2021; Gallagher et al., 2021), social communication and mental health (Elmer et al., 2020), depression and emotional disorders (Groarke et al., 2021) and psychological effects (Loslo-Roth et al., 2021). Further, the existing studies have examined intermediary models from time to time (Miranda et al., 2013; Padmanabhanunni & Pretorius, 2021). However, the samples in these studies are rather limited, and there are almost no studies that deal with cognitive, psychological, and motivational issues together, and there is no comparative study in the field of educational sciences at both high school and university level in this sense. Based on these research needs, the present study attempts to delve into the opinions of students and teachers at the high school and the higher education level in relation to further investigate the effects of the COVID-19 global pandemic on these student populations.

First, cognitive changes, psychological states (depression, anxiety) and motivation levels of high school students were studied. During this endeavor, some variables such as receiving psychological support (GPS), providing mentor support (Me-S), adaptation to the post-pandemic process (APPP), gender, digital competence (DC), and infrastructure competence (IC) were included. Next, teachers working at the high school level were analyzed in light of similar variables. Here, teachers were not given cognitive tests. This is because while it is oftentimes possible to compare students' academic achievements, for teachers there is no such valid or reliable assessment. In the second phase of the study, cognitive changes, psychological states (depression, anxiety) and motivational conditions of the students studying at university were explored. In doing so, variables like gender, GPS, Me-S, APPP, DC, and IC were investigated. Then, faculty members were inspected by means of similar variables.

Research Model

Plenty of branches of science have studied the permanent changes that have occurred in individuals due to the pandemic and those that transpired after the pandemic viz. throughout the post-pandemic period. The present study sought to inquire into the permanent problems within the framework of educational sciences rather than the perspectives of the medical or health sciences. Figure 9.1 portrays the research model analyzed for students and teachers at the high school level and students and faculty members at the tertiary level, accordingly.

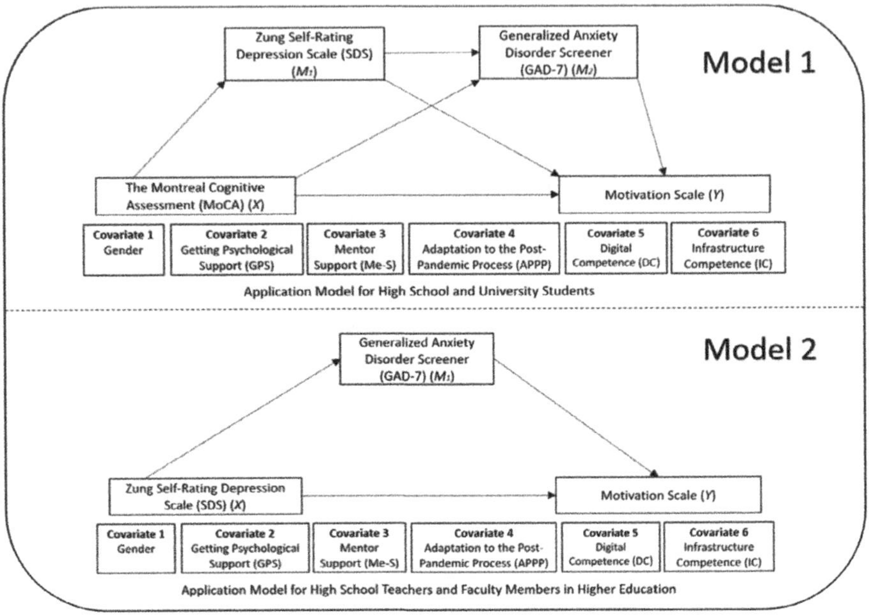

FIGURE 9.1. Research Model

Statement of the Problem

The primary purpose of the present research was to analyze the cognitive, psychological, and motivational problems that materialized in individuals during the post-COVID-19 global pandemic with regards to several different variables. Answers to the following sub-problems were sought within the parameters of the study:

1. What is the relationship among high school students' cognitive level, psychological states and motivational variables?
2. What is the relationship between the psychological states of high school teachers and their motivational variables?
3. What is the relationship among cognitive level, psychological state and motivational variables of university students?
4. What is the relationship between the psychological states of the faculty members and their motivational variables?
5. What are participant views regarding receiving psychological support, providing mentor support, adapting to the post-pandemic process, gender, digital competence and infrastructure adequacy?
6. How were the responses of the participants to the semi-structured interview questions categorized?

METHOD

In the present study, the cross-sectional design was utilized. To this end, the combination (variation) design, one of the mixed research methods, was used. There are two major reasons why the variation pattern was used. The first one is that studies deploying the quantitative paradigm cannot always-and fully-reveal cause-effect relationships. For this reason, using the qualitative paradigm is effective at the points where quantitative applications become insufficient. The second reason is that data diversity contributes positively to the validity and reliability of research. As a matter of fact, many studies in the literature stated that fostering data diversification reduces the number of errors involved in the research (Ayyıldız & Yılmaz, 2022; Fraenkel et al., 2011). In the combined design, qualitative and quantitative applications are carried out independently, and the results are combined and interpreted later. The research process consisted of two phases. In the first phase, quantitative applications were run. These applications related to the high school students, teachers and higher education students and faculty members. In the second phase, the interviews with the participants selected through the specific criteria took place with the help of open-ended semi-structured interview questions. The model that is pertinent to the implementation process is presented in the appendix.

After conducting a random sampling method, 428 high school students, 189 teachers of different branches, 673 university students and 105 faculty members participated in the research. Participants with diverse profiles were used within the scope of the research. The selection of the students and teachers, especially at the high school and university levels, is a strength of the current research. It has been emphasized in the literature that high school students and teachers experienced difficulty adapting to the instructional process after the COVID-19 pandemic. In addition, at the university level, which can be considered the continuation of high school education, cognitive, motivational and psychological difficulties were experienced after the COVID-19 pandemic. Therefore, the two aforementioned study groups were utilized in the present study.

Measures

The Montreal Cognitive Assessment (MoCA)

"The Montreal Cognitive Assessment (MoCA)" was utilized for measuring the cognitive levels of high school and university students. This test has been in use as part of numerous clinical and educational studies after the COVID-19 pandemic and has been translated into numerous different languages.

Zung Self-Rating Depression Scale (SDS)

"The Zung Self-Rating Depression Scale" was designed by Zung (1965). The widespread influence, the physiological equivalents, other abnormalities, and psychomotor activity are the four common aspects of depression that are measured

by the scale's 20 items. There are 10 questions with positive wording and ten with negative wording. A scale from 0 to 4 is used to grade each question viz. a little of the time, some of the time, good part of the time, most of the time. The range of scores is 25 to 49 normal range (NR), 50 to 59 mildly depressed (Mi-D), 60 to 69 moderately depressed (Mo-D), and 70 and above seriously depressed. (SD).

Generalized Anxiety Disorder Screener (GAD-7)

"Generalized Anxiety Disorder" Screener encompasses 7 items and is a 4-point Likert-type measurement tool. Scores of 5, 10, and 15 are taken as the cut-off points for mild, moderate, and severe anxiety, respectively. That being said, further evaluation is recommended provided the score is 10 or greater when used as a screening tool. GAD-7 total score for the seven items ranges from 0 to 21. 0–4: minimal anxiety (MA), 5–9: mild anxiety (Mi-A), 10–14: moderate (Mo-A) anxiety, 15–21: severe anxiety (SA). The GAD-7 was developed Spitzer et al. (2006).

Motivation Scale (MS)

The motivation scale was developed by Tulunay Ateş and İhtiyaroğlu (2019) to evaluate motivational levels of individuals. There are two dimensions in this scale, namely, Intrinsic Motivation (IM) and Extrinsic Motivation (EM). There are 21 items in total and it is a 5-point Likert-type scale. The statements in the scale are "1-Strongly Disagree, 2-Disagree, 3-Neither Agree nor Disagree, 4-Agree, 5-Strongly Agree".

Semi-Structured Interview Questions

Within the scope of the research, a semi-structured interview form consisting of 3 questions was created by the researchers to support the data obtained from quantitative applications and to be able to inquire into the participant views in depth. Trustworthiness and rigor were ensured for the interview form first, and it was then made ready for use.

Data Analysis

The quantitative data of the study were studied in two separate stages. First, descriptive statistics were utilized. At this stage, the mean and standard deviation values were calculated. Following this, the correlation between the variables was probed and presented with the reliability results. In addition, the normal distribution results of the application data were also examined. In the second stage, the structural relationships between the variables in the conceptual model were inspected. The quantitative data obtained within the scope of the research were reviewed through SPSS 25, AMOS, 24 and The PROCESS macro for the SPSS (Hayes, 2018) program.

Based on (?) the models developed by Hayes (2018), path analyses designated by the researchers were integrated into the study. A 95% confidence interval was used. As long as the confidence interval results do not include the zero value, it can be put forth that they are statistically significant (Deniz, 2021; Hayes, 2018). Plus, 5000 times, resampling was assured using the bootstrap method. Effect sizes were determined with confidence intervals for each path with 5000 bootstrapping samples. All the estimates were standardized to provide comparable effect sizes.

The qualitative data obtained were interpreted by subjecting them to content analysis. Prior to starting the coding and debugging process, a series of preliminary preparations were warranted to complete a high-quality coding process. The related preparations can be expressed as creating a coding guide, providing detailed training to coders, pre-testing, and developing management procedures to control the applicability and functioning of the very coding system (Özkan, 2019). Analyst triangulation was also chosen in the analysis of the interview data. This application is beneficial in preventing the occurrence of similar and controversial situations while coding. What is more, the levels of agreement and disagreement pertaining to the coders were calculated with the help of the formula determined by Miles and Huberman (1994), and this rate was defined as 91%. Since the consensus levels of the encoders were spotted within the ideal range, the Cohen Kappa Coefficient was identified, and the rate of cohesion and interoperability between encoders was found out as .82.

RESULTS

While presenting the research results, the results were planned to be reported in stages by considering the problem situations. Before proceeding to this stage, the correlation, reliability values, and normal distribution results between the variables can be observed from Table 9.1. The results belonging to the high school students, teachers, university students, and faculty members who constitute the research study group are expressed in a separate fashion.

Once Table 9.1 was viewed, it was apparent that the results of all study groups showed a normal distribution, and the reliability coefficients were .70 and above. With regards to the results coming from high school students, it was clear that there was a significant and positive correlation between MoCA and MS (r=.41, 95%CI=.23, .64). There was no significant difference between MoCA and SDS (r=-.32, 95%CI=-.46, -.11) and MoCA and GAD-7 (r=-.41, 95%CI=-.62, -.09) and there was a negative correlation. There was also a significant and positive correlation between SDS and GAD-7 (r=.35, 95%CI=.19, .52). There was no significant difference between MS and SDS (r=-.61, 95%CI=-.74, -.32) or MS and GAD-7 (r=-.48, 95%CI=-.56, -.29). A negative relationship was discovered. When the results of teachers working at the high school level were investigated, one can see that there is a significant and positive correlation between SDS and GAD-7 (r=.28, 95%CI=.15, .33). On the other hand, there was no significant difference between MS and SDS (r=-.39, 95%CI=-.51, -.22) or between MS and GAD-7 (r=-.20, 95%CI=-.33, -.16).

TABLE 9.1. Descriptive Statistics and Correlation Results for Variables

High School Students

Variable	1 [95% CI]	2 [95% CI]	3 [95% CI]	4 [95% CI]
1. MoCA	-			
2. SDS	-.32** [-.46, -.11]	-		
3. GAD-7	-.41** [-.62, -.09]	.35** [.19, .52]	-	
4. MS	.41** [.23, .64]	-.61** [-.74, -.32]	-.48** [-.56, -.29]	-
α	.701	.739	.802	.752
M	21.51	64.75	13.59	87.45
SD	2.69	4.71	3.56	8.17
Skewness	.041	-.128	.369	.096
Kurtosis	.899	.481	.663	.994

* $p < 0.05$, ** $p < 0.01$, *** $p < 0.001$

High School Teachers

Variable	1 [95% CI]	2 [95% CI]	3 [95% CI]
1. SDS	-		
2. GAD-7	.28** [.15, .33]	-	
3. MS	-.39** [-.51, -.22]	-.20** [-33, -.16]	-
α	.782	.796	.814
M	49.17	8.76	92.75
SD	1.86	3.58	5.96
Skewness	-.015	-.296	.186
Kurtosis	.368	.635	.87

1* $p < 0.05$, ** $p < 0.01$, *** $p < 0.001$

Higher Education Students

Variable	1 [95% CI]	2 [95% CI]	3 [95% CI]	4 [95% CI]
1. MoCA	-			
2. SDS	-.21** [-.35, -.06]	-		
3. GAD-7	-.34** [-.51, -.17]	.26** [.14, .38]	-	
4. MS	.55** [.32, .59]	-.49** [-.63, -.41]	-.34** [-.49, -.19]	-
α	.815	.836	.795	.896
M	25.82	53.17	9.26	90.14
SD	3.32	2.96	5.56	5.87
Skewness	.177	.369	.011	.178
Kurtosis	.762	.839	.552	.876

* $p < 0.05$, ** $p < 0.01$, *** $p < 0.001$

TABLE 9.1. Continued

Higher Education Faculty Members			
Variable	**1 [95% CI]**	**2 [95% CI]**	**3 [95% CI]**
1. SDS	-		
2. GAD-7	.19** [.11, .24]	-	
3. MS	-.22** [-.35, -.13]	-.16** [-25, -.07]	-
α	.832	.765	.906
M	33.22	6.14	101.25
SD	3.72	4.12	8.73
Skewness	.139	.174	-.132
Kurtosis	.889	.993	.452

* $p < 0.05$, ** $p < 0.01$, *** $p < 0.001$

α: Cronbach alpha, M: Mean, SD: Standard deviation.
MoCA: The Montreal Cognitive Assessment, SDS: Zung Self-Rating Depression Scale
GAD-7: Generalized Anxiety Disorder Screener, MS: Coronavirus Motivation Scale

With regards to the students' results at the university level, it would be fair to say that there was a significant and positive relationship between MoCA and MS (*r*=.55, 95%CI=.32, .59). There was no significant difference between MoCA and SDS (*r*=-.21, 95%CI=-.35, -.06) or between MoCA and GAD-7 (*r*=-.34, 95%CI=-.51, -.17). There was a negative correlation. It was found that there was a significant and positive correlation between SDS and GAD-7 (*r*=.26, 95%CI=.14-.38). Yet, there was no significant difference between MS and SDS (*r*=-.49, 95%CI=-.63, -.41) or MS and GAD-7 (*r*=-.34, 95%CI=-.49, -.19). A negative correlation was also found. The data from the faculty members working at the university level, suggest that there is a significant and positive relationship between SDS and GAD-7 (*r*=.19, 95%CI=.11, .24). There was no significant difference between MS and SDS (*r*=-.22, 95%CI=-.35, -.13) or MS and GAD-7 (r=-.16, 95%CI=-.25, -.07). It was detected that there is a negative relationship. The structural equation model and mediation analysis results for research groups are depicted in Figures 9.2, 9.3, 9.4, and 9.5. Bootstrapping results, on the other hand, are shared in Tables 9.2, 9.3, 9.4, and 9.5.

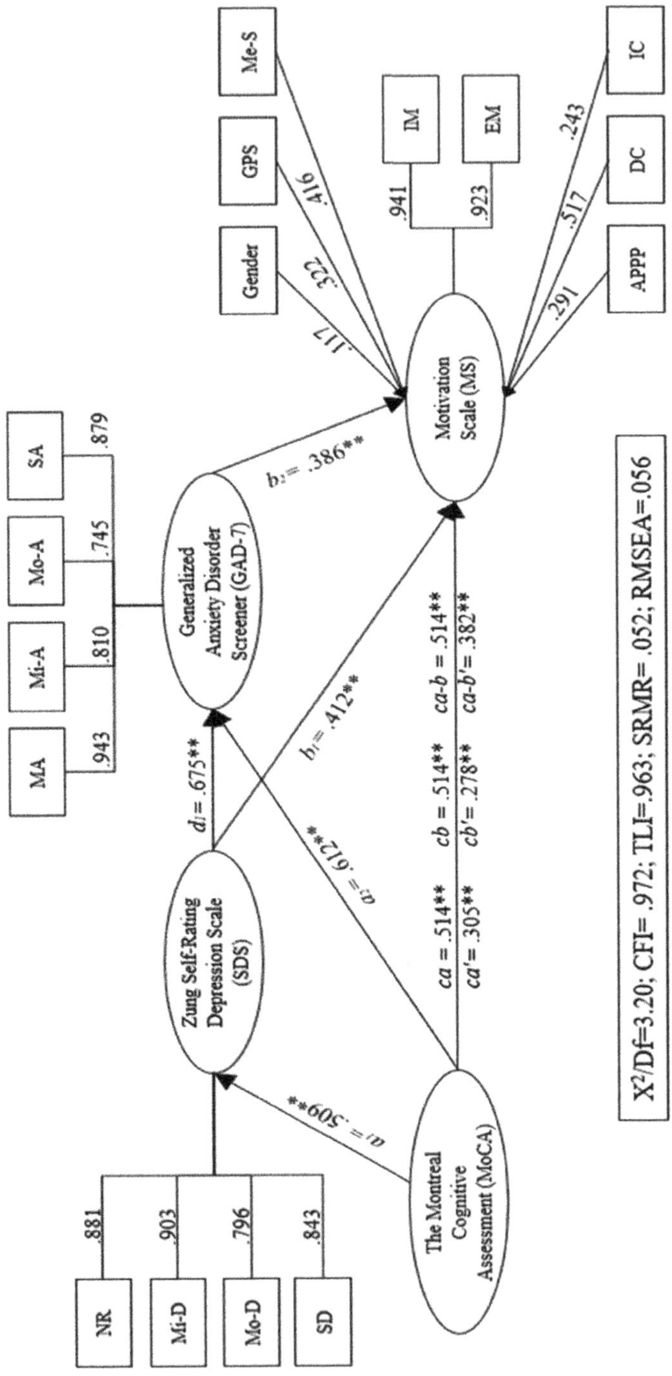

FIGURE 9.2. Mediation Model of MoCA and MS With the Mediating Role of SDS and GAD-7 (High School Students).

TABLE 9.2. Bootstrapping Results (High School Students)

	Coefficient	95% Bootstrap CI		*Sig (P)*
		LL	UL	
Standardized Direct Effects				
Gender→MS	.117			
GPS→MS	.322			
Me-S→MS	.416			
APPP→MS	.291			
DC→MS	.517			
IC→MS	.243			
MoCA→MS (*ca'*)	.305	.176	.396	**
MoCA→MS (*cb'*)	.278	.221	.401	**
MoCA→MS (*ca-b'*)	.382	.296	.532	**
MoCA→SDS	.509	.278	.771	**
MoCA→GAD-7	.612	.349	.638	**
SDS→MS	.412	.279	.481	**
SDS→GAD-7	.675	.501	.867	**
GAD-7→MS	.386	.139	.469	**
Standardized Total Indirect Effects				
MoCA→MS (*a'*)	.209	.174	.312	*
MoCA→MS (*b'*)	.236	.159	.308	**
MoCA→MS (*a-b'*)	.132	.049	.196	*
Standardized Total Effects				
MoCA→MS	.514	.332	.628	**

* $p < 0.05$, ** $p < 0.01$, *** $p < 0.001$
Note. CI: Confidence interval; LL: Lower limit; UL: Upper limit.

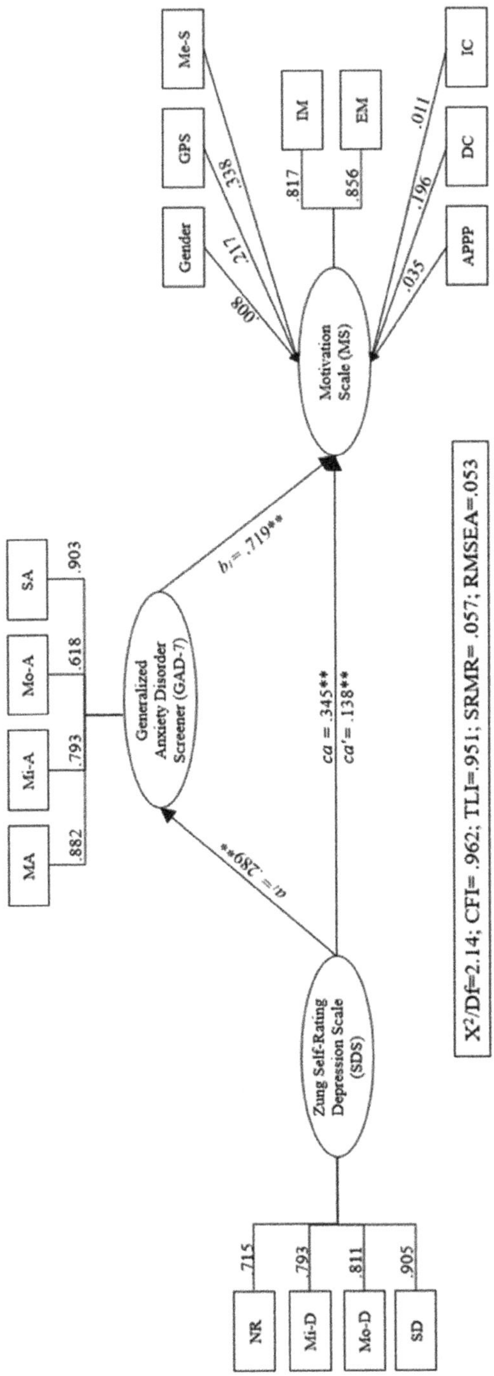

FIGURE 9.3. Mediation Model of SDS and MS With the Mediating Role of GAD-7 (High School Teachers).

TABLE 9.3. Bootstrapping results (High School Teachers)

		95% Bootstrap CI		
	Coefficient	**LL**	**UL**	**Sig (P)**
Standardized Direct Effects				
Gender→MS	.008			
GPS→MS	.217			
Me-S→MS	.338			
APPP→MS	.035			
DC→MS	.196			
IC→MS	.011			
SDS→MS (ca')	.138	.109	.195	**
SDS→GAD-7	.289	.074	.396	**
GAD-7→MS	.719	.551	.887	**
Standardized Total Indirect Effects				
SDS→MS (a')	.207	.119	.412	**
Standardized Total Effects				
SDS→MS	.345	.301	.423	**

* $p < 0.05$, ** $p < 0.01$, *** $p < 0.001$
Note. CI: Confidence interval; LL: Lower limit; UL: Upper limit.

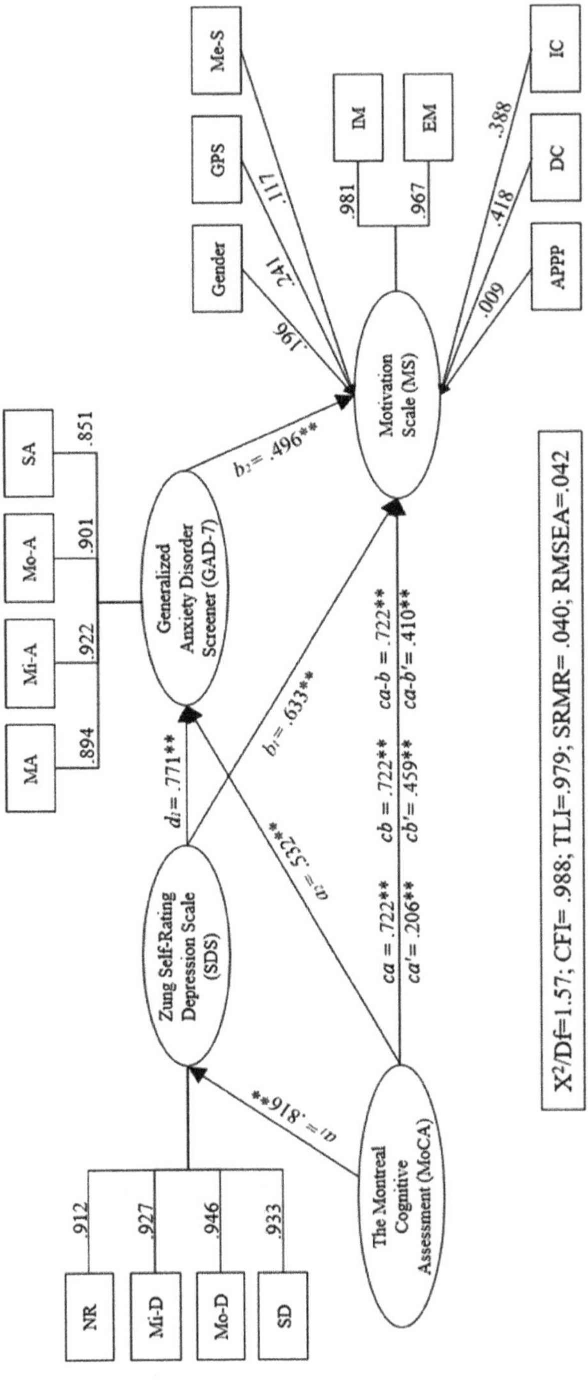

FIGURE 9.4. Mediation Model of MoCA and MS With the Mediating Role of SDS and GAD-7 (University Students).

TABLE 9.4. Bootstrapping Results (University Students)

	Coefficient	95% Bootstrap CI		Sig (P)
		LL	UL	
Standardied Direct Effects				
Gender→MS	.196			
GPS→MS	.241			
Me-S→MS	.117			
APPP→MS	.009			
DC→MS	.418			
IC→MS	.388			
MoCA→MS (ca')	.206	.105	.228	**
MoCA→MS (cb')	.459	.286	.502	**
MoCA→MS (ca-b')	.410	.336	.496	**
MoCA→SDS	.816	.547	.930	**
MoCA→GAD-7	.532	.441	.603	**
SDS→MS	.633	.117	.771	**
SDS→GAD-7	.771	.503	.809	**
GAD-7→MS	.496	.279	.519	**
Standardized Total Indirect Effects				
MoCA→MS (a')	.516	.441	.668	**
MoCA→MS (b')	.263	.169	.398	**
MoCA→MS (a-b')	.312	.137	.368	**
Standardized total effects				
MoCA→MS	.722	.556	.994	**

* $p < 0.05$, ** $p < 0.01$, *** $p < 0.001$
Note. CI: Confidence interval; LL: Lower limit; UL: Upper limit.

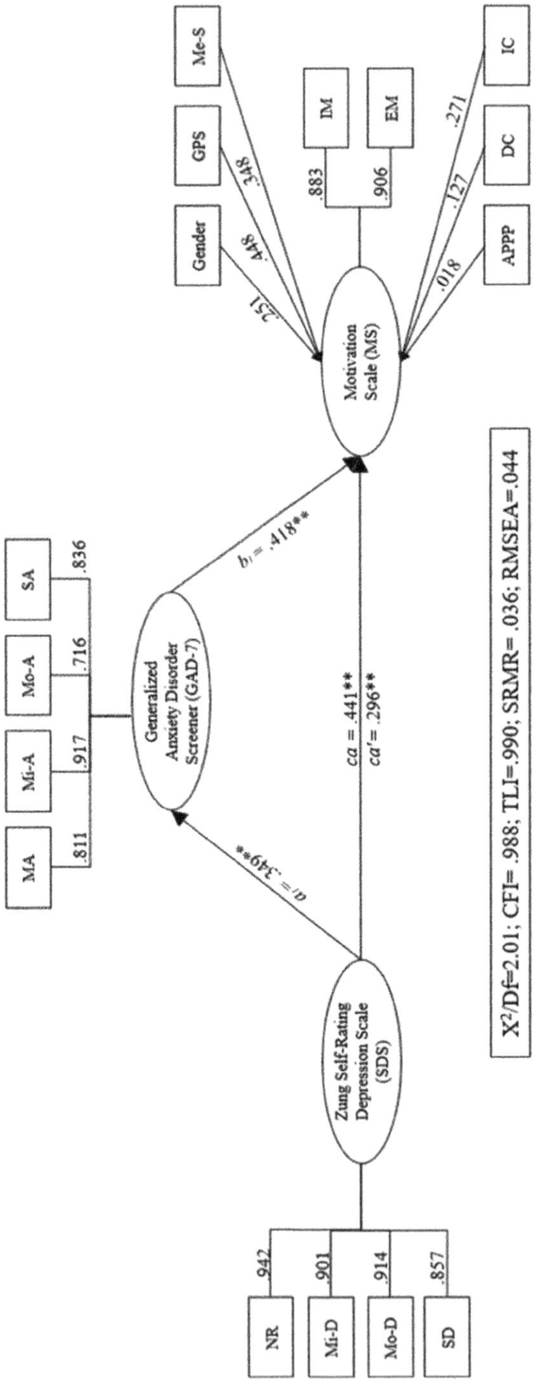

FIGURE 9.5. Mediation model of MoCA and MS with the mediating role of SDS and GAD-7 (Faculty Members).

TABLE 9.5. Bootstrapping results (Faculty Members)

	Coefficient	95% Bootstrap CI		Sig (P)
		LL	UL	
Standardized direct effects				
Gender→MS	.251			
GPS→MS	.448			
Me-S→MS	.348			
APPP→MS	.018			
DC→MS	.127			
IC→MS	.271			
SDS→MS (ca')	.296	.128	.307	**
SDS→GAD-7	.349	.265	.446	**
GAD-7→MS	.418	.379	.597	**
Standardized total indirect effects				
SDS→MS (a')	.145	.102	.189	**
Standardized total effects				
SDS→MS	.441	.339	.517	**

* $p < 0.05$, ** $p < 0.01$, *** $p < 0.001$
Note. CI: Confidence interval; LL: Lower limit; UL: Upper limit.

Upon closer inspection of the models for high school students and teachers, it was discerned that both models were significant, and that depression and anxiety had a mediating effect. Similar models were obtained amongst students and faculty members in higher education.

The models for university students and faculty members highlighted that both models had a mediating effect on depression and anxiety. In the latter part of the research, semi-structured interview questions directed to the participants were outlined by dividing them into themes and categories. Ten individuals from each of the groups took part in the study.

Based on the results displayed in Table 9.6, one can articulate that the post-COVID-19 pandemic effects cluster under three different themes. First, the most common problems in the theme of cognitive challenges were recognized as speech difficulties, stuttering, and decreased learning speed. Second, when psychological problems are analyzed, it can be argued that the behaviors of being pessimistic and prone to depression come to the forefront. Third, with respect to the motivational challenges, it was found that low concentration, disorientation, and distraction were frequently experienced. In conclusion, in light of the findings and results, the results of the present research suggested that individuals are affected by several different aspects of the post-COVID-19 pandemic period, which suggests that this is a unique time that has presented its own challenges.

TABLE 9.6. Content Analysis Results

Themes	Categories	(f)
Most common cognitive problems post-COVID-19 pandemic	Speech difficulties and stuttering	10
	Decreased learning rate	8
	Difficulty perceiving	7
	Brain fog (i.e., blurred memory)	5
	Missing or incorrect recall	3
	Mental confusion	2
	Decreased reasoning functions	2
	Difficulty making decisions	1
	Weakening of problem-solving skills	1
	The decline of abstract thinking skills	1
	Total	**40**
Most common psychological problems post-COVID-19 pandemic	Being a pessimist	12
	Being prone to depression	9
	Increased level of anxiety	7
	Questioning the source of information	5
	Needing more psychological support	3
	Difficulty empathizing	2
	Impatience and intolerance	1
	Fear of getting sick	1
	Total	**40**
Most common motivational problems post-COVID-19 pandemic	Low concentration	12
	Disorientation	8
	Distractibility	7
	Inability to focus for a long time	6
	Not enjoying life	2
	The weakening of entrepreneurship	2
	Being quiet	1
	Diminished socialization	1
	Spreading negative energy around	1
	Total	**40**

DISCUSSION

The present study, which investigated the cognitive, psychological, and motivational problems seen in individuals after the COVID-19 pandemic, utilized four different sample groups. The findings and results corroborated those of the accumulated literature, nonetheless, those that were novel were also elucidated.

First, the results of the analysis of the students at the high school level demonstrated that the cognitive test results of high school students were low, and that their motivation results were affected by depression and anxiety. These results confirm that model 1 is significant, and that motivation is affected by anxiety and depression. At the same time, it is natural that students' cognitive results decreased after the COVID-19 pandemic, and that this impacted motivation. Plentiful studies conducted after the COVID-19 pandemic pinpointed that individuals had difficulty speaking fluently, experienced learning difficulties, and performed cognitive functions with some difficulty (Bareket-Bojmel et al., 2021; Ekin Şahin & Töre, 2022). As a matter of fact, as a result of the MoCA test, the average of high school students was found to be 21.51. The fact that these results are 26 or below underpins that students possess cognitive problems at a certain level. These results have also been expressed in other studies in the literature focusing on the same subject (e.g., Jennings et al., 2022; Wu et al., 2021). At the same time, as a result of the interviews, the categories supporting the MoCA test results were constructed. These categories were actualized from the most common cognitive problems experienced by the participants. Another important finding that pertains to high school students is that depression levels and anxiety states have a positive relationship, which underlines a significant and highly negative relationship with motivation. Even though depression and anxiety cause a negative attitude in individuals under normal conditions, this does not directly impact their internal and external motivational states. Nevertheless, as a result of the structural equation analysis, the motivation of individuals was significantly affected by cognitive competence, depression, and anxiety. Apart from this, gender, GPS, Me-S, APPP, DC, and IC states influenced motivation levels significantly. These variables were the factors in model 1 that indirectly affected motivation. Among these variables, the DC variable had the greatest effect. One reason for this may be the high technology aptitude of the students at the high school level today. Further, these students have the capability to motivate themselves more easily since they spend a lot of time with technology.

When the analysis results of high school teachers are perused, it was found that they experienced a certain level of depression, anxiety, and loss of motivation during the post-COVID-19 pandemic period. Notwithstanding, this situation is not as high for students. Teachers' motivation levels were influenced by depression and anxiety, as with students' motivational levels (Carver & Scheier, 1990). These results suggest that Model 2 was validated and significant. Howbeit, the difference of Model 2 from Model 1 was that there was no MoCA test. But the variable of depression in teachers affected the motivation status more than the anxiety variable. The underlying reasons at this point for teachers' low anxiety levels can be attributed to age, experience, maturity, wisdom, experience, and the fact that a number of these variables may interact(Hullett & Witte, 2001). It is very possible that the factor affecting motivation is depression. After surveying the motivation of the teachers, it is acknowledged that there is a significant difference merely in three variables, unlike the situation of the students. It was interpreted that gender, APPP, and IC did not significantly affect teachers' motivation. At this point, a number of variables were disabled, unlike Model 1. That said, GPS, Me-S, and DC variables positively affected the motivation of teachers and students. Among them, other than the DC variable, variables can develop due to external support and cannot be regulated by intrinsic motivation (Milne et al., 2000; Yoon & Uysal, 2005).

Another sample group used in this research was university students. It was found that the cognitive test results (25.82) of university students were moderate, and that the variables of depression and anxiety influenced their motivational results. Amongst the variables specified in Model 1, for college students, the MoCA test results were higher than for high school students. These results also confirm Model 1. In this sample group, the motivational variable is also affected by the depression and anxiety variables. It is worth noting that the results for university students are more significant than those for high school students. This situation can be explained by various factors, namely, university students' personality development, age and experience along with self-efficacy. When one looks over the motivational status of university students, it is noticed that some factors make a significant difference. These lead to significant differences in variables like gender, GPS, Me-S, DC, and IC. In here, solely the APPP variable was not significant. Whereas this was a significant variable for high school students, it was not for university students. From here, we can deduce that university students adapted to normalization faster during the post-COVID-19 pandemic period than high school students.

When the results for faculty members in higher education were analyzed, the motivational variables were affected by depression and anxiety variables, and the depression and anxiety variables affected faculty members in higher education the least. These results suggest that Model 2 is significant. Faculty members were the least likely to affected by this process. The main reason for this may be their maturity status, higher specialization, training in psychology, time management, and their ability to cope with problems, perhaps as a function of their maturity (Hsu & Kang, 2009; Satıcı et al., 2020).

Depression and anxiety rates significantly affected motivation in all of the samples although this occurred at different levels. Unlike the high school teachers, the faculty members made more significant differences in gender, GPS, ME-S, DC and IC. The APPP variable was ineffective in all of the samples except for the high school students. This implied that faculty members in higher education, teachers, university students, and finally, high school students, adapted to the post-pandemic process. When the semi-structured interview results were analyzed, it was ascertained that after the COVID-19 pandemic, a general decline in overall cognitive, psychological and motivational levels was evident, a long-term fatigue came to the surface turning out to be permanent, and recurring problems in learning difficulties, and undesired consequences like cognitive disability, depression, anxiety and mood changes occurred.

CONCLUSION AND IMPLICATIONS

Below the results from the present study are summarized along with the implications for policy making and prospective studies.

1. The results based on cognitive assessments, have suggested that certain challenges were more prevalent amongst high school students during the post-COVID-19 pandemic period. These findings were valid for university students at a much lower level.
2. When it comes to the motivational variables, the APPP factor was significant only at the high school level. This result shows that the high school students can adapt to life after the pandemic. GPS, Me-S, and DC factors stand out as factors affecting motivation in almost all the sample groups. Psychological support needs to be widely provided after the pandemic. At the same time, feedback should be obtained by organizing orientation trainings and making applications at certain intervals.
    a. Students' and instructors' motivation (at any level) is impacted by the variables of depression and anxiety under all circumstances. This finding suggests the importance of the handling of external situations rather than the treatment of internal situations. This finding provided evidence that there is a need for the provision of applications along with content in the existing teaching programs after the COVID-19 pandemic.
    b. The analysis of the interviews demonstrated that the COVID-19 pandemic affected individuals at different levels and on different subjects cognitively, psychologically, and motivationally as well as created several overall challenges. This can be examined further viz. in detail by Republic of Türkiye Ministry of National Education (MoNE) and the Council of Higher Education (CoHE) and a systematic review can be recommended.

Limitations and Further Research Implications

This research has several limitations. First, the working groups should be expanded to cover the entire country and realistically should be expanded globally to cover the entire world. Because external factors may differ regionally, this may influence the internal variables. Another limitation of the present study is that it was conducted during a specific time period. Longer-term/longitudinal and regular follow-up studies might contribute more to further elucidate the psychological, cognitive and motivational challenges experienced as a function of the COVID-19 global pandemic. Model 1 and Model 2 were examined within the scope of the application. That being said, the components of these models can indeed be enhanced or changed. Losses that occurred particularly at the cognitive level can be investigated clinically. Again, apart from the phenomenon of motivational variables such as perseverance, determination and focus can also be integrated into the process.

AUTHOR NOTE

There is no funding associated with this work. There are no conflicts of interest associated with this work.

Correspondence should be directed to: Pinar Ayyildiz, Ankara Lokman Hekim University, Ankara, Türkiye. Email: pinarayyildiz @yahoo.com

Researching the Entangled: Post-COVID-19 Cognitive, Psychological and Motivational States

REFERENCES

Akdeniz, S., & Gültekin Ahçı, Z. (2023). The role of cognitive flexibility and hope in the relationship between loneliness and psychological adjustment: A moderated mediation model. *Educational and Developmental Psychologist, 40*(1), 74–85. https://doi.org/10.1080/20590776.2022.2050460

Ayyıldız, P., & Yılmaz, A. (2021). Putting things in perspective: The COVID-19 pandemic period, distance education and beyond. *Anemon Mus Alparslan University Journal of Social Sciences, 9*(6), 1631–1650. https://doi.org/10.18506/anemon.946037

Ayyıldız, P., & Yılmaz, A. (2022). Footprints of the COVID-19 Pandemic on higher education. *Journal of Uludag University Faculty of Education, 35*(3), 492–515. https://doi.org/10.19171/uefad.1080619

Bareket-Bojmel, L., Shahar, G., Abu-Kaf, S., & Margalit, M. (2021). Perceived social support, loneliness, and hope during the COVID-19 pandemic: Testing a mediating model in the UK, USA, and Israel. *British Journal of Clinical Psychology*, *60*(2), 133–148. https://doi.org/10.1111/bjc.12285

Carver, C. S., & Scheier, M. F. (1990). Origins and functions of positive and negative affect: A control-process view. *Psychological Review, 97*(1), 19.

Chang, E. C., Chang, O. D., Martos, T., Sallay, V., Zettler, I., Steca, P., D'Addario, M., Boniwell, I., Pop, A., Tarragona, M., Slemp, G. R., Shin, J.-E., de la Fuente, A., & Cardenoso, O. (2019). The positive role of hope on the relationship between loneliness and unhappy conditions in Hungarian young adults: How pathways thinking matters! *The Journal of Positive Psychology*, *14*(6), 724–733. https://doi.org/10.1080/17439760.2018.1545042

Demirtaş, A. S. (2021). Predictive roles of state hope and cognitive control/flexibility in state anxiety during COVID-19 outbreak in Turkey. *Thinking Man*, *34*(1), 89–96. https://doi.org/10.14744/DAJPNS.2020.00124

Deniz, M. E. (2021). Self-compassion, intolerance of uncertainty, fear of COVID-19, and well-being: A serial mediation investigation. *Personality and Individual Differences, 177*, 1–5. https://doi.org/10.1016/j.paid.2021.110824

De Pedraza, P., Guzi, M., & Tijdens, K. (2020). *Life dissatisfaction and anxiety in COVID-19 pandemic (No. 544)*. GLO Discussion Paper. https://www.econstor.eu/handle/10419/217053

Diamond, A., & Ling, D. S. (2019). Review of the evidence on, and fundamental questions about, efforts to improve executive functions, including working memory. In

J. M. Novick, M. F. Bunting, M. R. Dougherty, & R. W. Engle (Eds.), *Cognitive and working memory training: Perspectives from psychology, neuroscience, and human development* (pp. 143–431). Oxford University Press. https://psycnet.apa.org/record/2019-63579-008

Ekin Şahin, E., & Töre, B. (2022). Fear of COVID-19 and subjective well-being: The sequential mediating role of cognitive flexibility and Psychological resilience. *Current Approaches in Psychiatry, 14*(1), 92–99. https://doi.org/10.18863/pgy.1067626

Elmer, T., Mepham, K., Stadtfeld, C., & Capraro, V. (2020). Students under lockdown: Comparisons of students' social networks and mental health before and during the COVID-19 crisis in Switzerland. *Plos One, 15*(7), 1–15, e0236337. https://doi.org/10.1371/journal.pone.0236337

Fraenkel, J. R., Wallen, N. E., & Hyun, H. H. (2011). *How to design and evaluate research in education* (8th ed.). McGraw-Hill Education.

Gallagher, M. W., Smith, L. J., Richardson, A. L., D'Souza, J. M., & Long, L. J. (2021). Examining the longitudinal effects and potential mechanisms of hope on COVID-19 stress, anxiety, and well-being. *Cognitive Behaviour Therapy, 50*(3), 234–245. https://doi.org/10.1080/16506073.2021.1877341

Genç, E., & Aslan, G. (2021). Optimism and dispositional hope to promote college students' subjective well-being in the context of the COVID-19 pandemic. *Journal of Positive School Psychology, 5*(2), 87–96. https://doi.org/10.47602/jpsp.v5i2.255

Grey, I., Arora, T., Thomas, J., Saneh, A., Tohme, P., & Abi-Habib, R. (2020). The role of perceived social support on depression and sleep during the COVID-19 pandemic. *Psychiatry Research, 293*, 1–6, 113452. https://doi.org/10.1016/j.psychres.2020.113452

Groarke, J. M., McGlinchey, E., McKenna-Plumley, P. E., Berry, E., Graham-Wisener, L., & Armour, C. (2021). Examining temporal interactions between loneliness and depressive symptoms and the mediating role of emotion regulation difficulties among UK residents during the COVID-19 lockdown: Longitudinal results from the COVID-19 psychological wellbeing study. *Journal of Affective Disorders, 285*, 1–9. https://doi.org/10.1016/j.jad.2021.02.033

Hayes, A. F. (2018). *Introduction to mediation, moderation, and conditional process analysis: A regression based approach.* Guilford Publications.

Horigian, V. E., Schmidt, R. D., & Feaster, D. J. (2021). Loneliness, mental health, and substance use among US young adults during COVID-19. *Journal of Psychoactive Drugs, 53*(1), 1–9. https://doi.org/10.1080/02791072.2020.1836435

Hsu, C., & Kang, S. (2009). Chinese urban mature travelers' motivation and constraints by decision autonomy. *Journal of Travel & Tourism Marketing,* 26(7), 703–721.

Hullett, C., & Witte, K. (2001). Predicting intercultural adaptation and isolation: Using the extended parallel process model to test anxiety/uncertainty management theory. *International Journal of Intercultural Relations, 25*(2), 125–139.

Jennings, G., Monaghan, A., Xue, F., Duggan, E., & Romero-Ortuño, R. (2022). Comprehensive clinical characterization of brain fog in adults reporting long COVID Symptoms. *Journal of Clinical Medicine, 11*(12), 1–16. https://doi.org/10.3390/jcm11123440

Loslo-Roth, R., George Levi, S., & Margalit, M. (2021). Hope during the COVID-19 outbreak: Coping with the psychological impact of quarantine. *Counselling Psychology Quarterly*, 1–15. https://doi.org/10.1080/09515070.2021.1881762

Miles, M. B., & Huberman, A. M. (1994). *Qualitative data analysis: An expanded sourcebook* (2nd ed.). Sage Publications, Inc.

Milne, S., Sheeran, P., & Orbell, S. (2000). Prediction and intervention in health-related behavior: A meta-analytic review of protection motivation theory. *Journal of Applied Social Psychology, 30*, 106–143.

Miranda, R., Valderrama, J., Tsypes, A., Gadol, E., & Gallagher, M. (2013). Cognitive inflexibility and suicidal ideation: Mediating role of brooding and hopelessness. *Psychiatry Research, 210*(1), 174–181. https://doi.org/10.1016/j.psychres.2013.02.033

Mondelli, V., & Pariante, C. M. (2021). What can neuroimmunology teach us about the symptoms of long-COVID? *Oxford Open Immunol*, 2, iqab004.

Özkan, U. B. (2019). *Document review method for educational sciences research* (1st ed.). Pegem Academy Publishing.

Padmanabhanunni, A., & Pretorius, T. (2021). The loneliness–life satisfaction relationship: The parallel and serial mediating role of hopelessness, depression and ego-resilience among young adults in South Africa during COVID-19. *International Journal of Environmental Research and Public Health, 18*(7), 1–10, 3613. https://doi.org/10.3390/ijerph18073613

Rumas, R., Shamblaw, A. L., Jagtap, S., & Best, M.W. (2021). Predictors and consequences of loneliness during the COVID-19 pandemic. *Psychiatry Research, 300,* 1–8, 113934. https://doi.org/10.1016/j.psychres.2021.113934

Satıcı, B., Gocet-Tekin, E., Deniz, M. E., & Satıcı, S. A. (2020). Adaptation of the fear of COVID-19 scale: Its association with psychological distress and life satisfaction in Turkey. *International Journal of Mental Health and Addiction, 19,* 1980–1988. https://doi.org/10.1007/s11469-020-00294-0

Spitzer, R. L., Kroenke, K., Williams, J. B., & Lowe, B. (2006). A brief measure for assessing generalized anxiety disorder: The GAD-7. *Archives of Internal Medicine, 166*(10), 1092–1097.

Stokes, A. C., Xie, W., Lundberg, D. J., Glei, D. A., & Weinstein, M. A. (2021). Loneliness, social isolation, and all-cause mortality in the United States. *SSM-Mental Health, 1*, 1–8, 100014. https://doi.org/10.1016/j.ssmmh.2021.100014

Torjesen, I. (2021). COVID-19: Long COVID symptoms among hospital inpatients show little improvement after a year, data suggest. *British Medical Journal BMJ,* 375, n3092.

Tulunay Ateş, A., & İhtiyaroğlu, N. (2019). Adult motivation scale: A scale development study. *Kastamonu Education Journal, 27*(2), 611–620. https://doi.org/10.24106/kefdergi.2612

Wu, X., Wang, Z., Zhang, H., Yuan, P., Yu, Q., Zhou, Z., & Zhao, Q. (2021). Effects of Internet language related to COVID-19 on mental health in college students: The mediating effect of cognitive flexibility. *Frontiers in Psychology, 12*, 1–9, 600268. https://doi.org/10.3389/fpsyg.2021.600268

Yoon, Y., & Uysal, M. (2005). An examination of the effects of motivation and satisfaction on destination loyalty: A structural model. *Tourism Management, 26*(1), 45–56.

Zung, W. W. (1965). A self-rating depression scale. *Archives of General Psychiatry Arch Gen Psychiatry, 12*, 63–70.

CHAPTER 10

K–12 TEACHER SUPPORT DURING THE COVID-19 PANDEMIC

Velma D. Menchaca and Alejandro Garcia
The University of Texas Rio Grande Valley

A qualitative study was conducted with forty-two teachers who are also graduate students enrolled in the Master of Education Principal program in a Texas Hispanic Serving Institution. The purpose of this qualitative study was to discover teachers' perceptions of their preparation and support from their school districts and campus principals during the COVID-19 pandemic. After analyzing the focus group interview data, the following three themes emerged: inadequate preparation for teaching online, a need for technological support, and a need for social/emotional support.

INTRODUCTION

The novel coronavirus, otherwise known as COVID-19, first appeared in Wuhan, China, in late December 2019. Several months later, the situation become grim, and the entire globe was stricken by the pandemic (Hopkins Medicine, 2020). United Nations Educational, Scientific and Cultural Organization (UNESCO) reported in March 2020 that in just a few months, millions of students had tran-

Instructional Survival in the Midst of the Perfect Storm:
The Experiences of K–12 Teachers During the COVID-19 Global Pandemic, pages 169–189.

Published under exclusive licence by Emerald Publishing Limited
ISBNs: 978-1-83708-502-6 HB, 978-1-83708-503-3 PB,
978-1-83708-504-0 EPDF, 978-1-83708-505-7 EPUB

sitioned to alternate methods of teaching and learning worldwide. Schools shut down completely for approximately two weeks with governments mandating new safety protocols such as social distancing, mask wearing, closing of all non-essential businesses and stay at home orders (Johnson et al., 2020).

Public schools and universities across America followed suit with face-to-face classes being affected by this virus. By the end of February 2020, the Texas Education Agency (TEA) was closely monitoring the reports being shared by the Center for Disease Control (CDC) as growing concerns of the novel coronavirus (COVID-19) were beginning to surface (Texas Education Agency, 2020). Of utmost concern to the schools was that all individuals were to follow protocol issued by the CDC (2019). The Texas Education Agency (TEA) was also in full gear creating guidance for the 1,200 districts so that all receive accurate information (Texas Education Agency, 2020).

Most schools and universities had scheduled the Spring Break holiday for the second and third weeks of March 2020. During the second week of March, even though there were few known COVID infected individuals in Texas, school districts began to meet to discuss how to move forward. School districts and universities that had spring break the second week of March extended the spring break another week and cancelled classes. This gave the school districts and universities an extra week to plan how to best move forward with online instruction.

During a span of two weeks, public schools and universities were faced with a sudden shift of offering online instruction, otherwise known as distance learning. State Education Agencies, school administrators, teachers, students, and parents faced a major challenge of adapting to a new mode of teaching and learning. (R. Ayala, Principal BISD, personal communication May 23, 2020). Working families with small children had to quickly find help at home or find places to drop off children. This really became a crisis as families scrambled to find relatives, friends or make other accommodation for their children.

On March 19, 2020, Governor Abbott closed all school districts from March 20- April 3, 2020 (BallotPedia, 2020). However, on March 31, 2020, Governor Abbott extended the state-wide school closure through May 4, 2020. On April 17, 2020, the Governor closed schools for the remainder of the academic year (Swaby, 2020). With the closure of schools being inevitable, districts were ordered to transition to online instruction (Oprysko, 2020; Tabachinik, 2020). School superintendents soon began to send emails to families of students with information that classes would be transitioning to online instruction. School principals found themselves navigating areas that were very unfamiliar to them, transitioning to online instruction with little to no knowledge of how to proceed (Herold, 2020).

Most principals used the extended spring break in mid-March 2020, to meet with teachers and to strategize on how to proceed with instruction from home. Teachers began to identify students who did not have laptops or Wi-Fi at home. These home situations for students and teachers became more challenging. Also, parents began to look for friends or relatives who could come to their home and help with their children, or to find places where the children could be dropped off and cared for.

Principals had dealt with challenges such as fights, drugs, bomb threats, and school shootings. However, dealing with COVID-19 brought forth a crisis that had not been experienced in over 100 years with the N1H1 virus also known as the Spanish flu (CDC, 2019). As districts began to strategize how to ensure that instruction would continue despite the many challenges, they tackled each challenge as it came. Districts began to distribute laptops to students and in remote areas, school buses were utilized as hubs to provide internet services to those neighborhoods.

A study by Marshall et al., (2020) found that many teachers had not taught online before and few had received any training from their campuses or districts. Not all teachers felt comfortable using technology and more specifically, for teaching lessons online (Saad & Sankaran, 2020). Other teachers shared that they had limited resources to transition to online learning (Anderson & Hira, 2020; Beese & Mlakar, 2020; Kelley, 2020). Teachers were unfamiliar with online platforms in that many did not have the training for teaching remotely.

Some schools opted for a hybrid or blended model of instruction. In this instance, schools would send packets of work, whether it be worksheets or handouts, to homes where students did not have access to the internet or did not have technology such as computers or laptops (Marshall et al., 2020). Not all students were able to learn remotely because too many obstacles prevented online learning. This is a well-written, interesting historical account of this time.

Chapter Objectives

1. To discuss how teachers felt about their preparation in dealing with distance learning during the COVID-19 pandemic.
2. To describe the type of distance learning support that teachers reported receiving during the COVID-19 pandemic.

Statement of the Problem

The COVID-19 global pandemic forced K–12 schools across the United States to quickly switch from face-to-face instruction to online teaching and learning (Butcher, 2020; Francom et al., 2021; Gallagher, 2020) "Many teachers were unprepared for this transition and faced great challenges associated with delivering quality instruction in an online format" (Francom et al., 2021, p.589). There was minimal guidance and direction provided from Texas at first. The uncertainty was unreal and many school districts were faced with many challenges. Many K–12 teachers who were accustomed to teaching in a face-to-face modality were forced to rapidly transition to teaching fully online in a crisis mode (Butcher, 2020). For example, within a matter of days, teachers needed to learn how to teach online and use various technologies. Not all teachers felt comfortable using technology and more specifically, teaching lessons online (Saad & Sankaran, 2020). Teachers throughout the state shared that they had limited resources to transition to online instruction (Anderson & Hira, 2020; Beese & Mlakar, 2020; Kelley, 2020). In addition, many educators felt unprepared and felt that a greater amount of support was needed from their districts, principals, and parents. "Despite the need for preparation, a review of the literature reveals that many K–12 institutions are not prepared for academic continuity in the face of a pandemic" (Francom et al., 2021, p. 590). Support for teachers was inconsistent, and support varied from school district to school district.

REVIEW OF THE LITERATURE

Technology in Schools

Webber (2003) argued, "...technology pervades almost everything in our lives—online banking, shopping, text messaging, movies-on-demand, coordinated traffic flow, light rapid transit scheduling, mobile telephone networks, climate control systems, and medical information access" (p.119). It could be argued that during the twenty-first century, technology has become omnipresent and inescapable. Cell phones, laptops, electronic readers, and other portable devices such as the Nintendo Switch are part of student life inside and outside the classroom (Luckin et al., 2009). Although students are using these devices frequently, the methods of teaching and delivering instruction remained much the same during the 20th century. The development of recent technology has vastly changed the way we communicate, learn, and engage with one another, and as a result, the 21st century educational landscape has also been altered. One of these changes has been the addition of online distance education (Archambault & Crippen, 2009). With the pandemic in 2020, this became a priority in K–12 education and across Universities (Kelley, 2020).

Online Learning

According to Hrastinski (2008), online learning is a web-based educational method which is a form of distance learning that delivers learning to K–12 and university students remotely, no matter the distance. To be classified as online learning, all content must be virtually delivered at least 80% of the time (Allen & Seaman, 2006). The model for online learning, which was once the main stay for universities, is now a customary practice in many K–12 schools (Hill, 2002).

The two principle modalities of online learning, asynchronous and synchronous learning, are now commonplace in both K–12 and university classrooms. Asynchronous learning happens when students log on to Learning Management Systems such as Google Classrooms, Canvas or Blackboard at their own pace and at their own times to interact with instructor. Conversely, synchronous learning takes place with the instructor directly guiding the lessons with all students being actively present and engaged in the Learning Management Systems at the same time. Often, synchronous learning takes place with live video conferencing software such as Zoom or Microsoft Teams. (Hrastinski, 2008).

It should be noted that online learning and face-to-face learning are unique modalities with their own distinct differences and challenges. For example, Shaw (2001) stated that problems develop when traditional teaching practices are quickly adjusted to distance learning. Kim (2020) documented that even though many similarities exist between face-to-face and online learning, there are also different social experiences between them. Additionally, teachers should "…take account of children's developmental levels, as well as find online learning tools which are appropriate, and that can promote children's participation and learning (Kim, 2020, p. 148).

Teachers' Support for Teaching Online

Teachers also require a support system for learning modern technologies such as in Learning Management Systems (LSM). Online learning has been a concept that has profoundly affected the delivery of instruction for K–12 students. Teacher training programs for supporting the implementation of technology developed teaching approaches have usually centered on teachers' individual abilities and attitudes (Twining et al., 2013). Zhao (2007) asserted that acquiring the skills of newer technologies requires proper training and a definite change in teaching and learning methods.

When confronted by the change in modality during the pandemic, teachers felt unprepared and incapable of switching to online instruction. (Butcher, 2020; Francom et al., 2021; Wu, 2021). The type of planning and development that online teaching needs was not done during the pandemic due to a lack of time and resource limitations (Hodges et al., 2020). "As a result, teachers and students have had to quickly alter their teaching methods, regardless of whether they were experienced in and prepared for online education. Because of this situation, a proper term has appeared in the academic domain: emergency remote education" (Wu, 2021, p. 2).

Eslaminejad et al., (2009) postulated that it is irrational to expect teachers to switch their existing teaching practices without adequate and appropriate staff development in newer technologies. The COVID-19 pandemic, required of K–12 schools, forced both teachers and students to quickly switch from face-to-face, the known, to online teaching and learning, the unknown (Gallagher, 2020). Furthermore, Kirkwood and Price (2005) found that the better trained, the more assured about using modern technologies, the more effective teachers were at supporting the learning of their students.

THEORTICAL FRAMEWORK

This study is based on the theoretical framework of social support systems. Studies on social support theories and models have been prevalent in academic studies since the 1980s (Drennon-Gala, 1995; Racino, 2006; Vaux, 1986). Social support is the perception and actuality that one is cared for, has assistance available from other people, and most popularly, that one is part of a supportive team or network (Wasserman & Faust, 1994). Support can be acquired from various sources, and these theories study the relationships between family, friends, neighbors, colleagues, organizations, and societies (Taylor, 2011). Cockrell and Shelley (2010) found significant relationships among different indicators for the support system. House (1981) reviewed Tandy's work on social support that focused on how best to understand the meaning of social support through recognizing and discussing issues. Tandy (1985) identified five types of support: Direction, Disposition, Description/Evaluation, Content and Network (Tandy, 1985). Cutrona and Suhr (1992) define a social support category system, which involves five categories of social support: (a) informational, (b) emotional, (c) esteem, (d) social network support, and (e) tangible support. The theoretical framework for this study is centered on Tandy's (1985) work on Social Support. According to Tandy (1985), "Support availability refers to the quantity and quality of the support to which people have access" (p. 188).

Support sources can be informal, such as with family or close friends, or more formal, such as with colleagues or community organizations (Hogan et al., 2002). Sources of social support are extremely important for coping with different situations. Of the relationships studied, the "teacher and school personnel support have been shown to be stronger than other relationships of support." Relationships on school settings tend to be more stable than family and friend social relationships because the latter relationships tend to experience more conflicts; therefore, are more unstable (Chu et al., 2010).

METHOLOGY

This study used a qualitative research design that gives meaning to social phenomena and makes it understandable (Strauss & Corbin, 1998). Ideally qualitative research aids in providing meaning to areas in which there is little information. Qualitative studies typically focus upon naturally occurring ordinary events in natural settings, thus, places emphasis on people's everyday lives (Miles & Huberman, 1994). This study utilizes an emic focus in which the participants' viewpoints are taken rather than an etic focus where the participants viewpoints are represented by the researchers' preexisting knowledge of the study (Schutt, 2017).

Sample Population and Setting

Purposeful sampling was used in this study and should be used to "...indicate that interviewees or participants are selected based on their knowledge and verbal eloquence to describe a group or (sub)culture to which they belong" (Patton, 2015, p. 353). In this study, the inclusion criteria consisted of only graduate students who are presently classroom teachers, and who are enrolled in the Master of Educational Leadership degree program in several South Texas school districts. For this study, only participants who were certified classroom teachers and who taught before and during the pandemic were in the sample of this study. Out of the one hundred students enrolled in the principalship master's program, only sixty-four students had agreed and responded to the online questionnaire. The other participant source consisted of two recorded focus group interview sessions via Zoom facilitated by the same researcher. From the sample of the sixty-four graduate student participants who completed the online questionnaire, only twenty-four had agreed to participate in the focus group interviews.

Data Collection Procedures and Instrumentation

The primary data source for this study consisted of an online questionnaire. The online questionnaire consisted of four demographic questions and six questions which explored the participants' perceptions on their level of support and preparation during COVID-19. The other source of data is two focus group sessions which were recorded using Zoom. The focus group questions consisted of ten open-ended questions. Open ended questions were administered because "… open ended questions typically involve an inductive approach to discover what meanings and influences are and how they are involved in these events and activities" (Maxwell, 2008, p. 232). The advantage for this approach is that the "…inquirer asks general questions of participants, and the participants shape the response possibilities" (Creswell, 2012, p. 19). "Participants can best voice their experiences while being unconstrained by any perspectives of the researcher or past research findings" (Creswell, 2012, p. 218).

Validity and Reliability

To maintain validity and reliability and to minimize risks to participants, the present study followed some initial steps as guidelines (Miller & Crabtree, 1999). These guidelines included: knowing your biases and preconceptions, seeking others, asking for alternative interpretations, and knowing what your questions are seeking (ok). The first data set used in this study was from an online questionnaire and maintained a high degree of confidentiality by not identifying the participants. The focus group interviews also minimized risk by not having the participants identify themselves by removing their names for the Zoom interviews.

Other techniques used in this study were respondent validation also known as member checking and triangulation to develop both validity and reliability. Respondent valuation is one of the possible methods that research can take to avoid misinterpretation of the participant's discussions (Bryman & Burgess, 2002). This is accomplished by soliciting feedback from the participants sampled and if done thoroughly, will eliminate the researchers' biases or misunderstandings. The researchers used member checking to verify the themes identified from their groups. All participants agreed on the themes identified by the researchers.

The other method taken in this study to establish validity and reliability was with triangulation of data, which according to Fielding and Fielding (1986), is a method that uses a variety of data sources. Its purpose is to reduce biases and allows for researchers to ensure "that the study will be accurate because the information draws on multiple sources of information, individuals, or processes" (Creswell, 2012, p. 259). In this study, triangulation was achieved through memos, an online questionnaire, and focus groups. Taking memo notes was done from the "...researcher's field notes recording what the researcher hears, sees, experiences and thinks while collecting and reflecting on the process" (Miles & Huberman, 1984, p. 428).

Research Questions

1. How prepared did a sample of teachers perceive themselves to be for distance learning during the COVID-19 pandemic?
2. What type of distance learning support did a sample of teachers perceive that they received from their principals during the COVID-19 pandemic?

Data Analysis

This study follows the tenet of qualitative research in which data analysis is based upon focusing on meaning rather than on quantifiable phenomena, and a collection of data based on a few cases rather than minimal data on many cases (Denzin & Lincoln, 2000). The analysis of this study began in the field with an online questionnaire, observations (memos), and focus group interviews. Furthermore, data analysis attached codes to a set of notes drawn from the interviews identify the patterns and create themes (Miles & Huberman, 1994). The following six steps were conducted in this this study: preparing and organizing data, exploring codes, coding to build themes, representing and reporting the findings, interpreting the findings, and validating the accuracy of the findings (Creswell, 2012, p. 262).

The first step was in the preparation and organization of data which involved downloading the online questionnaire results. Then the other data source, the focus group interviews, were transcribed. Both data sources were saved in a secure location to be accessed by both researchers. The data was analyzed by hand and with the aid of word processing software.

Secondly, exploration of the data was conducted by primary reading and note taking of the data so that both researchers could gain a general understanding of what the data was revealing. The process of coding followed several readings of both data sources.

Next, codes were verified, and coding led to the reduction of the recorded and transcribed text into the categorization of themes. This process involved using line-by-line reading, note taking, and analysis of the text. These themes were constructed so that the pheromone being studied could be better understood.

In the fourth step, the data and themes were transformed into narrative which represented and was reported into findings. This process included writing the results and reporting them with some data tables and an explanation of their meaning. The fifth step, interpretation of findings, followed and involved constructing meaning of the discovered themes. This stage calls for taking some ideas from the review of literature and making connections to the findings.

The ultimate step, according to Creswell (2012) requires the researchers to validate the accuracy of findings. In this study's case, this was accomplished by asking peers to review the data and having some participants review the transcribed focus group data. The intent of the last step is to have external reviewers validate the accuracy of the findings.

RESULTS

After analyzing the focus group interview data, the following three themes were discovered: 1) inadequate preparation for teaching online, 2) a need for technological support and 3) a need for social/emotional support.

Inadequate Preparation for Teaching Online

It is important to have an adequate understanding and command of all the tools teachers use in the classroom. Effective professional development for teachers should be sustained over time and connected to classroom instruction, while requiring active participation from teachers (Belland et al., 2018). Online teaching teacher training has ranged from official certification courses and professional development sessions to informal mentoring and on-the-job training (Dereshiwsky, 2013).

With the advent of the COVID-19 pandemic, a condition for urgency to transition to online teaching became paramount. Districts knew the urgency to create workshops for teachers and determine their technological gaps to determine how to proceed. "Leaders hurriedly set up workshops to enhance the skill gaps of teachers, although it is a necessary step, cannot replace the need for sustained training in both the pedagogical and technical areas" (Wu, 2021, p.2).

The data from the study's questionnaire revealed that of the forty-two teachers' responses to the questionnaire, 23.81 percent reported that they felt that their campuses had prepared them to teach online prior to the pandemic. The remaining 76.1 percent felt that they were unprepared to teach online prior to the pandemic. The same participants stated that they did not feel prepared at all. One stated that she was "especially not prepared because at the lower grades, we really don't use technology, even within the regular academic school setting." Another participant echoed this sentiment of unpreparedness and stated that,

> I was not prepared whatsoever. Not even a little bit. I am not tech savvy; I don't know anything about Twitter, Facebook, or anything like that. I do not use computers. So, trying to learn these programs was difficult, and then to figure out a way for the students to be engaged and to show what they are learning, when they are used to having hands on instruction.

When asked about challenges in teaching online during the pandemic, one participant was quoted as saying "...when we went out for spring break, and we did not come back, there was zero communication for about a month. And there was so much uncertainty about what was going on, especially where we're going to log in, what the medium was, how we were going to conduct things from there." Most of the study's participants felt uncomfortable and stressed since that felt that they were isolated from their campus and students. One participant stated the message that was received was "you're on your own, and you don't get to see the kids. So, figure it out. But God help you if you fail a student. What am I supposed to do?"

Furthermore, when asked about their preparation from their campuses or districts, most of the teachers, or 83.3 percent surveyed, reported that they received professional development during the pandemic to teach online. According to the participants, most of the professional development received consisted of working with Google Classroom or Microsoft Teams. The remaining 16.7 percent reported that they had not received any professional development during the pandemic on how to teach online, yet they were required to do so. "All too often, the training offered was based on a transfer of knowledge and acquisition of skills approach which left teachers with a mountain to climb in terms of fully understanding and appropriating the new tools in their own teaching" (Kirkwood & Price, 2005, p. 228).

The Need for Technological Support

Teachers require a support system for learning modern technologies such as in Learning Management Systems. Online learning has been a concept that has profoundly affected K–12 students. Since the early 1990s, distance teaching via the Internet has become a global trend, and software, hardware and educational training have been evolving. "Nouns related to e-learning have emerged such as online learning, distance teaching, digital learning, mobile learning, and more recently, massive open online courses (MOOCs) have shown a trend of learning via the Internet" (Wu, 2021, p. 1).

Teacher training programs that support the implementation of technology had developed teaching approaches that were usually centered on teachers' individual abilities and attitudes (Twining et al., 2013). Learning about the use of newer technologies requires proper training and a definite change in teaching and learning methods (Zhao, 2007). Furthermore, when confronted by the change in modality during the pandemic, teachers felt unprepared (Wu, 2021). Most of the participants who participated in the focus group interviews reflected that they were not "tech-savvy" and did not know anything about Twitter, Facebook, or anything like that." One participant stated that, "trying to learn these programs one was difficult, and then two (sic) trying to figure out a way for the students to be engaged and to show what they are learning, when they are used to having hands on. Technology support personnel were needed according to a few participants since they felt it was "extremely difficult to mentally prepare to switch to online where all that their lessons that they had created for years had to be switched and it seemed "like wow it's another job, like a totally different job."

Unfamiliarity with the software is a big issue in terms of needing support. One participant stated that, "I did not know any of those programs, so trying to learn those programs, and then trying to set them up for students that didn't know how to use those programs and trying to teach the parents how to use those programs was very difficult." They further explained that in addition to preparation and training, a lot of support in the form of assistance was needed for teachers like themselves. For example, when working with Canvas, a commonly used Learning Management System, one participant stated that, they had quite a few questions about it and that "it was difficult to use when they introduced it; it was a monster and had a lot of HTML coding. Another participant said that "it was very confusing since Canvas has its own gradebook and a lot of teachers were old school and did not know a lot about technology. Many had lingering questions about adding the gradebook features."

Not only must teachers teach content, but they also must ensure that students are able to effectively apply online resources as part of their learning. Technologies that students are using outside of school have the power to improve education if they are employed correctly, and if students are instructed in proper academic uses. Students, both those in the brick-and-mortar and the online schools, often must "power down and feel disconnected when they come to school" (Schrum & Levin, 2009, p. 29). During the pandemic, teachers were overwhelmed by familiarizing themselves with many modern technologies and tools in a brief time. Therefore, they focused their efforts on the immediate problem of mastering the tools for online instruction instead of understanding the pedagogical possibilities of those tools.

The Need for Social/Emotional Support

In terms of social or emotional support, sources of support can be informal such as with family or close friends, or more formal such as with colleagues or community organizations (Hogan et al., 2002). The source of social support is extremely important in coping with different or demanding situations, like the pandemic. Of the different relationships studied, the support between teachers and school personnel has been shown to be stronger than other relationships of support. This could be that teachers and school personnel tend to spend at least 7–8 hours a day in the same environment for about five days out of the week. Consequently, these relationships tend to be more stable than relationships with family where conflicts could arise; therefore, more unstable (Chu et al., 2010).

Cobb (1976) defines social support as "information leading the subject to believe that s/he is cared for and loved, esteemed, and a member of a network of mutual obligations" (p. 300). Kaplan et al. (1977) view support as how much an individual's social needs for affection, security, approval, or belonging are met through social interactions.

In this study, 26.19 percent of the participants strongly agreed that they had received some emotional support from their campus principals. In addition, 38.10 percent agreed as well. Some participants stated that, "…on our campus, through a lot of our Zoom meetings, we received a lot of emotional support; our principal acknowledged the fact that we were all experiencing something very emotional. Some people on our campus lost family members. Due to this, we had to have emotional networks going on." Furthermore, others stated that "Our principal was supportive emotionally and technology wise. If we needed some more training on a certain program, they would provide the necessary means that we needed for learning something new; so, they were supportive. Administration was cognizant of the emotional rollercoaster that many of us were on and were supportive." One participant said, "Several colleagues lost loved ones, family, or friends, so having our leaders provide them with food, extra help, or time needed was extremely helpful. "Another participant noted that their campus principal was sympathetic and emphatic to the situation, since many of the decisions were based upon what central office was mandating during the pandemic. This participant stated that,

My principal was at least emotionally supportive; as much as we felt like the kids needed us, and in a lot of ways, we needed them (campus principals) too because a lot of us are, this is our identity, you know, teaching (sic). It's not what I do, it's who I am. You know (sic), and not being able to do that, it's, it's incredibly frustrating.

Overall, most study participants expressed the need for emotional support during the pandemic from their campus principals and peers. Teachers should not have to experience confusion or anxiety when teaching online. Districts and campus leaders should have a set of clear expectations for teaching online, provision of learning resources, levels of student performance and fair grading (Francom et al., 2021).

DISCUSSION

Inadequate Preparation for Teaching Online

Although teaching online is not entirely a new practice, many teachers have still not been adequately prepared for online teaching. Previous studies have shown that adoption of innovative teaching practices is challenging for teachers

(Webb & Cox, 2004). Being ready for newer teaching modalities is crucial for success. Borotis and Poulymenakou (2004) defined e-learning readiness as the mental or physical preparedness of an organization for some e-learning experience or action. One condition that establishes a lack of meaningful technological integration is an absence of professional development (Zhao, 2007).

"Nothing about adapting to the newfound requirements of online instruction in a post- COVID-19 world is easy, including sifting through the various solutions and suggestions that have emerged because of moving most instruction away from classrooms and into the homes of students" (Aguilar, 2020, p. 309). Success of any type of change such as the initiation of online teaching and learning is partly due to how well teachers deal with and implement online teaching (McPherson & Nunes, 2004). In other words, a critical factor is for teachers to feel confident and comfortable in teaching online, all of which can never happen without adequate support and preparation. "Professional development programs have an important effect, especially if they focus on the teachers and applying it in the work context" (Ley et al., 2021, p. 550).

The Need for Technological Support

In addition to adequate professional development, teachers also need technological support for proper implementation of online teaching. "Technical problems have long created challenges with the use of technology for learning. Indeed, it is important to minimize the issues as much as possible from the beginning of the learning experience" (Hill, 2002, p. 67). An important initiative such as online learning needs adequate technical support. "While professional development is important, there is a need for systemic support to launch and sustain new forms of teaching and learning that may be required" (Johnson et al., 2020, p.17). "The provision of hurriedly set up workshops to enhance the skill gaps of teachers, although it is a necessary step, cannot replace the need for sustained support in both the pedagogical and technical areas" (Wu, 2021, p.19).

Participants in this study expressed that they needed to ask questions about many sides of teaching online. "Teachers who are using computer technologies in their classrooms need sufficient support from computer experts and should learn different software programs" (Pourhosein, 2013, p. 263). For most of them, technical support was key to getting started (Baran & Correia, 2014). Teachers need technical support in "making sure technologies work, troubleshooting when problems occur, helping students with their technology issues, and setting up the technological infrastructure" (Baran & Correia, 2014, p 98). Providing teachers "...with technical support that is appropriate for their own level of technical proficiency, and guiding them as they explore new tools, are both crucial for enhancing excellence in online teaching" (Baran & Correia, 2014, p. 98). Without the proper type of support, technology initiates will fall short of expectations and will lose teacher momentum. Sandholtz (2001) notes that, even when teachers leave teacher development programs with specific plans for using technology in their classrooms, they often abandon or alter these plans when they meet technical constraints coupled with inadequate support.

Transitioning from face-to-face instruction to fully online instruction created a sense of urgency and professionalism on the part of teachers. Part of the challenges faced by the teachers was learning to use online tools quickly. Therefore, by having adequate technical support, many of the teachers in this study reflected that this was an essential element that led to success in teaching online.

The Need for Social/Emotional Support

The third support needed by teachers is social/emotional support. Social/emotional support is typically defined as "interpersonal exchanges intended to enhance the well-being of the individual being helped" (Gottlieb & Bergen, 2010, p. 512). Much of the research in this area shows that the role of a teacher can be emotionally demanding involving multiple stressors such as learning a new teaching modality such as teaching online (Conley & You, 2014; Somech, 2016). Without adequate social or emotional support, there could be negative consequences to the classroom and students (Frenzel et al., 2009). Researchers emphasize the need for social and emotional support to prevent negative effects on campus (Almeida et al., 2016).

Workplace sources of support are considered the most significant factors in improving a teacher's emotional well-being. This type of support can come from diverse groups such as fellow teachers or campus principals. For example, support from peers or fellow teachers can vary depending on the culture of the campus and the needs of the teachers (Baran & Correia, 2014). Tatar (2009) polled teachers and discovered that the second most used source of support was the campus principal, right after the teachers' colleagues. Peers could support teachers by being paired with an experienced online teacher who could build a mentoring relationship with them while sharing their best practices (Baran & Correia, 2014; Pas et al., 2012). "In the natural environment, social support arises from the conduct of personal relationships. Indeed, the relationship itself gives supportive meaning to behavior and, conversely, supportive behaviors can bring meaningful relationships to interactions" (Gottlieb & Bergen, 2010, p. 512).

Russell et al., (1987) found that teachers who received some support from their campus principals were less likely to be emotionally drained; so, they had more positive experiences with students. In addition to these outcomes, it was found that teachers' sense of job satisfaction and personal health also improved. (Littrell et al., 1994).

CONCLUSION

"As a result of the pandemic, teachers and students have had to quickly alter their teaching methods, regardless of whether they were experienced in and/or prepared for online instruction. Because of this situation, a proper term has appeared in the academic domain: emergency remote education" (Wu, 2021, p. 2). Teachers' successes in handling e-learning depends on their prior technical experience in information technology (Boakye & Banini, 2008). The diverse ways in which the online curriculum is being delivered are new to many and are often quite different from the traditional approaches. A major factor influencing the success of e-learning is a teacher's technological competency. Instructors must be educated or must educate themselves to take advantage of these updated teaching methods. The way that teachers teach is a product of their own schooling, training, and experiences.

In addition, without a supportive network of campus administrators, colleagues and/or parents, many educators would not have been as successful in overcoming the obstacles and challenges presented by the COVID-19 pandemic. Teachers felt that the emotional support that they received during the pandemic was authentic and stronger than it ever had been before. Even though many teachers reported that they were teaching from their homes for several months or several semesters, they said that they were encouraged and supported via Zoom or via email on a regular basis. For online learning to continue to thrive, the necessary supports of professional development, technical aid and social/emotional support must be present to keep and support an online teaching and learning environment (Wolf, 2006).

Implications for the Future

Teachers who have been reluctant to learn newer skills remained in the classroom despite the obstacles that the pandemic and its conditions brought forth. One lesson that all stakeholders must keep in mind is that the duty of teaching students with technology does not solely rely upon the classroom teachers. A support network of instructional trainers, IT support staff, and principals needs to be in place for instructional support, technical support, and social/emotional support (Luckin et al., 2009).

Any new or existing technologies will require adequate and sustainable professional development from support staff who themselves are teachers. Professional development must be ongoing and available throughout the school year and be made available to teachers before frustration sets in. The same can be said about technical support for teachers. School districts must ensure that both hardware and software are running optimally and that networks are properly functioning and kept so that instruction can be conducted without downtime. Finally, social/emotional support should be provided by peers and leaders. Leaders should be available to listen empathically and to empower teachers (Sims, 2017; Zhang & Bartol, 2010). By listening empathically and empowering teachers, teachers can be motivated and supported (Zhang & Bartol, 2010). Messages which empower teachers will often result in self-confidence and inspire teachers and other staff to take the initiative in moving forward with online learning. (Choi, 2006).

Summary—Challenges and Opportunities

One challenge for school districts is to ensure adequate planning, training and support for teachers' and students' digital literacy and readiness for online teaching and learning. The COVID-19 global pandemic provided teachers and administrators with a chance to evaluate the readiness of their schools for distance education as well as readiness for future emergency situations (Francom et al., 2021). Working in crisis mode is not a practical long-range solution for districts, campuses, and teachers, although many districts were able to successfully implement virtual learning during the pandemic (Johnson et al., 2020). A second challenge is for teachers to adapt their online lessons, so students' interactions may increase between the teachers and their peers. Whether done synchronously or asynchronously, fostering this interaction may be challenging for some teachers. Common methods include working with electronic bulletin boards, discussion boards, e-mails, or synchronous chat rooms (Frazer et al., 2017).

A stronger interaction is tied directly to the potential opportunity for creating a stronger instructor presence. Creating a stronger instructor presence, "facilitates student learning, aims to create connection with students in the classroom, creates shared experiences, establishes mutual comfort, and is responsive to students" (Frazer et al., 2017, p. 3). All of these are vital skills that require preparation, training, and support for teachers and educators. There is also an opportunity for teachers to create flipped classroom experiences with their students. Flipped classrooms are known for, "inverting the classroom which means that events that have traditionally taken place inside the classroom now take place outside the classroom and vice versa" (Lage & Platt, 2000, p.32). According to Bishop and Verleger (2013), the flipped classroom can be defined as an educational technique that consists of two parts: interactive group learning activities inside the classroom, and direct computer-based individual instruction outside the classroom" (p. 5). For example, students could read, research, and view instructional materials such as videos outside the instructional time, and interact with the teacher and peers during instructional time. This creates a more student-centered instructional environment. (Bishop & Verleger, 2013).

AUTHOR NOTE

There is no funding associated with this work. There are no conflicts of interest associated with this work.

Correspondence should be directed to: Velma Menchaca, Ph.D. The University of Texas Rio Grande Valley, 1201 W University Drive, Edinburg, TX 78539, United States of America.

REFERENCES

Aguilar, S. J. (2020). A research-based approach for evaluating resources for transitioning to teaching online. *Information and Learning Sciences, 121*(5/6), 301–310. https://doi.org /10.1108/ILS-04-2020-0072

Allen, E., & Seaman, J. (2006). *Making the grade: Online education in the United States.* Sloan Consortium.

Almeida, D. M., Davis, K. D., Lee, S., Lawson, K. M., Walter, K. N., & Moen, P. (2016). Supervisor support buffers daily psychological and physiological reactivity to work-to-family conflict. *Journal of Marriage and Family, 78*(1), 165–179.

Anderson, E., & Hira, A. (2020). Loss of brick-and-mortar schooling: How elementary educators respond. *Information and Learning Sciences, 121*(5/6), 411–418. https://doi.org/10.1108/ILS-04-2020-0085

Archambault, L., & Crippen, K. (2009). Examining TPACK among K–12 Online Distance Educators in the United States. *Contemporary Issues in Technology and Teacher Education, 9*, 71–88. http://www.citejournal.org/vol9/iss1/general/article2.cfm

BallotPedia. (2022). https://ballotpedia.org/School_responses_in_Texas_to_the_coronavirus_(COVID-19)_pandemic

Baran, E., & Correia, A. (2014). A professional development framework for online teaching. *TechTrends, 58*, 95–101.

Beese, J., & Mlakar, M. (2020). An administrator's perception on the novel coronavirus. *Journal of Educational Leadership in Action, 7*(1), Article 6.

Belland, B. R., Kim, N. J., & Walker, A. E. (2018). Effectiveness of computer-based scaffolding in the context of problem-based learning for stem education: Bayesian meta-analysis. *Educational Psychology Review, 30*(2), 397–429. https://doi.org/10.1007/s10648-017-9419-1

Bishop, J., & Verleger, M. A. (2013, June), *The flipped classroom: A survey of the research.* Paper presented at 2013 ASEE Annual Conference & Exposition, Atlanta, Georgia. 10.18260/1-2—22585

Boakye, K. B., & Banini, D. A. (2008). Teacher ICT readiness in Ghana. In K. Toure, T. M. S. Tchombe, & T. Karsenti (Eds.), *ICT and changing mindsets in education*. Langaa.

Borotis, S., & Poulymenakou, A. (2004). E-learning readiness components: Key issues to consider before adopting E-learning interventions. In J. Nall & R. Robson (Eds.), *Proceedings of E-Learning 2004—World Conference on E-Learning in Corporate,Government, Healthcare, and Higher Education* (pp. 1622–1629). Association for the Advancement of Computing in Education (AACE).

Bryman, A., & Burgess, R. G. (2002). Reflections on qualitative data analysis. In A. Bryman & R. G. Burgess, (Eds.), *Analyzing qualitative data,* (pp. 216–226). Routledge.

Butcher, J. (2020). *Public-private virtual-school partnerships and federal flexibility for schools during COVID-19* (Mercatus Center Research Paper Series) [special edition policy brief]. Mercatus Center.

Center for Disease Control. (2019). *Pandemic influenza.* https://www.cdc.gov/flu/pandemic -resources/1918-pandemic-h1n1.html

Choi, J. (2006). A motivational theory of charismatic leadership: Envisioning, empathy, and empowerment. *Journal of Leadership and Organizational Studies, 13*(1), 24–43. https://doi.org/10.1177/107179190701300105O1

Chu, P. S., Saucier, D. A., & Hafner, E. (2010). Meta-analysis of the relationships between social support and well-being in children and adolescents. *Journal of Social and Clinical Psychology.*, *29*(6), 624–645. https://doi:10.1521/jscp.2010.29.6.624

Cobb, S. (1976). Social support as a moderator of life stress. *Psychosomatic Medicine, 38,* 300–314.

Cockrell, C., & Shelley, K. (2010). The relationship between academic support systems and intended persistence in doctoral education. *Journal of College Student Retention: Research, Theory and Practice, 12*(4), 469–484. https://doi: 10.2190/CS.12.4.e

Conley, S., & You, S. (2014). Role stress revisited: Job structuring antecedents, work outcomes, and moderating effects of locus of control. *Educational Management Administration & Leadership, 42*(2), 184–206.

Creswell, J. W. (2012). *Educational research: Planning, conducting, and evaluating quantitative and qualitative research* (4th ed.). Pearson.

Cutrona, C. E., & Suhr, J. A. (1992). Controllability of stressful events and satisfaction with spouse support behaviors. *Communication Research*, *19(*2), 154–174.

Denzin, N. K., & Lincoln, Y. S. (2000) The discipline and practice of qualitative research. In: N. K. Denzin, & Y. S. Lincoln, (Eds.), *Handbook of qualitative research*, (pp. 1–32). SAGE Publications.

Dereshiwsky, M. (2013*). Continual engagement: Fostering online discussion*. LEARN Books.

Eslaminejad, T., Masood, M., & Ngah, N. A. (2009). Identifying instructors' readiness factors on e-learning for the continuing medical education programs in Iran. In *E-Learn: World Conference on E-Learning in Corporate, Government, Healthcare, and Higher Education (*pp. 238–243). Association for the Advancement of Computing in Education (AACE).

Fielding, N. G., & Fielding, J. L. (1986). *Linking data.* SAGE Publications.

Francom, G. M., Lee, S. J., & Pinkney, H. (2021). Technologies, challenges and needs of K–12 teachers in the transition to distance learning during the COVID-19 pandemic. *TechTrends, 65,* 589–601. https://doi.org/10.1007/s11528-021-00625-5

Frazer, C., Sullivan, D. H., Weatherspoon, D., & Hussey, L. (2017) Faculty perceptions of online teaching effectiveness and indicators of quality. *Nursing Research and Practice,* Article 9374189. https://doi.org/10.1155/2017/9374189

Frenzel, A. C., Goetz, T., Lüdtke, O., Pekrun, R., & Sutton, R. E. (2009). Emotional transmission in the classroom: Exploring the relationship between teacher and student enjoyment. *Journal of Educational Psychology, 101*(3), 705–716.

Gallagher, K. S. (2020, April 13). *Supporting online learning in a time of pandemic.* Policy Analysis for California Education. https://edpolicyinca.org/newsroom/supporting-online-learning-time-pandemic

Gottlieb, B. H., & Bergen, A. E. (2010). Social support concepts and measures. *Journal of Psychosomatic Research, 69*(5), 511–520.

Herold, B. (2020, March 27). The scramble to move America's schools online. *Education Week.* Retrieved https://www.edweek.org/ew/articles/2020/03/26/the-scramble-to-move-americas-schools-online.html

Hill, J. R. (2002). Overcoming obstacles and creating connections: Community building in Web-based learning environments. *Journal of Computing in Higher Education, 14*(1), 67–86.

Hodges, C., Moore, S., Lockee, B., Trust, T., & Bond, A. (2020). The difference between emergency remote teaching and online learning. *EDUCAUSE Review.* https://er.educause.edu/articles/2020/3/the-*difference-between-emergency-remote-teaching-and-online- learning*

Hogan, B., Linden, W., & Najarian, B. (2002). Social support interventions: Do they work? *Clinical Psychology Review, 22*(3), 381–440. https://doi:10.1016/s0272-7358(01)00102-7.

Hopkins Medicine. (2020). *What is coronavirus?* https://www.hopkinsmedicine.org/health/conditions-and-diseases/coronavirus

House, J. S. (1981). *Work stress and social support.* Addison-Wesley Publishing Company.

Hrastinski, S. (2008). Asynchronous and synchronous e-learning. *EDUCAUSE Quarterly, 31*(4), 51–55.

Johnson, N., Veletsianos, G., & Seaman, J. (2020). U.S. faculty and administrators' experiences and approaches in the early weeks of the COVID-19 pandemic. *Online Learning, 24*(2), 6–21. https://doi.org/10.24059/olj.v24i2.2285

Kaplan, B. H., Cassel, J. C., & Gore, S. (1977). Social support and health. *Med Care, 15*(5), 47–58.

Kelley, E. (2020). Reflections on three different high school chemistry formats during COVID-19 remote learning. *Journal of Chemistry Education, 97(9), 2606–2616.* https://doi.org/10.1021/acs.jchemed.0c00814

Kim, J. (2020). Learning and teaching online during COVID-19: Experiences of student teachers in an early childhood education practicum. *International Journal of Early Childhood, 52*, 145–158. https://doi.org/10.1007/s13158-020-00272-6

Kirkwood, A., & Price, L. (2005). Learners and learning in the twenty-first century: What do we know about students' attitudes towards and experiences of information and communication technologies that will help us design courses? *Studies in Higher Education, 30*(3), 257–274.

Lage, L., & Platt, G. (2000). The internet and the inverted classroom. *The Journal of Economic Education, 31*(1), 11.

Ley, T., Tammets, K., Sarmiento-Márquez, E., Leoste, J., Hallik, M., & Poom-Valickis, K. (2021). Adopting technology in schools: Modeling, measuring, and supporting knowledge appropriation. *European Journal of Teacher Education, 45*(4), 548–571. https://doi:10.1080/02619768.2021.1937113.

Littrell, P. C., Billingsley, B. S., & Cross, L. H. (1994). The effects of principal support on special and general educators' stress, job satisfaction, school commitment, health, and intent to stay in teaching. *Remedial and Special Education, 15*(5), 297–310.

Luckin, R., Clark, W., Graber, R., Logan, K., Mee, A., & Oliver, M. (2009). Do web 2.0 tools really open the door to learning? Practices, perceptions and profiles of 11–16-year-old students. *Learning, Media, and Technology, 34(*2), 87–104. https://doi:10.1080/17439880902921949

Marshall, D. T., Shannon, D. M., & Love, S. M. (2020). How teachers experienced the COVID-19 transition to remote instruction. *Phi Delta Kappan, 102,* 46–50.

Maxwell, J. A. (2008). Designing a qualitative study. In *The SAGE handbook of applied social research methods* (Vol. 2, pp. 214–253). Sage.

McPherson, M., & Nunes, M. B. (2004). *Developing innovation in online learning: An action research framework.* RoutledgeFalmer.

Miles, M. B., & Huberman, A. M. (1994). Data management and analysis methods. In N. K. Denzin, & Y. S. Lincoln (Eds.), *Handbook of qualitative research* (pp. 428–444). SAGE Publications.

Miller, W., & Crabtree, B. (Eds.). (1999). *Doing qualitative research* (2nd ed.). SAGE Publications.

Oprysko, C. (2020, April 16). More than a dozen states have extended stay-home orders past White House deadline. *Politico.* https://www.politico.com/news/2020/04/16/coronavirus-stay-home-orders-extended-190889

Pas, E. T., Bradshaw, C. P., & Hershfeldt, P. A. (2012). Teacher-and school-level predictors of teacher efficacy and burnout: Identifying potential areas for support. *Journal of School Psychology, 50*(1), 129–145.

Patton, M. Q. (2015). *Qualitative research & evaluation methods: Integrating theory and practice* (4th ed.). SAGE Publications.

Pourhosein, G. A. (2013). Factors contributing to teachers' use of computer technology in the classroom. *Universal Journal of Educational Research, 1,* 262–267. 10.13189/ujer.2013.010317

Racino, J. (2006). Social support. In G. Albrecht (Ed.), *Encyclopedia on disability* (pp. 1470–1471). SAGE Publications.

Russell, D. W., Altmaier, E., & Van Velzen, D. (1987). Job-related stress, social support, and burnout among classroom teachers. *Journal of Applied Psychology, 72*(2), 269–274.

Saad, S., & Sankaran, S. (2020). Technology proficiency in teaching and facilitating. In *Oxford research encyclopedia of education.* Oxford University Press. https://doi.org/10.1093/acrefore/9780190264093.013.591

Sandholtz, J. H. (2001). Learning to teach with technology: A comparison of teacher development programs. *Journal of Technology and Teacher Education, 9*(3), 349–374.

Schrum, L., & Levin, B. B. (2009). *Leading 21st century schools: Harnessing technology for engagement and achievement.* Corwin.

Schutt, R. K. (2017). *Investigating the social world* (9th ed.). SAGE Publications.

Shaw, R. (2001). *Information design and distance learning for international development.* Water Engineering and Development Centre. Loughborough University.

Sims, C. M. (2017). Do the big-five personality traits predict empathic listening and assertive communication? *International Journal of Listening, 31*(3), 163–188.

Somech, A. (2016). The cost of going the extra mile: The relationship between teachers' organizational citizenship behavior, role stressors, and strain with the buffering effect of job autonomy. *Teachers and Teaching, 22*(4), 426–447.

Strauss, A., & Corbin, J. (1998). *Basics of qualitative research techniques.* SAGE Publications.

Swaby, A. (2020, April 17). Governor Greg Abbott keeps Texas classrooms closed for the remainder of school year. *The Texas Tribune.* https://www.texastribune.org/2020/04/17/gov-greg-abbott-keeps-texas-classrooms-closed-remainder-school-year/.

Tabachinik, S. (2020, March 24). Coronavirus stay-at-home orders in Colorado. *The Denver Post.* https://www.denverpost.com/2020/03/24/coronavirus-stay-at-home-orderscolorado/

Tandy, C. H. (1985). Social support measurement. *American Journal of Community Psychology, 13,* 187–202. 10.1007/BF00905728

Tatar, M. (2009). Teachers turning for help to school counsellors and colleagues: Toward a mapping of relevant predictors. *British Journal of Guidance & Counseling, 37(2)*, 107–127.

Taylor, S. E. (2011). Social support: A review. In H. S. Friedman (Ed.), *The Oxford handbook of health psychology* (pp. 189–214). Oxford University Press.

Texas Education Agency. (February 28, 2020). *TEA Annual Report 2021.* https://tea.texas.gov/about-tea/news-and-multimedia/correspondence/taa-letters/tea-is-closely-monitoring-novel-coronavirus-COVID-19

Twining, P., Raffaghelli, J., Albion, P., & Knezek, D. (2013). Moving education into the digital age: The contribution of teachers' professional development. *Journal of Computer Assisted Learning, 29*(5), 426–437. https://doi:10.1111/jcal.12031

Vaux, A. C., Phillips, J., Holly, L., Thomson, B. C., Williams, D., & Stewart, D. (1986). The social support appraisals (SS-A) scale: Studies of reliability and validity. *American Journal of Community Psychology, 14*, 195–218.

Wasserman S., & Faust, K. (1994). *Social network analysis: Methods and applications.* Cambridge University Press. https://doi.org/10.1017/CBO9780511815478

Webb, M., & Cox, M. (2004). A review of pedagogy related to information and communications technology. *Technology, Pedagogy and Education, 13*(3), 235–286. https://doi:10.1080/ 14759390400200183.

Webber, C. F. (2003). New technologies and educative leadership. *Journal of Educational Administration, 41*(2), 119–123.

Wolf, P. D. (2006). Best practices in the training of faculty to teach online. *Journal of Computing in Higher Education, 17*, 47–78. http://dx.doi.org/10.1007/BF03032698

Wu, S-Y. (2021). How teachers conduct online teaching during the COVID-19 pandemic: A case study of Taiwan. *Frontiers in Education, 6,* https://doi:10.3389/feduc.2021.675434

Zhang, X., & Bartol, K. M. (2010). Linking empowering leadership and employee creativity: The influence of psychological empowerment, intrinsic motivation, and creative process engagement. *Academy of Management Journal, 53*(1), 107–128.

Zhao, Y. (2007). Social studies teachers' perspectives of technology integration. *Journal of Technology and Teacher Education, 15*(3), 311–333.

CHAPTER 11

ATTACHMENT, ATTENTION, AND ACHIEVEMENT DURING THE COVID-19 PANDEMIC

A Conceptual Literature Review

Romona F. Banks, Mahaliah Bowman Campbell, Dana M. Dillard, and Joseph A. Torres
University of Arizona Global Campus

The COVID-19 pandemic brought with it uncertainty, stress, and multiple challenges as individuals worldwide attempted to cope with rapid changes occurring in multiple domains, including occupational status, financial stability, academic progress, and social support systems at the expense of attending to ongoing, but perhaps less cognitively demanding, tasks. Previous research demonstrates that unmitigated stressors and threats to coping share a relationship with physical, mental, and academic outcomes and that early relationships correspond with the ability to attend to and cope with stress.

In the current conceptual literature review, synthesis of existing research on attachment theory, cognitive load theory, and attention mechanisms provides a framework

Instructional Survival in the Midst of the Perfect Storm:
The Experiences of K–12 Teachers During the COVID-19 Global Pandemic, pages 191–212.

Published under exclusive licence by Emerald Publishing Limited
ISBNs: 978-1-83708-502-6 HB, 978-1-83708-503-3 PB,
978-1-83708-504-0 EPDF, 978-1-83708-505-7 EPUB

for examining academic achievement under time heightened stress, such as during the COVID-19 pandemic. This framework may provide a means for modeling future research to predict academic losses and explore interventions in environments that may be characterized by insecure attachment, uncertainty, and high stress.

Keywords: COVID-19, Pandemic, Stress, Coping, Academic Achievement, Attachment Theory, Cognitive Load Theory, Attention Mechanisms, Uncertainty, Intervention.

INTRODUCTION

Early work with attachment styles has provided a theoretical foundation for examining how infants and children interact with the world. Based on a child's perception of support and safety, the world becomes a playground that can be seen as an exciting adventure in exploration or as a terrifying foray into the unknown. While much of the early work on attachment focused on experiences in childhood, contemporary researchers have concluded that attachment styles have relationships with learning and achievement across the lifespan; however, they also appear to correspond with distress and anxiety (Read et al., 2018; Vaughn et al., 2009), suggesting opportunities for intervention to improve both wellbeing and academic success during uncertain times, such as the COVID-19 pandemic. In the following conceptual literature review, the authors reviewed and synthesized existing empirical research with attachment theory and cognitive load theory to identify possible relationships between attachment, attention, and academic success during times of stress.

Research Question and Search Strategy

The guiding question for this literature review was: What, if any, relationships between attachment style, cognitive load, attention, and academic achievement have been identified in contemporary research? To accomplish this, the authors conducted a search of available databases, including EBSCOhost, PsycARTICLES, PubMed Central, ProQuest, ResearchGate, and Google Scholar, using key terms and Boolean operators to identify studies with intersecting themes, including attachment, attention, cognitive load, academics, achievement, COVID, online learning, uncertainty, and belonging.

Goals and Objectives

The overarching goal of this conceptual literature review was to investigate and synthesize the existing body of empirical research at the intersection of attachment theory and cognitive load theory. With this goal, we worked to identify theoretical relationships between attachment styles, attention mechanisms, and academic achievement, with a specific focus on how these dynamics manifested during times of heightened stress and uncertainty, such as the COVID-19 pandemic.

The authors' objectives were.

1. To provide a comprehensive overview of attachment theory, emphasizing its development, various attachment styles, and its foundational role in shaping individuals' emotional responses and interpersonal relationships,
2. To explore cognitive load theory and its implications for attentional processes, emphasizing how cognitive load and attachment styles might impact an individual's capacity to focus and sustain attention,
3. To review and synthesize empirical studies linking attachment styles and attentional mechanisms, particularly during periods of heightened stress and uncertainty, such as the COVID-19 pandemic,
4. To assess the influence of attachment styles and attentional processes on academic success, aiming to uncover patterns and potential mechanisms through which attachment may impact learning outcomes, and
5. To identify potential areas for intervention and propose strategies that can be employed to mitigate the negative impact of insecure attachment styles on attention and academic success during stressful times, contributing to both enhanced well-being and improved educational outcomes.

ATTACHMENT THEORY

Attachment theory arose from the partnership of Mary Salter Ainsworth and John Bowlby (1991), who separately sought to examine personality development but joined to build a unified ethological approach. Although Bowlby's original interest in attachment arose from observations of maternal separation, deprivation, and loss and Ainsworth's focus began in Blatz's security theory, both theorists came to an agreement on the situational and biological contexts which interact to influence parent-child relationships. Of interest for both theorists was the process of restoration of secure attachment following distress or upheaval in the environment.

Bowlby (1969) asserted in his theory that each child is born with innate motivating forces to seek contact with a primary caregiver. The child may or may not be completely dependent on their caregiver and may develop effective or ineffective attachments. Catherall (2014) found that effective attachment, or having greater levels of secure dependence, fostered greater levels of confidence, which can act as a source of security for the child. For instance, a caregiver may serve as a secure base, allowing the child to explore an environment with the knowledge that the caregiver will be close by to attend to the needs of the child when needed. As Sampaio and Lifter (2014) discussed, children with secure attachments may display distress when unable to access their caregiver. Therefore, in times of fear, the need for attachment is activated in the child. Outside of the secure base, Catherall (2014) reported that the attachment theory assumed that there are two ways that insecure attachment can occur. First, anxiety can develop when the connection between the child and caregiver is threatened. Attachment behaviors, such as becoming clingy or seeking a response from the caregiver, may be displayed. Second, avoidance can develop when the child realizes that the connection with the caregiver may be lost. As an attempt to cope with the loss, the child may begin to ignore the need for the connection and may engage in other activities.

Development of Attachment Bonds

Bowlby (1988) found that providing an optimal environment through healthy interactions would result in healthier attachment patterns. Given this, the attachment that is developed with the caregiver is an important part of the child's survival. Although historically the child's attachment to their mother has been emphasized, contemporary work reiterates the importance of responsive, sensitive, and reflective caregiving from providers, including fathers, co-parents, and other parenting figures (Flaherty & Sadler, 2011; Hong & Park, 2012).

In addition to attachments with caregivers, children may also develop attachments with others (Bowlby, 1988). Bowlby found that attachment was an important process that had lifelong social implications. The attachment style developed during childhood may carry on with the child throughout their adulthood and influence how they relate to society. In essence, the earliest interactions between a child and a caregiver create an internal working model for the child about the nature of relationships (Flaherty & Sadler, 2011). The attachment bond emerges as a mental representation of the expectations of interactions with emotionally close others, which is foundational for healthy emotional expression and communication, self-regulation, and resilience across the lifespan (Flaherty & Sadler, 2011). The child achieves independence through a process of internalizing security in their closeness (Hong & Park, 2012). Promoting the development of effective attachment patterns and bonds becomes paramount in physical and socioemotional health.

Describing Attachment Patterns

According to Bowlby (1982), four concepts describe the formation of attachment patterns. These interrelated concepts are a safe haven, secure base, proximity maintenance, and separation. Bowlby (1988) reported that a safe haven refers to when the child seeks out the attachment figure when they are faced with perceived danger. In this case, crying is an attachment behavior that serves as a form of communication when trying to satisfy safety and security needs. According to Faris and McCarroll (2010), crying would discontinue when the child finds that the action or behavior was not successful in achieving their needs.

Levesque (2012) reported that as the child ages, the use of an attachment figure as a safe haven lessens, and the child may begin to view the attachment figure as a secure base. According to Bowlby (1982), having identified a secure base, a child may explore the world with an understanding that the attachment figure will be available when needing protection from perceived danger. The child may become aware that the attachment figure can respond to their needs when necessary and be confident that the attachment figure can help. Bowlby (1982) asserted that the child may take the attachment figure for granted, relying on safety and security being present. However, if the attachment figure is not available, the stability of the child may become threatened.

Proximity maintenance refers to a need to be around people who will provide a safe haven and minimize separation (Bowlby, 1988). The idea is that emotions can motivate a direct behavior toward certain anxiety and depression when individuals fear separation from those who provide care and protection. Pairing students with a sibling, childhood friend, or family member that may be employed where the child is attending school may decrease anxiety, fear, and separation, providing a safe haven of comfort and safety (Mattanah et al., 2004).

According to Bowlby (1982), separation distress may arise when the child becomes separated from the attachment figure. For instance, the child may cry when the attachment figure leaves them at the daycare center. Bowlby (1969) reported that the child's experience of separation distress was compared to that of an adult in mourning. The primary attachment approach to proximity maintenance is to ensure safety and minimize the anxiety due to separation during transitions (Dewitte & De Houwer, 2008). Therefore, during times of separation and uncertainty, such as during the COVID pandemic, youth, teenagers, and adults may surround themselves with familiar environments to diffuse the distressing feelings of change or abandonment (Collins & Feeney, 2000).

Ainsworth and Bowlby (1991) reported that attachment theory is an approach for children forming connections, which occurs between early problems and issues with forming connections in life. To assess these qualities of attachment empirically, Ainsworth developed a controlled laboratory paradigm called the Strange Situation study, in which researchers observed children as they navigated unusual conditions of caregiver play, caregiver absence, stranger presence, and caregiver reunion. Children identified as displaying secure attachments would engage in active exploration of the environment before the attachment figure leaves the room, distress at separation, relief at the reunion, and a return to baseline behavior (Ainsworth & Bowlby, 1991). Secure attachment refers to a child who has a balance between attachment and exploratory behaviors (Ainsworth & Bowlby, 1991). In this case, parents are a secure base that children may return to when they sense danger. Ramsauer et al. (2014) found that securely attached children were warm when the mother returned. The caregiver's ability to attend to the needs of the child influences the consistency of the child's attachment, highlighting the importance of responsive and contingent parenting.

However, not all children displayed these patterns associated with secure attachment. Differences in attachment styles emerged during the play, absence, and reunion periods of the Strange Situation (Ainsworth & Bowlby, 1991; Ainsworth et al., 1978/2015), leading to the categorization of insecure attachment types. Whereas securely attached infants became distraught when caregivers left the room and sought out their caregiver for comfort upon return, some children appeared unaffected by separation and would avoid attempting contact with the caregiver when they returned, a pattern of attachment categorized as insecure-avoidant or anxious-avoidant (Ainsworth et al., 1978/2015). Insecure-avoidant attachment refers to a child who suppresses the need for safety, being more self-reliant and believing their needs would never be met (Ainsworth & Bowlby, 1991).

Some children appeared ambivalent to the presence of a caretaker during playtime but would become severely distressed when the caregiver separated; paradoxically, the return of the caregiver did not soothe these children. Indeed, these children often seemed torn between desiring and resisting comfort. This pattern of responding to the Strange Situation was labeled insecure-resistant, anxious-ambivalent, or anxious-resistant (Ainsworth et al., 1978/2015; Hong & Park, 2012). Insecure-resistant attachment refers to the child being distressed by the parent's departure and having difficulty settling down when the parent returns (Ainsworth & Bowlby, 1991).

A fourth pattern of responding later identified as insecure-disorganized attachment occurred when children seemed disoriented, confused, or dazed during the different phases of the Strange Situation (Hong & Park, 2012). Insecure-disorganized attachment refers to an attachment pattern that may be characterized by profound trauma or loss, causing severe confusion (Ainsworth & Bowlby, 1991). The parent may be the source of distress.

Cultural Differences in Attachment

The original conceptualizations of the attachment theory and its subsequent styles developed as the result of a series of studies conducted in Baltimore, Maryland, United States. Waters et al. (2015), in their preface to Ainsworth et al. (1978/2015), highlighted the importance of considering culture and family dynamics in interpreting and applying attachment constructs. Independence, for example, can become a culture-laden word and may carry different connotations for infant behaviors depending on the values, beliefs, and mores espoused by cultural tradition. In this way, the role of the situation is not always addressed in contemporary applications of attachment theory or in how these contexts affect parenting and attachment. Cultural and social differences may exist in attachment and development outcomes.

Stern et al. (2022) highlighted this disparity by recognizing that Black youth development often becomes contextualized within sociocultural stressors, including systemic discrimination, inequality and inequity in education and economic opportunities, family systems disruption, and limited potential for socioeconomic gain, and cultural strengths, including support from extended family relationships and positive racial socialization. Attachment security can provide a window into the health protective effects of positive socialization derived from attachment theory while recognizing the social and cultural factors that correspond with diverse family dynamics (Mikulincer & Shaver, 2020).

Attachment security comprises two dimensions that describe an attachment orientation (Bowlby, 1973, as cited in Mikulincer & Shaver, 2020). Attachment avoidance is one dimension in which an individual fails to seek or even rejects others in times of need and distrusts the motivations of others; attachment anxiety is the other dimension, representing a belief of unavailability of others during times of need, which may cooccur behaviorally with a need for approval (Mikulincer & Shaver, 2020). Attachment security occurs when individuals demonstrate low attachment avoidance and low attachment anxiety. For individuals with attachment security, there is an innate belief that loved ones can be counted on to assist when in need and will be supportive, that the emotional or tangible support they may be able to provide will relieve the distress, and that the distressed individual can return to a previous, undistressed state. Individuals with attachment security who believe and receive care and validation are reinforced in that belief, a process Mikulincer and Shaver (2016, as cited in Mikulincer & Shaver, 2020) called the broaden-and-build cycle of attachment security. Attachment security becomes a cornerstone for resilience in adversity.

Adult Attachment

As individuals transition from childhood to adulthood, attachment figures began to shift from caretakers to peers or romantic partners. According to Cooper et al. (1998), adolescents and young adults begin to encounter new relationships, in which the representations of the self and others continue to change. Similar to the theories of Bowlby, affectionate bonds may involve various emotional dynamics and stability. For instance, Sperling and Berman (1994) reported that adult attachment is described as the stable tendency of an individual in making substantial efforts to seek and maintain proximity to other individuals who provide physical or psychological safety and security. According to Hazan and Shaver (1987), adult attachment was characterized by three discrete attachment style categories that mirror Ainsworth et al.'s (1978/2015) designations. These attachment style categories are secure, insecure: anxious/ambivalent, and insecure: anxious/avoidant. Those who are securely attached may be more self-confident and socially competent, which means they may be more likely to establish stable and long-term relationships. However, those who are anxious/ambivalent may lack confidence and may be concerned about abandonment. These individuals may be more likely to be jealous or experience frequent breakups and reunions. Those who are avoidant may not be interested in close relationships and uncomfortable with self-disclosure. They may be socially inept and less likely to become involved in long-term relationships.

According to Bartholomew and Horowitz (1991), adult attachment is based on four categories, which have two continuously partitioned dimensions. These dimensions include views of the self and views of others. For instance, if an individual's view of self is positive, they may view themselves as worthy of love and support. However, if the view of self is negative, they may view themselves as not worthy of love and support. Now, if the individual's view of others is positive, they may view others as being reliable and trustworthy, but if the view of others is negative, they may view others as unreliable and untrustworthy. Although discussed within the context of romantic relationships, these attachment patterns may also have implications in other social contexts, such as between students and teachers.

ATTACHMENT AND STUDENT ACHIEVEMENT

The relationship between social and emotional contexts and student learning provides key insight to developing supportive learning environments. A supportive learning environment considers the needs of the student as they relate to additional interactions with the student's family, community, and classroom (Darling-Hammond et al., 2020). Capable instructors adapt to these needs to promote attachment security and optimal growth in classrooms where students feel safe, secure, and supported to explore ideas.

Several factors impact student achievement as a function of the learning environment (Darling-Hammond et al., 2020; Duncan et al., 2007; Ghanbari et al., 2020; Kelleher, 2022; Rapanta et al., 2020). Parents and educators play an intricate role in providing a safe and engaging learning environment for the student. Their roles can have a significant influence on the student's achievement level that can be impacted interchangeably by transparency and attachment. Darling-Hammond et al. (2020) highlighted that development can be influenced by the student's interactions with their family, community, and classroom experience and that based on the student's individual needs, they may require a more stylized instructional format or support system to achieve success. Furthermore, student success is predicated on the status of their attachment and the ability of the instructor to anticipate and deliver resources to assist the student in achieving their goals. For example, community-based organizations such as PepsiCo Educational Technology (n.d.) and Betabox (2022) seek to provide resources that may assist in student engagement and achievement while also specifically addressing the emotional and social context that impact human cognition. The relationship between attachment security and student achievement appeared in Kurland and Siegel's (2020) longitudinal study as well, in which students with secure attachments graduated at a higher rate and with a higher GPA than students with insecure attachments. Female participants were overrepresented (75.3% of the sample) in Kurland and Siegel's work, but this presents an additional compelling factor to examine in future work looking at attachment security and student achievement in college settings, though Mikulincer and Shaver (2007, as cited in Kurland & Siegel, 2020) indicated that gender is not predictive of attachment style. Interestingly, students with insecure attachments who dropped out of school tended to have lower GPAs than students with insecure attachments who were retained. This may serve as an intervention point in identifying at-risk students who may require emotional and social support in addition to access to educational resources.

Likewise, learning dispositions found in different attachment personalities predicted achievement (Larose et al., 2005). Individuals with dismissing attachment styles had lower grade averages than autonomous and preoccupied individuals. Autonomous individuals had more stable learning dispositions, such as quality of exam preparation, priority of studies, attention, and willingness to seek help from a teacher. Dismissing and preoccupied individuals showed a decreased quality of learning dispositions over time. Preoccupied individuals also had a greater fear of failure than autonomous individuals. Transition into the first year of college depends significantly on a maintained focus on individual studies and achievement.

COGNITIVE LOAD THEORY AND ATTENTION

First proposed in the late 1980s, Sweller (1988) reported that cognitive load theory was an instructional theory that considers the capacities and limitations of human cognition. Within cognitive load theory, attention is focused on the schema acquisition and its association with different types of cognitive processes and problem-solving approaches. Additionally, Moreno and Park (2010) reported that cognitive learning theory focused on the individual learning complex tasks. According to Clark and Clark (2010), learning is the process of constructing new knowledge by observing prior experience and incorporating it with new information to form schemas. These schemata may facilitate the retention and retrieval of knowledge from one's long-term memory to be used for future understandings. From this perspective, cognitive load theory assumes that the schema formation is the foundation of performance and requires attention to be focused on problem-solving. However, Moreno and Park (2010) reported that any mental activity that distracts from the schema formation must be limited so that learning is not diminished because of cognitive overload. For instance, an individual's distracting and inattentive actions or behaviors may impose extraneous cognitive load by diverting attention away from the learning material and causing them to activate a selective attention process.

Types of Cognitive Load

Intrinsic, extraneous, and germane load are three types of cognitive load variables, associated with cognitive load theory, which determines the level of demand on an individual's capacity-limited processing. According to Moreno and Park (2010), the three cognitive load variables involve the inherent complexity of information to be learned, how information is presented, and the mental effort required given an individual's prior experience and knowledge.

When concerning intrinsic load, the load may vary from one individual to another because of the interactivity of elements that is associated with the individual's prior knowledge. The interpretation of intrinsic load may be conceived as not only the content of an individual's message but on how those individuals express themselves. According to Mayer and Moreno (2010), extraneous load refers to cognitive processing that does not contribute to an individual's learning. This typically occurs from the inclusion of non-essential material and poor presentations. In this case, the information may be harder to learn because of the information being confusing. For instance, Moreno and Park (2010) reported that extraneous loads are defined as cognitive processing that does not contribute to the comprehension of the individual's message, internalization of content, and the interpretation of skills. Moreno and Park (2010) reported that germane load refers to cognitive processing that is devoted to schema formations. In other words, the processing is directed at the organization of mental representations of essential information and integrating it with existing knowledge (Mayer & Moreno, 2010). For instance, Moreno and Park (2010) reported that germane load is the processing capacity devoted to automating and building knowledge.

Attention and Distractions

According to Chandler and Sweller (1992), cognitive load theory suggested that educators remove competing stimuli to avoid split attention. This should allow individuals to focus on a single source of information. Just like listening to a lecture should not be interrupted by competing explanations, Chandler and Sweller (1992) demonstrated that the learning experience can be improved when competing stimuli were merged into one source of information. Presenting audio and visual stimuli simultaneously can enhance an individual's learning experience precisely because of distinct processing pathways (Chandler & Sweller, 1992), but this must be done carefully because, as Jones and Macken (1993) reported, split attention can impact an individual when the distraction is presented in the learning environment. For instance, light from someone's phone can pull someone's attention elsewhere. The removal of the distraction (i.e., non-relevant stimuli) can reduce the extraneous cognitive load imposed on an individual.

Cognitive Load, Anxiety, and Attachment

In addition to competing stimuli, individuals face increasing cognitive load in the form of stressors, and these stressors may correspond with attachment processes. Anxiety, specifically, contributes to extraneous cognitive load, which can impact learning perceptions (Fredericks et al., 2021). Forrest (2008), although related to sports performance, identified the influence of adult attachment in attention-mediated performance processes, such as self-regulation, competition anxiety, and choking under pressure. The conditions identified by Forrest may correspond with adult learning situations and intrinsic and extraneous cognitive load. Specifically, unexpected conditions, fear of failure, and fatigue may correspond with pressures experienced in the online learning environment for returning adult learners, while coach stress may be viewed similarly as instructor stress in which a learner sees a coach (or instructor) as an attachment figure that may trigger attachment anxiety or avoidance in individuals with these attachment patterns.

For example, McWilliams and Brodeur (2016), who examined the hypothesis that adult attachment style correlated with attention, identified a positive relationship between attachment anxiety and orientation to threat. The implications suggested that individuals who are anxious in their attachments are quicker to attend to stimuli that may be perceived as a threat. This has implications in education and learning as attention to information may be influenced by threat and relevance assessments and distractibility.

Cognitive Load, Self-Regulation, and Attachment

Continuing with this, Silva et al. (2012) highlighted the intimate role between attachment and self-regulation, particularly in processing information with emotion-based content. This may suggest that attentional processes are differentially triggered based on subject content with information that has individual salience being attended to differently than information that does not trigger an emotional connection. In self-regulating responses to threat information that compete with learning, individuals potentially experience increasing intrinsic, extraneous, and germane cognitive load (Seufert, 2018). While Silva et al. did not assess attention to information, they did examine the impact of distracters. They found that negative distractors impacted accuracy overall and that individuals with anxious attachment patterns tended to show more interference and arousal in response to distractions. Individuals with avoidant attachment tended to perform similarly to individuals with secure attachment patterns. The increased demands to self-regulate an emotional response to a negative distractor for individuals with anxious attachments may create an environment in which new learning is not sustainable, which may also correspond with Kurland and Siegel's (2020) finding that students with lower GPA and insecure attachment were less likely to be retained across four years. This has particular relevance when considering a possible mediated effect of attachment patterns on attention in adult learners during COVID-19. With an abundance of emotionally charged media serving as possible negative distractors, attention may be diverted away from a target (in this instance, schoolwork) toward emotionally arousing material that interferes with studies (i.e., media).

THE ROLES OF ATTACHMENT, COGNITIVE LOAD, AND ATTENTION ON ACADEMIC PERFORMANCE DURING TIMES OF UNCERTAINTY

In the past decade, American society has faced many challenges. Social and political upheaval have introduced significant stressors into everyday life, which are layered on top of existing cultural norms that may place the dream of attaining higher education out of reach for some individuals. For example, during slavery, African Americans were forbidden to learn how to read or write, and those who tried, and if it was revealed, were beaten, jailed, or killed for gaining knowledge that would free them from the bondage of achieving equality and prosperity that an education would provide (Patton & McClure, 2009). Despite efforts to increase diversity, inclusion, equity, and belongingness, African American college students continue to face challenges because of their race, financial status, reduced exposure to world history, campus environment, systemic and institutionalized racism, and not having faculty and staff members who look like them (Rose, 2013). In addition, African American students may experience attachment security differently, which may complicate help-seeking when new information is confusing, thus activating both cognitive load and attachment anxiety. Historically Black Colleges and Universities (HBCUs) may alleviate some cognitive load because of their support systems, lack of stigmas, and the ability to provide emotional, social, and cultural understanding attachment in the form of academic support from faculty and staff members who "look like" them. For example, teachers influential with African American students use various approaches, including culturally responsive and "vervistic" instructional techniques (Young, 2017). Culturally responsive pedagogy is a major concept that stresses the ability of teachers to respond to their students by incorporating elements of students' culture into their teaching (Ladson-Billings, 2006). Therefore, the use of this approach reduces anxiety and cognitive load. Culturally responsive teaching, as defined by Gay (2000), uses "the cultural knowledge, prior experience, frames of reference, and performance styles of ethnically diverse students to make learning encounters more relevant" (p. 29).

Colleges and universities that incorporate social and academic integration play an essential role in the motivation, achievement, and retention of students, especially African American students. For example, first-generation students' social involvement and engagement help them meet peers with similar backgrounds. For instance, Claflin University, an HBCU, provides a social involvement and engagement event every other week on campus for students to have fun and decompress. The activities include music, food, and booths from different programs, sororities, fraternities, and access to academic resources. An interview with Claflin University, HBCU's director Dr. Bridget Dewees, who oversees the Student Retention and Quality Assurance Department, found that the activities positively relate to the student's academic success. The Social melt-down reduces students' anxiety when they realize that they are not alone about how they feel ... lonely or misfit (Claflin University, 2022).

Aligning with the approach taken by Claflin University, Cabrera et al. (1999) identified that positive transitions into college on academic, social, and personal levels are facilitated through secure attachment and the ease of separation-individuation. Loneliness in first-year college students impedes separation-individuation and increases negative feelings and anxiety toward the transition into college. Recent research found loneliness to be negatively correlated with secure attachment styles and perceived parental care and predicted by self-criticism and ambivalence (Wiseman et al., 2006). Low self-criticism in secure individuals may lead to a higher perception of social networks or individuals with high levels of self-induced isolation. Social and emotional factors, arising from attachment insecurity, may contribute to cognitive load and impede student success.

The transition to the college environment may serve as an emotional distractor under ideal circumstances; however, college students in the 2020s faced less than ideal circumstances. Beginning in late 2019 and accelerating in 2020, the COVID-19 pandemic destabilized lives across the world as individuals struggled to cope with changes in multiple domains (Marmarosh et al., 2020; Xing et al., 2023). Financially, in the United States, the unemployment rate rose from 4.4% in March 2020 to 14.7% in April 2020 (U.S. Bureau of Labor Statistics, 2020a, 2020b). While unemployment rates stabilized, some workers continued to telework due to the pandemic, with 7.8% of the population over the age of 24 working remotely in June 2022 (U.S. Bureau of Labor Statistics, 2022), resulting in disruptions to home routines. For parents who did not telework (92.3% of the population in June 2022 [U.S. Bureau of Labor Statistics, 2022]), the uncertainties of school closures may have contributed to household pandemic stressors. Academically, students in traditional educational settings found themselves in states of uncertainty as they could not be sure that their schools would remain open. Institutions with online programs may have offered more stability in their course offerings and status, but these institutions are staffed and attended by people who were juggling the multi-pronged attack of an international pandemic. During this time, individuals with non-secure attachment styles may have been particularly at-risk to the effects of an uncontrollable event that reinforced the belief that the world is not a safe place and that there are no safe bases to return to.

This risk is evidenced in the work of Larose et al. (2005) who identified that the transition to college may activate challenges to personal systems that threaten adjustment to college expectations and academic success. Students with secure attachments may find it easier to develop support networks and build resilience with the knowledge of an accessible support system if it becomes necessary to activate it (Mahama et al., 2021). Students with insecure attachments may be less prepared to meet the demands and challenges of college and may feel incompetent to address these changes (Larose et al., 2005). With threats to emotional systems activated by increasing cognitive load, students with insecure attachments may find themselves less successful in coping with additional stressors (Marmarosh, 2022). As additional stressors continue to overtax the systems, individuals with insecure attachments face the burden of prioritizing, appraising, and responding to information and may find themselves attending to information that is perceived as most salient, which may not be classroom materials necessary for achieving academic success. This aligns with the cognitive load theory (Sweller, 2011, as cited in Kalsi et al., 2022), which, in part, proposes that distractions in the environment prevent students from attending to learning material. Distractions may have different pathways to disruption. They may occur indirectly by requiring students to allocate attention resources to ignore distractions, such as the noises of cohabitants moving around the house while trying to study, or they may occur directly when they require that students identify if a distraction warrants an immediate threat perception, such as cry for help from someone in the household. Identifying risk and resilience in academic achievement through a lens of attachment and attention may provide an actionable approach to addressing diverse student needs.

CHALLENGES AND AREAS OF OPPORTUNITY DURING COVID-19

The pandemic has resulted in many organizational and educational systems adapting to online communication, but not all efforts have addressed the multiple and sometimes competing needs of students. Perceived effectiveness of the online environment may be further influenced by perceptions of engagement and attention. Kalsi et al. (2022) specifically addressed attention and interaction based on engagement within a learning environment (i.e., webcam interaction) by examining the impact of attention contagion, defined as the spread of inattentiveness between students in virtual classrooms when students have their webcams on. Based on the data, students having their webcams on does have an influence on attention contagion and engagement (Kalsi et al., 2022). Other factors (i.e., stating that "this lecture is important") also influence attention contagion. The most influential factor seems to be the attentiveness that is provided through webcam engagements.

Since the inception of the pandemic, some organizations implemented "Social Hours" as a means for associates to stay connected; this concept was not only beneficial for strengthening connections during the pandemic but also possibly impacting work performance (Parker et al., 2020). However, the sudden shift from face-to-face instruction to a fully remote learning environment, without regard to the student's adaptability and acceptability may have impacted their learning behavior. Student motivation to learn or ability to assimilate to a new learning method or environment may have been hindered by the sudden shift as it represented another threat to cognitive load in an already uncertain time (Mayer & Moreno, 2003). Additional evidence that unexpected changes to the learning environment impede learning appeared as Kalsi et al. (2022) found that students' academic performance was better within a hybrid environment compared to that of a fully online environment.

Connections and attachment impact work and academic performance, leading to the individual's overall self-confidence, self-esteem, and self-growth (Bernier et al., 2004; Bowlby, 1988; Kalsi et al., 2022). However, the connections and attachments must be mutual and intentional to be effective (Kalsi et al., 2022). Calma-Birling and Zelazo (2022) have indicated in their study that the COVID-19 pandemic has impacted the social lives of high school and college students. Furthermore, the researchers indicated that some studies reported increased emotional distress among adolescents and young adults, while other studies reported an increase followed by a decrease in emotional distress. The researchers were interested in the resilience factors that may impact high school and college students' emotional well-being (Calma-Birling & Zelazo, 2022), finding that conflict with parents is a risk factor that may influence negative affect and feeling less supported throughout the pandemic. Perceptions of support and anxiety may intersect, increasing cognitive load and reducing the ability to retain and apply new knowledge and information. Calma-Girling and Zelazo indicated many COVID-19 factors (i.e., staying home, not seeing friends in-person, parent conflict, taking online classes) influence negative affect (i.e., feeling disconnected, disoriented, lonely, stressed). However, mindfulness and self-compassion may be two factors associated with emotional well-being during the pandemic (Banks & Dillard, 2021). Although Calma-Girling and Zelazo indicated that conflict with parents and taking online classes were the least impacted by active, appreciative, determined, optimistic, and supported positive affect, affect had some significant impact on the other COVID-19 factors. The factors that the researchers indicated (mindfulness, self-compassion, self-control) provide a general reference to how attachment theory, cognitive load, and attention can influence an individual's emotion/well-being, which could eventually impact their behavior or performance.

Engagement, within the learning environment, is defined as an approach to motivate through collaboration. Based on Kuh (2001) and Dixson's (2010) assessment of how factors impact learning, engagement does not differ from motivation, self-regulation, interest, expectancy value, self-determination. collaboration, or class participation, they are all intertwined and correlated. The only limitation to a lack of engagement within the learning environment is the exclusion of a student's ability to learn based on their abilities or culture (Young, 2017); otherwise, there are no limitations regarding the application of engagement as a construct to classroom practice (Dixson, 2010; Kuh, 2001), especially within an online classroom setting. Rapanta et al. (2020) indicate that online teaching and learning should imply pedagogical content knowledge (PCK), used in designing and organizing to enhance learning experiences and creating distinctive learning environments through digital technologies. An instructor may be able to ensure this construct of learner-centeredness by eliminating cognitive distractions within the classroom environment (Dixson, 2010; Mayer & Moreno, 2003). Doing so provides a voice and elicits creativity from individuals in that environment. Therefore, the application of engagement within the course is necessary based on Kuh (2001) and Dixson's (2010) observations. Based on both studies, a classroom environment should be open to different approaches to student engagement activities that enhance the student's quality of learning to further motivate them and reduce distractions and stressors that can impede success. Ghanbari et al. (2020) indicate that high levels of cognitive load can negatively impact learning and performance. Kelleher (2022) has provided two areas of treatment that may be beneficial in reducing the cognitive load on students: "(1) Provide clear instructions for assignments, while improving the work environment, presenting information more effectively, and nurturing each student's sense of belonging, and (2) use scaffolds to reduce demands on working memory" (p. 1).

The constructs of engagement are very necessary to bridge the gap between theories that have been explored in relevance to real-life examples that may be meaningful to understanding students and their achievement. Students' self-regulated learning can be positively or negatively impacted by motivation and passion. Most importantly, self-regulated learning can be influenced by connection, trust, and reflection – where secure attachment provides a secure base to explore learning, the self-regulation-induced cognitive load may be tempered by connection and trust. Those factors then expand into an ability to think critically.

To confront existing boundaries in education, an educator must meet students where they are—in their own communities with their own experiences. Technology has increasingly impacted social interactions and education with many factors that continue to influence how individuals connect with one another and how they learn. A few of the factors that may influence social interactions and learning are both nature and nurture-based (i.e., the environment/surroundings, biology, family/friends, understanding/knowledge). This conceptual literature review analyzed attachment and attention and the impact of those factors on student achievement during the COVID-19 pandemic. Cognitive load theory provided a lens for examining the role of anxiety and distractors on attention. The appraisal of these stressors appears to coincide with attachment security, making students with insecure attachments vulnerable to the negative cognitive effects of disruption, distraction, and unexpected change that may, in turn, correspond with poorer academic outcomes. Through this lens, educators may be tasked with identifying solutions to promote engagement by establishing social connections and trust and reducing non-relevant stimuli that may compete with existing cognitive resources. Future research would benefit from exploring cultural and gender differences in attachment security, cognitive load, and student achievement, particularly during times of upheaval and social unrest.

FUTURE IMPLICATIONS

As a result of this literature review, the following implications emerged:

1. Cognitive load theory provides a framework for predicting relationships between attachment and attention during stressful times, including the COVID-19 pandemic.
2. Cognitive load explains demands on individuals' attention capacity. Additional demands on cognitive capacities reduce ability to attend to non-relevant stimuli, which may include coursework and course concepts.
3. Evidence from other universities demonstrates that offering social support opportunities for individuals who may not be securely attached creates engagement and a sense of belonging, particularly during stressful times, including potentially for students that have been impacted by COVID-19.

4. Marginalized groups may be more susceptible to cognitive load as a consequence of high stress and high uncertainty via the role of insecure attachment on attention.

CONCLUSION

This conceptual literature review sought to synthesize existing empirical research regarding attachment styles and cognitive load theories and how they impact attention and academic success during times of stress. Ainsworth and Bowlby's (1991) research parallels with the synthesis of this review. Bowlby's interest in attachment extended from observations of maternal separation, deprivation, and loss while Ainsworth's focus arose from Blatz's security theory, the two concepts merged into a theme of situational and biological context that provided a parent-child relationship perspective. Both theorists' interests concerned the process of restoration of secure attachment following distress or upheaval in the environment, the focus of this conceptual literature review.

As Bowlby (1988) has indicated, an analysis of the literature suggests that an optimal environment, inclusive to healthy interactions, results in healthier attachment patterns. The author continues to reiterate research which indicates that responsive, sensitive, and reflective caregiving from providers is imperative to the child's survival, as it could carry on with the child throughout their adulthood and influence how they relate to society. Bowlby (1982) shared four concepts that describe the formation of attachment patterns and were the foundation for this conceptual literature review: safe haven, secure base, proximity maintenance, and separation. In addition to the previously mentioned factors, cognitive load and attention were also analyzed to gain a greater understanding of how they are impacted by attachment. The research indicates that individuals are continuously impacted by increasing cognitive load (in the form of stressors, such as COVID-19) and these stressors may influence the attachment process. For example, anxiety may contribute to extraneous cognitive load, this can impact learning perceptions (Fredericks et al., 2021).

If there is ever a need to suddenly shift from face-to-face instruction to a fully remote learning environment, the student's adaptability/acceptability should be considered in relation to their learning behavior, this could impact their assimilation to a new learning method or environment as experienced during the COVID-19 pandemic. Rapanta et al. (2020) suggest that online teaching and learning should integrate pedagogical content knowledge (PCK), this process implements designing and organizing to enhance learning experiences that create distinctive learning environments through digital technologies. Marmarosh et al. (2020) also indicate the importance of cohesion, specifically when isolation is a factor such as due to the COVID-19 pandemic. Each of the factors that have been discussed throughout this conceptual literature review is relevant, however, Kalsi et al. (2022) suggest that the connections and attachments must be mutual and intentional to be effective. Additionally, Calma-Birling and Zelazo (2022) indicated that a student's connection could impact their emotional wellbeing, therefore, mindfulness, self-compassion, and self-control could all be influenced by their attachment, cognitive load, and attention that could influence their behavior or performance, especially during stressful times like the COVID-19 pandemic.

REFERENCES

Ainsworth, M. D. S., Blehar, M. C., Waters, E., & Wall, S. N. (2015). *Patterns of attachment: A psychological study of the Strange Situation* (Classic ed.). Psychology Press. (Original work published 1978) https://doi.org/10.4324/9780203758045

Ainsworth, M. S., & Bowlby, J. (1991). An ethological approach to personality development. *American Psychologist, 46*(4), 333–341. https://doi.org/10.1037/0003-066x.46.4.333

Banks, R., & Dillard, D. (2021). Coping and relaxation during the COVID-19 pandemic. *The UAGC Chronicle, 1*, 17–19. https://online.flippingbook.com/view/713129899/20/

Bartholomew, K., & Horowitz, L. M. (1991). Attachment styles among young adults: A test of a four-category model. *Journal of Personality and Social Psychology, 61*(2), 226–244. https://doi.org/10.1037/0022-3514.61.2.226

Bernier, A., Larose, S., Boivon, M., & Soucy, N. (2004). Attachment state of mind: Implications for adjustment to college. *Journal of Adolescent Research, 19*(6), 783–806. https://doi.org/10.1177/0743558403260096

Betabox. (2022). *North Carolina partners with Betabox Learning to address learning loss.* https://betaboxlearning.com/betabox-learning-partners-with-state-of-north-carolina-to-launch-pilot-program/

Bowlby, J. (1969). *Attachment and loss: Vol. 1. Attachment*. Basic Books.

Bowlby, J. (1982). *Attachment and loss: Vol. 1. Attachment* (2nd ed.). Basic Books.

Bowlby, J. (1988). *The secure base: Parent-child attachment and healthy human development*. Basic Books.

Cabrera, A. F., Nora, A., Terenzini, P. T., Pascarella, E., & Hagedorn, L. S. (1999). Campus racial climate and the adjustment of students to college: A comparison between White students and African American students. *Journal of Higher Education, 70*, 134 –160. doi:10.2307/2649125

Calma-Birling, D., & Zelazo, P. D. (2022). A network analysis of high school and college students' COVID-19-related concerns, self-regulatory skills, and affect. *American Psychologist, 77*(6), 727–742. https://doi.org/10.1037/amp0001023

Catherall, D. R. (2014). *Handbook of stress, trauma, and the family*. Routledge. https://doi.org/10.4324/9780203644157

Chandler, P., & Sweller, J. (1992). The split-attention effect as a factor in the design of instruction. *British Journal of Educational Psychology, 62*(2), 233–246. https://doi.org/10.1111/j.2044-8279.1992.tb01017.x

Claflin University. (2022). *Academic Success Center: Mission statement*. https://www.claflin.edu/about/vision-mission-and-guiding-principles

Clark, R. E., & Clark, V. P. (2010). From neo-behaviorism to neuroscience: Perspectives on the origins and future contributions of cognitive load research. In J. L. Plass, R. Moreno, & R. Brünken (Eds.), *Cognitive load theory* (pp. 203–228). Cambridge University Press. https://doi.org/10.1017/CBO9780511844744.012

Collins, N. L., & Feeney, B. C. (2000). A safe haven: An attachment theory perspective on support seeking and caregiving in intimate relationships. *Journal of Personality and Social Psychology, 78*(6), 1053–1073. https://doi.org/10.1037/0022-3514.78.6.1053

Cooper, M. L., Shaver, P. R., & Collins, N. L. (1998). Attachment styles, emotion regulation, and adjustment in adolescence. *Journal of Personality and Social Psychology, 74*(5), 1380–1397. https://doi.org/10.1037/0022-3514.74.5.1380

Darling-Hammond, L., Flook, L., Cook-Harvey, C., Barron, B., & Osher, D. (2020). Implications for educational practice of the science of learning and development. *Applied Developmental Science, 24*(2), 97–140, https://doi.org/10.1080/10888691.2018.1537791

Dewitte, M., & De Houwer, J. (2008). Proximity and distance motives in adult attachment. *European Journal of Personality, 22*(8), 1–20. https://doi.org/10.1002/per.696

Dixson, M. D. (2010). Creating effective student engagement in online courses: What do students find engaging? *Journal of the Scholarship of Teaching and Learning, 10*(2), 1–13

Duncan, G. J., Dowsett, C. J., Claessens, A., Magnuson, K., Huston, A. C., Klebanov, P., Pagani, L. S., Feinstein, L., Engel, M., Brooks-Gunn, J., Sexton, H., Duckworth, K., & Japel, C. (2007). School readiness and later achievement. *Developmental Psychology, 43*(6), 1428–1446.

Faris, M., & McCarroll, E. (2010). Crying babies: Answering the call of infant cries. *Texas Child Care, 35*(2), 14–21. https://www.childcarequarterly.com/fall10_story2a.html

Flaherty, S. C., & Sadler, L. S. (2011). A review of attachment theory in the context of adolescent parenting. *Journal of Pediatric Health Care, 25*(2), 114–121. https://doi.org/10.1016/j.pedhc.2010.02.005

Forrest, K. A. (2008). Attachment and attention in sport. *Journal of Clinical Sport Psychology, 2*, 242–257. https://doi.org/10.1123/jcsp.2.3.242

Fredericks, S., ElSayed, M., Hammad, M., Abumiddain, O., Istwani, L., Rabeea, A., Rashid-Doubell, F., & Bella, A. M. E. (2021). Anxiety is associated with extraneous cognitive load during teaching using high-fidelity clinical simulation. *Medical Education Online, 26*(1), 1994691. https://doi.org/10.1080/10872981.2021.1994691

Gay, G. (2000). *Culturally responsive teaching. Theory, research, and practice.* Teachers College Press.

Ghanbari, S., Haghani F., Barekatain M., & Jamali A. (2020). A systematized review of cognitive load theory in health sciences education and a perspective from cognitive neuroscience. *Journal of Education and Health Promotion, 28*(9), Article 76. https://doi.org/10.4103/jehp.jehp_643_19

Hazan, C., & Shaver, P. R. (1987). Romantic love conceptualized as an attachment process. *Journal of Personality and Social Psychology, 52*(3), 511–524. https://doi.org/10.1037/0022-3514.52.3.511

Hong, Y. R., & Park, J. S. (2012). Impact of attachment, temperament, and parenting on human development. *Korean Journal of Pediatrics, 55*(12), 449–454. https://doi.org/10.3345/kjp.2012.55.12.449

Jones, D. M., & Macken, W. J. (1993). Learning memory, and cognition. *Journal of Experimental Psychology, 19*(2), 369–381.

Kalsi, S. S., Forrin, N. D., Sana, F., MacLeod, C. M., & Kim, J. A. (2022). Attention contagion online: Attention spreads between students in a virtual classroom. *Journal of*

Applied Research in Memory and Cognition. Advance online publication. https://doi.org/10.1037/mac0000025

Kelleher, I. (2022, September 16). How to reduce the cognitive load on students during lessons. *Edutopia.* https://www.edutopia.org/article/how-reduce-cognitive-load-students-during-lessons/

Kuh, G. D. (2001). *The national survey of student engagement: Conceptual framework and overview of psychometric properties.* University of Indiana Center for Postsecondary Research.

Kurland, R. M., & Siegel, H. I. (2020). Attachment and college academic success: A four-year longitudinal study. *Open Journal of Social Sciences, 8*(12), 45–55. https://doi.org/10.4236/jss.2020.812005

Ladson-Billings, G. (2006). Yes, but how do we do it? Practicing culturally relevant pedagogy. In J. Landsman & C. Lewis (Eds.), *White teachers/diverse classrooms: Building inclusive schools, promoting high expectations and eliminating racism* (pp. 29–42). Stylus.

Larose, S., Bernier, A., & Tarabulsy, G. M. (2005). Attachment state of mind, learning dispositions, and academic performance during the college transition. *Developmental Psychology, 41*(1), 281–289.

Levesque, A. (2012). Influences of family of origin and relationship closeness on romantic attachment security. *Psi Chi Journal of Psychology Research, 17*(4), 145–153. https://doi.org/10.24839/2164-8204.jn17.4.145

Mahama, I., Asante, F. L., Mensah, J. K., Kwaw, R., Amponsah, M. A., Nartey, P., & Oopuk, E. B. (2021). Attached or not attached: Does different learning styles exist among students with or without sense of belonging amidst COVID-19? *Journal of Educational Technology and Online Learning, 4*(2), 175–193. https://doi.org/10.31681/jetol.905277

Marmarosh, C. L. (2022). Attachments, trauma, and COVID-19: Implications for leaders, groups, and social justice. *Group Dynamics: Theory, Research, and Practice, 26*(2), 85–102. https://doi.org/10.1037/gdn0000187

Marmarosh, C. L., Forsyth, D. R., Strauss, B., & Burlingame, G. M. (2020). The psychology of the COVID-19 pandemic: A group-level perspective. *Group Dynamics: Theory, Research, and Practice, 24*(3), 122–138. http://dx.doi.org/10.1037/gdn0000142

Mattanah, J. F., Hancock, G. R., & Brand, B. L. (2004). Parental attachment, separation, individuation, and college student adjustment: A structural equation analysis of mediational effects. *Journal of Counseling Psychology, 51*(2), 213–225. https://doi.org/10.1037/0022-0167.51.2.213

Mayer, R., & Moreno, R. (2003). Nine ways to reduce cognitive load in multimedia learning. *Educational Psychologist, 38*(1), 43–52.

Mayer, R., & Moreno, R. (2010). Techniques that reduce extraneous cognitive load and manage intrinsic cognitive load during multimedia learning. In J. L. Plass, R. Moreno, & R. Brünken (Eds.), *Cognitive load theory* (pp. 131–152). Cambridge University Press. https://doi.org/10.1017/CBO9780511844744.009

McWilliams, L. A., & Brodeur, D. (2016). Adult attachment and performance on an attentional orienting task. *Canadian Journal of Behavioural Science/Revue Canadienne des Sciences du Comportement, 48*(4), 286–295. http://dx.doi.org/10.1037/cbs0000055

Mikulincer, M., & Shaver, P. R. (2020). Broaden-and-build effects of contextually boosting the sense of attachment security in adulthood. *Current Directions in Psychological Science, 29*(1), 22–26. https://doi.org/10.1177/0963721419885997

Moreno, R., & Park, B. (2010). Cognitive load theory: Historical development and relation to other theories. In J. L. Plass, R. Moreno, & R. Brünken (Eds.), *Cognitive load theory* (pp. 9–28). Cambridge University Press. https://doi.org/10.1017/CBO9780511844744.003

Parker, K., Menasce-Horowitz, J., & Minkin, R. (2020). *How the Coronavirus outbreak has and hasn't changed the way Americans work*. Pew Research Center. https://www.pewresearch.org/social-trends/2020/12/09/how-the-coronavirus-outbreak-has-and-hasnt-changed-the-way-americans-work/

Patton, L. D., & McClure, M. L. (2009). Strength in the spirit: A qualitative examination of African American college women and the role of spirituality during college. *The Journal of Negro Education, 78*(1), 42–54. https://www.jstor.org/stable/25608717

PepsiCo Educational Technology. (n.d.). *PepsiCo Educational Technology*. https://community.duke.edu/program/pepsico-k-12-technology-mentor-program/

Ramsauer, B., Lotzin, A., Muhlhan, C., Romer, G., Tobias, N., Fonagy, P., & Powell, B. (2014). A randomized controlled trial comparing Circle of Security Intervention and treatment as usual as interventions to increase attachment security in infants of mentally ill mothers: Study protocol. *BMC Psychiatry, 14*(1), 24–35. https://doi.org/10.1186/1471-244x-14-24

Rapanta, C., Botturi, L., Goodyear, P., Guardia, L., & Koole, M. (2020). Online university teaching during and after the COVID-19 crisis: Refocusing teacher presence and learning activity. *Postdigital Science Education, 2*, 923–945. https://link.springer.com/article/10.1007/s42438-020-00155-y

Read, D. L., Clark, G. I., Rock, A. J., & Coventry, W. L. (2018). Adult attachment and social anxiety: The mediating role of emotion regulation strategies. *PLoS ONE, 13*(12), e0207514. https://doi.org/10.1371/journal.pone.0207514

Rose, S. (2013). The value of a college degree. *Change, 45*(6), 24–33. https://doi.org/10.1080/00091383.2013.842101

Sampaio, A., & Lifter, K. (2014). Neurosciences of infant mental health development: Recent findings and implications for counseling psychology. *Journal of Counseling Psychology, 61*(4), 513–520. https://doi.org/10.1037/cou0000035

Seufert, T. (2018). The interplay between self-regulation in learning and cognitive load, *Educational Research Review, 24*, 116–129. https://doi.org/10.1016/j.edurev.2018.03.004

Silva, C., Soares, I., & Esteves, F. (2012). Attachment insecurity and strategies for regulation: When emotion triggers attention. *Scandinavian Journal of Psychology, 53*, 9–16. https://doi.org/10.1111/j.1467-9450.2011.00924.x

Sperling, M. B., & Berman, W. H. (Eds.). (1994). *Attachment in adults: Clinical and developmental perspectives*. Guilford Press.

Stern, J. A., Barbarin, O., & Cassidy, J. (Eds.). (2022). Attachment perspectives on race, prejudice, and anti-racism: Introduction to the special issue. *Attachment & Human Development, 24*(3), 253–259. https://doi.org/10.1080/14616734.2021.1976920

Sweller, J. (1988). Cognitive load during problem solving: Effects on learning. *Cognitive Science, 12*, 257–285.

U.S. Bureau of Labor Statistics. (2020a, April 3). *Economic situation news release* [USDL-20-0521]. https://www.bls.gov/news.release/archives/empsit_04032020.htm

U.S. Bureau of Labor Statistics. (2020b, May 8). *Economic situation news release* [USDL-20-0815]. https://www.bls.gov/news.release/archives/empsit_05082020.htm

U.S. Bureau of Labor Statistics. (2022, July). *Employed persons who teleworked or worked at home for pay at any time in the last 4 weeks because of the coronavirus pandemic by selected characteristics* [Table]. https://www.bls.gov/cps/effects-of-the-coronavirus-COVID-19-pandemic.htm

Vaughn, L. M., Battle, J. V., Taylor, T., & Dearman, L. (2009). Learning styles and the relationship to attachment styles and psychological symptoms in college women. *College Student Journal, 43*(3), 723–735. https://www.thefreelibrary.com/Learning+styles+and+the+relationship+to+attachment+styles+and...-a0206687065

Waters, E., Bretherton, I., & Vaughn, B. E. (2015). Preface. In Ainsworth, M. D. S., Blehar, M. C., Waters, E., & Wall, S. N., *Patterns of attachment: A psychological study of the Strange Situation* (Classic edition, pp. x–xxxvi). Psychology Press. https://doi.org/10.4324/9780203758045

Wiseman, H., Mayseless, O., & Sharabany, R. (2006). Why are they lonely? Perceived quality of early relationships with parents, attachment, personality predispositions and loneliness in first-year university students. *Personality and Individual Difference, 40*, 237–248.

Xing, F., Malik, M., Dershewitz, S., Hedlund, S., Gedo, P., Woods, K. M., & Marmarosh, C. (2023). Online supervision during COVID-19: Supervisor's perspective during a time of crisis. *Professional Psychology: Research and Practice*. Advance online publication. https://doi.org/10.1037/pro0000532

Young, J. R. (2017). Vervistic instruction as a vehicle to mathematics competency for African American girls. In *Cultivating achievement, respect, and empowerment (CARE) for African American girls in prek-12 settings* (pp. 69–90). https://www.researchgate.net/publication/313143920_Vervistic_instruction_as_a_vehicle_to_mathematics_competency_for_African_American_girls

CHAPTER 12

THE IMPACT OF THE CORONAVIRUS COVID-19 GLOBAL PANDEMIC ON K–12 STUDENTS, TEACHERS, AND SCHOOLS IN THE U.S.

Daniel W. Wong
Professor Emeritus, Mississippi State University

Lucy Wong Hernandez
University of Southern Maine

INTRODUCTION

The effects of the COVID-19 global pandemic both in the U.S. and globally will be felt for many years to come. This unprecedented health-related pandemic kept families sheltered in place in their homes for months. As the result of this unprecedented event, relationships with the government, the outside world, our communities, and each other had to be reoriented. In comparison, although COVID-19,

Instructional Survival in the Midst of the Perfect Storm:
The Experiences of K–12 Teachers During the COVID-19 Global Pandemic, pages 213–232.

Published under exclusive licence by Emerald Publishing Limited
ISBNs: 978-1-83708-502-6 HB, 978-1-83708-503-3 PB,
978-1-83708-504-0 EPDF, 978-1-83708-505-7 EPUB

January 2020, and the terrorist attack of September 11, 1991, were different crises, their impact on society will linger as tragic, defining historical moments. Unfortunately, society must be aware that tragic events like these unforgettable experiences could happen again.

The consequences of COVID-19 in the U.S. caused schools to be closed, and work responsibilities were performed remotely in an effort to prevent the spread of the COVID-19 coronavirus. Parents, teachers, and schools struggled to keep children healthy and occupied. Social-emotional skills are at the core of all meaningful learning and are critical to overall well-being. While children may not always have access to ideal instruction for their academic subjects, they can still learn essential emotional literacy skills that will benefit them.

School-age children between 6 and 12 and teenagers who attend middle schools and high schools are incredibly vulnerable to these unexpected life-threatening events, and most likely, they will remember these experiences forever. Teaching them how to endure a crisis and to be resilient may be the most important lesson that they ever learn (Wong et al., 2021). According to the Centers for Disease Control and Prevention (CDC, 2024), parents, family members, school staff, and other trusted adults can play an essential role in helping children to make sense of what they hear in a way that is honest, accurate, and that minimizes anxiety and fear.

The Impacts of the COVID-19 Pandemic on K–12 Learners

During the height of the pandemic in 2020, the CDC created specific guidance to help parents, teachers, school district leaders, and school counselors converse with children about the COVID-19 pandemic. The CDC guidance included: 1) to remain calm and reassuring and remember that children will react to both what you say and how you speak; 2) to make yourself available to listen and to talk to and to be sure that children know that they can come to you when they have questions and to avoid language that might blame others and lead to stigma; 3) to remember that viruses can make anyone sick, regardless of a person's race or ethnicity and to avoid making assumptions about who might have COVID-19; 4) to reduce the amount of screen time focused on COVID-19 because too much information on one topic can lead to anxiety; 5) to provide information that is honest and accurate and give children information that is truthful and appropriate for the age and developmental level of the child and 6) to talk to children about how some stories on COVID-19 on the Internet and social media may be based on rumors and inaccurate information.

It is entirely understandable to be anxious and worried when we are trying to cope with crisis and uncertainty, but how we manage that anxiety has a significant impact on our children. In a crisis, keeping worries in check will help the students and their families navigate this uncertain situation as efficiently as possible. Many schools had to use Skype, FaceTime, and Zoom to stay connected with the students and their parents. This communication can help children feel connected to their schools and classmates and mitigate some of the stress from being away from school and friends. Communicating with children reasonably is the best way to help them understand, and parents and counselors should be mindful of what kind of information they want to share. Experts highly recommend that if teachers find themselves feeling anxious and nervous, they should try to avoid showing these feelings to their students. When feeling overwhelmed and exhausted, they should take a deep breath, step away to take a moment to think, and collect their composure to resume their tasks (Child Mind Institute, 2020).

The Pandemic Necessitates Instructional Methods

The COVID-19 pandemic forced teachers to implement new methods and new tools for remote teaching and forced students to learn through remote learning. This new method of teaching and learning was troubling for most. There was less teacher-student interaction, and the students with the greatest need often received the most minor lesson instructions. These dynamics had profound implications as schools planned to reopen the following semester. However, although the picture of diminished instruction was clear, this hopeful plan was not simple. Academic learning, at any level, during an emergency pandemic is complex and contradictory.

Some students received live video lessons for hours daily and stayed in close contact with their teachers, while others received no real-time instruction and heard from their teachers maybe once a week. Many teachers worked 12-hour days, while many others worked less than they used to. Some parents angrily demanded more robust academic support during home learning, while others demanded relief, saying they could not handle home-schooling and other obligations during the brutal pandemic. This situation created questions between teachers and educational leaders: How can they maintain high-quality instruction while providing the flexibility that families need to survive a national crisis? That is a critical question of whether remote learning or some version of it could continue in many school districts next semester due to the coronavirus.

Interviews with teachers, however, surface a host of dynamics that have reduced teachers' work hours and led them to focus on review instead of new teaching materials. Some of these actions arose from state and district directives. Retrieved from https://www.edweek.org/research-center/

This edited book "Instructional Survival in the Midst of the Perfect Storm: The Experiences of K–12 Teachers During the COVID-19 Global Pandemic," has compiled a variety of different research studies conducted by committed scholars in an effort to investigate the impact of the COVID-19 pandemic on K–12 students, parents, teachers, school administrators, and stakeholders.

Elementary Teachers' Instructional Experiences: Teaching Remotely and Concurrently During COVID-19

As presented in this book, Chapter 2 entitled *Instructional Survival: A Qualitative Case Study of Elementary Teachers' Experiencing: Teaching Remotely and Concurrently during COVID-19* Ladendorf (Chapter 2) conducted a qualitative case study to investigate the experiences of elementary school teachers as they navigated both remote and concurrent instruction during the 2020–2021 school year.

This qualitative case study aimed to understand the lived experiences of elementary teachers teaching remotely during the COVID-19 pandemic. The following research questions guided this study: 1) How did elementary teachers describe the impact that COVID-19 had on their work in and out of the classroom? Moreover, 2) What observed and described changes did elementary teachers make during remote and concurrent instruction due to COVID-19?

Three elementary teachers were recruited for this study. The procedure for this study was that these teachers had to complete two interviews and were observed three times during remote and concurrent instruction. The data was analyzed over three cycles for emergent themes. The impact COVID-19 had on teachers fell into two categories: instructional and emotional effects. Instructionally, teachers utilized previously created lessons and adapted them to deliver to a digital video format. Teachers did not incorporate much new technology and relied on teacher-led instruction. The instructional impact was connected to the emotional effects that COVID-19 had on these teachers. They experienced shock, fear, and isolation while navigating remote instruction. Teachers focused on instructional survival throughout the year, measuring their success by their ability to survive to the last day of school. Recommendations for remote and blended teaching were explored, and lessons can be gleaned from these three teachers' navigation of emergency remote instruction.

The results of this study established emergent themes that fell into two categories: instructional impacts and emotional impacts of COVID-19 on elementary school teachers. Instructional impacts focused on how the teachers approached their instruction during remote and concurrent teaching. These themes also explored the types of resources and instructional practices teachers utilized throughout the 2020–2021 school year. Emotional impacts focused on how the teachers reacted emotionally to COVID-19, their teaching situation, and how their students adapted to this situation.

Educators' Burnout and Career Dissatisfaction

Educators' job burnout and many leaving their profession have been well-researched and documented. Many K–12 teachers considered quitting or resigning from their academic position after the 2021–22 school year, during the pandemic and the post-pandemic years. According to the Merrimack College Teacher Survey (2022), a nationally representative poll of more than 1,300 teachers conducted by the EdWeek Research Center (2022) in January and February of 2022, 20 percent of respondents indicated that they were "very likely" to leave the teaching profession within the next two years, and an additional 24 percent reported being "fairly likely" to do so (Retrieved from: https://www.edweek.org/research-center/reports/teaching-profession-in-crisis-national-teacher-survey.

In Chapter 3, Camp et al.'s chapter entitled *Educators' Job Burnout and Intentions to Leave During the COVID-19 Pandemic*, (Chapter 3) investigated nationally representative samples of teachers and school leaders from the RAND American Educator Panels to document K–12 teachers' and leaders' levels of concern about job-related burnout and stated consideration of leaving the profession. This study also investigated factors associated with teachers' and administrators' significant concerns about job burnout and teachers' considerations about leaving their jobs. Approaching retirement age (being 55 or older), changing instructional modes, hybrid teaching, COVID-19-related health concerns, and high levels of job burnout all appeared to be significant predictors of teachers' probability of considering leaving or retiring from teaching. Health concerns and switching instruction modes were also associated with higher levels of concern about teacher burnout. This research study indicates a potential disconnect between factors that affect administrators and those that affect teachers. Leaders, especially those in larger education systems, may not be acutely aware of the impacts that shifting modes of instruction have on teachers and thus underestimate the stress that doing so puts on teachers. The analysis from the first full academic year (2020 –2021) in the pandemic raises concerns about potential increases in teacher turnover due to high levels of job burnout, which aligns with recent reports of increased teacher turnover entering the third academic year during the pandemic. The survey research results could be used to monitor teachers' considerations to leave and levels of job burnout during times of crisis and to help inform timely strategies for better-retaining teachers.

The analysis from this study indicated that the first full academic year of the pandemic raised concerns about a potential increase in teacher turnover because of high levels of job burnout during the pandemic. Although teacher turnover remained relatively stable during the first two pandemic school years, recent reports from several states show an uptick in teacher turnover entering the third pandemic academic year 2022–2023. The lasting impacts of any changes in teacher turnover are yet to be seen; however, even low rates of teacher turnover could be problematic if concentrated in areas with teacher shortages (e.g., rural areas or in specific fields like math, science, or special education). Finally, higher levels of job dissatisfaction could affect teacher effectiveness and harm student academic progress even if teachers decide not to leave.

The Effects of the COVID-19 Pandemic on Teachers' Stress, Burnout, and Mental Health

In Chapter 4—*A Perfect Storm: COVID-19 as a Demotivating Factor Contributing to Teacher Stress, Burnout, and Mental Health*, Jones et al. (Chapter 4) conducted a study based on the data derived from the second phase of a mixed-methods study examining the impact of COVID-19 on teachers. At the end of 2021 and the beginning of 2022, a survey was administered to 3,982 participants. Following the study, focus groups and 25 semi-structured interviews were conducted. The survey consisted of the Oldenburg Burnout Inventory (OBI; Demerouti et al., 2003). Perceived Stress Scale (PSS; Cohen et al.,1983), and PHQ-8 (Patient Health Questionnaire depression scale; Kroenke & Spitzer, 2002). The investigation of how COVID-19 impacted teachers indicates a significant rise in teacher stress, burnout, and issues related to mental health. Data from the PHQ-8 indicated moderate levels of depression across the participants. In contrast, OBI data found above-average burnout levels within both subscales of disengagement and exhaustion and a moderate rise in stress levels from the PSS. Data from qualitative questionnaires, focus groups, and interviews support these findings, with participants identifying the following factors as contributing significantly to their mental health: unmanageable increases in workload, inconsistency in school/district policies, decreases in teacher autonomy, and lack of support for student's mental health. According to these findings, both challenges and opportunities were identified for state legislatures, boards of education, and local school districts to assist teachers and to ameliorate experiencing demotivation. There is a strong emphasis that teachers' needs must be met. It would benefit administrators and teachers to work together to solve school issues post-pandemic and in the future. Teachers are with students all day, so their knowledge and perspective on solving problems within the schools should be respected and utilized. Teachers also need more time to plan curriculum, grade students' work, and attend professional development opportunities. A four-day school week was suggested to serve students best and to provide teachers with the necessary planning time. As students continue to exhibit the trauma, they experienced both during and before the pandemic, teachers need increased administrative and parental support that assists in the teachers' work with students. Teachers' working conditions will impact students' learning conditions, making it a priority for local district officials to improve. Teacher retention must be necessary for federal, state, and local leaders to improve. While much attention is paid to attracting new teachers to the field, working to retain current teachers will go much further. To attract and retain teachers, the federal government may consider providing additional grants for teachers who remain in the profession for at least five years. The teaching profession is not among the highest-paid fields, but in many states, the credentialed career does not even garner a livable wage to support a family. Increasing retirement contributions would also retain educators. It was highlighted that many states increase individuals' contributions, increase qualifying years, and reduce monthly payment amounts, which leads teachers to leave the profession since they will not see the pensions they were once promised. States should also improve the health-care benefits and work to reduce teacher costs. While these challenges present opportunities, we owe it to teachers to change the profession to one that is respected, adequately compensated, and autonomous. Until these changes are made, we will see demotivated teachers who want to leave the profession.

Elementary Teacher Morale and Mental Health Following the COVID-19 Pandemic

As schools entered the 2021–2022, teachers were asked to close the learning loss gap, maintain the same standards as a typical school year, implement COVID-19 safety protocols, and teach to grade-level standards. The study by Marshall et al. (Chapter 5) used the theoretical framework of teacher demoralization to explore teacher morale and mental health at the end of the 2021–2022 school year. The sample included 459 PK–12 elementary teachers from across the United States. The results found that teacher autonomy and administrative support significantly influenced teacher morale and mental health, and teacher morale and mental health suffered during the crisis. This study found that administrative support, teacher autonomy, and parent support all positively predicted teacher morale and mental health. Teachers receiving more support from parents and school leaders reported higher morale and better mental health. These results are significant as states and schools continue to see an exodus of teachers leaving the profession. School leaders can use the results from the current study as a starting point to support teachers and their well-being moving forward.

There are some limitations associated with this study that are worth noting. First, the Phase 1 survey participants were drawn from a voluntary sample, mostly from social media. Teachers who frequent education-related social media sites may differ in essential ways from those who do not. Those who saw the invitation to participate in this research and decided to participate may differ from those who elected not to do so. The same limitations apply since Phase 2 participants were a subset of the Phase 1 sample. Additionally, it is possible that teachers who elected to participate in a focus group also differed systematically from those who completed the survey but opted not to participate in the second phase of this work. Second, a strength of this work is the triangulation of three types of data from two sources (survey quantitative, survey open-ended qualitative, and focus group qualitative). Participants responded similarly in the closed-response items comprising scales, in the open-ended item generically asking teachers about the challenges they faced, and in the focus groups that were conducted, strengthening our findings' validity.

The researchers identified that the teacher morale model they tested explained only about 30% of the variance, and their mental health model explained approximately 20%. Both models suggest that other factors contributing to teacher morale and mental health are worth exploring. The researchers recommended that future work attempt to understand other factors that impact teachers in these ways, especially those within a school leader's locus of control. Furthermore, it is essential to protect dedicated planning time for teachers, allowing them opportunities to plan the lessons, communicate with other stakeholders, and get a break during the day. Finally, school leaders must proactively ensure that teachers are compensated. Teachers dedicated extensive time to teaching throughout the pandemic without receiving adequate compensation. School leaders and policymakers must prioritize appropriate compensation for teachers if they wish to retain them in the classroom beyond the pandemic.

Social Support, COVID-19, and Teachers' Stress

Teachers have experienced heightened stress during the COVID-19 pandemic, with a significant number of the workforce resigning since the pandemic's onset. The pandemic has presented teachers with additional stressors such as lesson conversion, health concerns, increased negative emotions, and social distancing, likely increasing attrition.

In Chapter 6, entitled *Social Support and COVID-19: How U.S. K–12 Teachers Were Impacted by Gratitude and Mentoring During the COVID-19 Pandemic*, Mosley et al. (Chapter 6) conducted a quantitative study on teacher support by conducting modified grounded theory research to explore, resulting in 23 participants of varying vulnerability to stress based on a prior study phase. Forty teachers were recruited from a stratified random sample of 300 public school teachers in a large southwestern district.

Although there is a high correlation between teacher's occupational health and pandemic-related stress, not all teachers experienced pandemic-related stress in the same way, nor did their stress present uniform impacts on their occupational health. The current study aimed to understand how social support experiences during the COVID-19 pandemic assisted teachers working during this turbulent time. Findings revealed a modified grounded theory of how social support sustains teachers and sustains them in the turbulent pandemic episode. Research conducted before the COVID-19 pandemic showed the promise of practices facilitating social support in education, such as beginning teacher mentoring. However, the disruptions due to social distancing during the pandemic posed questions about how previously identified support practices may persist in the face of new working environments. This study presented evidence that social support for teachers can be given and received in the face of ever-changing and uncertain workplace demands. Such support enables teachers to sustain their work. Social support was particularly salient for teachers during this challenging time, as they felt they were risking their lives each day and receiving little concern from others for their well-being.

School leaders must prioritize teacher well-being when navigating broad changes or new obstacles, such as coping with the impact and necessary changes due to the pandemic. The current study's findings illustrate how the presence of social support, especially in the form of gratitude and mentoring, is a viable way to ensure that teachers can sustain their jobs in the face of new challenges such as the COVID-19 pandemic.

Teacher Self-Efficacy During the Pandemic

A teacher's belief in their capability to engage students in learning, even when students are difficult or unmotivated, has been labeled "teacher self-efficacy" in the context of social learning and social cognitive theory developed by Albert Bandura. Research shows that teachers with high levels of self-efficacy are more open to new teaching methods, set more challenging goals, and adjust their teaching strategies when faced with difficulties, especially during complex and challenging times, like teaching during the pandemic.

In Chapter 7 *Teacher Self-Efficacy During COVID-19: A Qualitative Study on Experienced High School Teachers*, Conley (Chapter 7) conducted a qualitative study focused on teachers' experiences within the four sources that have been observed to impact self-efficacy, including mastery experiences, vicarious experiences, social persuasion, and physiological states (Usher & Pajares, 2006). Seven teachers with at least ten or more years of experience in a public high school were interviewed for this research. This study observed that each teacher was impacted, to varying degrees, by each of the four sources of self-efficacy between March 2020 and June 2022. The most impacted sources of self-efficacy among all participants were mastery experiences, social persuasion, and personal physiological state. This study's findings suggested that the amount of support from schools and leadership played a significant role in how well teachers could regain their self-efficacy to where they were pre-COVID-19. In addition, teachers with an adaptable growth mindset toward teaching were more likely to rebound from self-efficacy loss quickly. Based on these findings, school districts should evaluate what kind of support they provide to teachers pre- and- post-COVID-19. While some schools and communities could turn quickly to virtual classes, other schools had more difficulty reaching that point due to internet connectivity issues and a lack of technology devices for students (United Nations Educational, Scientific and Cultural Organization (UNESCO), 2020a). School closures prompted immediate concerns, including learning loss, low-income students not receiving meals, and students being home alone or caring for siblings. Moreover, long-term concerns about teachers and how they adapted to the changes are still being identified two years later. This study seeks to observe and explore COVID-19's impact on teachers' self-efficacy beliefs as educators. A specific focus was on experienced high school teachers with at least ten or more years of teaching experience when the pandemic began. While this current study provided several insights into how experienced teachers adjusted during COVID-19, there are many directions where this research can continue. Future COVID-19-related research could be conducted on how teachers' self-efficacy changed among teachers with five or fewer years of experience. This study suggested that emotional flexibility is a skill that can be developed through mindfulness training and strategies that help workers focus on what is important to them and not on negative behaviors in the workplace. This emotional flexibility training could be valuable for teachers rebuilding their self-efficacy beliefs and combating a fixed mindset. With many teachers leaving the profession, it is essential to take a closer look at what teachers went through during these past few years to hopefully prevent teachers from leaving education due to burnout, a consequence of low self-efficacy. This study suggests that classroom experience is often insufficient to protect teachers from emotional and mental stressors in their workplace. The teachers who ended the interviews saying they were at the prime of their careers were the same teachers who said they received support when needed. Even though it appears that the worst of COVID-19 changes are in the past, schools still must take the time to evaluate the needs of their teachers and observe the sources that impact their self-efficacy, including mastery experiences, vicarious experiences, social persuasion, and physiological state. By reviewing and considering teacher's self-efficacy, school districts can provide teachers with the support they need to adapt and grow as educators. If students going through school hope to get a quality education, they must be taught by confident, skilled, and supported educators.

How the Pandemic Impacted Students with Special Needs and Their Parents

The COVID-19 pandemic impacted school systems and students in the U.S. and worldwide. It shut down schools without the necessary preparation for teachers to plan and organize online teaching, leaving students and parents struggling to figure out how to continue their children's education without the support of school facilities. Further, maintaining daily routines was challenging for all students, especially those with special needs. These students who needed routine and additional support found themselves without routines, and those who needed additional support in adaptive behaviors were at a loss. This period of schools being shuttered left students with a void in their regular learning opportunities. As COVID-19 interfered with schooling, teachers were concerned with how remote learning and even the results of missing time in school would impact students with special needs.

As the pandemic continued in 2021–22, new evidence on the experiences of students with disabilities has raised more challenges and provided few concrete answers. The impact on students with disabilities during the pandemic deserves more studies. We still know very little about how the pandemic has impacted academic, behavioral, social-emotional, and post-school outcomes for students with disabilities. It is evident that less than a third of rigorous analyses on the pandemic's academic impacts disaggregated outcomes for students with disabilities. When research outcomes are presented, students with disabilities are often treated as a monolith, which likely masks critical variation in outcomes depending on students' intensity of special education services, race, socioeconomic status, and English learner status.

What we know about students' experiences during the pandemic suggests that the pandemic will exacerbate existing inequities. Questions around compensatory services, delays in and questions surrounding eligibility for special education services, disrupted transition planning, and reliance on underqualified educators are complicating efforts to accelerate support for students with disabilities. (Retrieved from Center for Reinventing Public Education (CRPE) 2022. https://crpe.org/)

As discussed in Chapter 8, Wood and Wood (Chapter 8) conducted a sequential mixed-methods study to gather teachers' perceptions of how the pandemic and resulting loss of in-person education impacted students with special needs and how it might have also affected parent involvement. The study used a sequential mixed-methods approach within one high school in a Midwestern state.

This sequential mixed-methods study conducted in one Midwestern high school with special education teachers utilized a mixed-methods approach to determine the teachers' perceptions and concerns regarding the impact COVID-19 had on their students and the lasting results they now face. The quantitative data focused on how the school provided needed services and whether this shutdown created any positives. In the qualitative analysis, three themes emerged. These themes focused on loss of academic skills, lack of student accountability, access to services such as the Internet, and lack of attendance, attention, and social-emotional stability. Not only did the teachers feel that their students had lost ground academically, but they also found that their students had forgotten how to "do school." This rapid move to distance education surprised most schools because policies were not in place or designed for teachers to work remotely, nor were students or families prepared for this type of school. Further, teachers were not prepared with the pedagogical structures, plans, or expectations for students, and communication systems were not in place to provide quality communication with parents, students, and staff (Hood, 2020). The problem focus was whether students with special needs exhibited gaps in their learning and how losing months of in-person instruction affected their ability to function well academically, socially, and emotionally in the school setting upon their return to school. Further, the present study sought to investigate how this gap in school learning may have changed parental involvement.

The research questions that guided the investigation included the following: 1. How well did the school provide services to students with special needs during the COVID-19 global pandemic? 2. What changes have teachers seen in students with special needs following COVID-19 as they returned to school? 3. How has the switch to technology impacted parent involvement? Additionally, based on the findings from this study, it is clear that schools must be better prepared for using technology if a future pandemic or disaster should occur. With the changing climate issues, it would appear more likely that a disaster could happen, causing schools to close. Thus, they must be better prepared and not caught without plans and processes, including an online curriculum and teacher preparation. Further, more research is needed to investigate the long-term effects of the pandemic.

Further, future research should be conducted to determine the best and most appropriate way to train teachers to address the social-emotional needs of students and what curricula provide the best support. With the findings from this research, a follow-up study could interview teachers at schools using the most appropriate social-emotional training and curriculum to gather their perceptions of the effects on students. While teachers have begun to recognize those areas where schools have not risen to the level of service needed by the students who experienced the gap in their academics and social-emotional development, schools and districts will also need to investigate how to best provide services that have been missing during the pandemic. Changes must begin if schools and districts are to graduate students who can become independent citizens. To remedy the issues created and left behind by the COVID-19 pandemic and the shuttering of schools, it will take a joint effort among teachers, administrators, parents, and the community to ensure that students regain what was lost.

Post-COVID-19: Cognitive, Psychological, and Motivational States

The COVID-19 pandemic will continue to impact educational services for a considerably long time. Students, teachers, educators, and other stakeholders continue to struggle with the pandemic's permanent effects. Ayyildiz and Yilmaz conducted a study entitled *Researching the Entangled: Post-COVID-19 Cognitive, Psychological and Motivational States* (Chapter 9). This research aimed to investigate the opinions of students and teachers at the high school and the tertiary level while investigating some key variables. A combination (variation) design, one of the mixed research methods, was deployed in this regard. This research employed a random sampling method, including 428 high school students, 189 teachers of different branches, 673 university students, and 105 faculty members. The Montreal Cognitive Assessment (MoCA), Zung Self-Rating Depression Scale (SDS), Generalized Anxiety Disorder Screener (GAD-7), Motivation Scale (M.S.), and Semi-Structured Interview Questions were utilized as data collection instruments.

The data obtained within the scope of the research were analyzed using SPSS 25, AMOS 24, and The PROCESS macro for the SPSS program. In addition, path analyses produced by the current study researchers were also referred to. In the end, it was determined that the cognitive test results of high school students were low, and their motivation results were affected by the variables of depression and anxiety. These variations appear to create significant differences in variables such as gender, receiving psychological support, providing mentor support, adaptation to the post-pandemic process, digital competence, and infrastructure competence. Since the outbreak of the COVID-19 pandemic, individuals have been experiencing cognitive, psychological, motivational, and other severe challenges of varying nature. Long-term fatigue has arguably led to numerous permanent and characteristic problems. Individuals with COVID-19 have started to show persistent and unknown symptoms such as mental confusion, muscle pain, weakness, learning difficulties, cognitive impairment, depression, anxiety, myalgia, fatigue, insomnia, and mood disorders. In addition to these challenges, low energy and brain exercise are frequently encountered through concentration problems, disorientation, inability to focus, and difficulty finding the right words while communicating. Long-term psychological, cognitive, or adverse mental health conditions have resulted. Thus, the effects of the COVID-19 pandemic have negatively affected different spheres of human lives. Amongst the spheres in question, education has a unique place considering its societal connections along with its links to the development of persons at a rather micro level and with its links to development at a relatively more macro level. Education is a service that must be accomplished continuously and consistently, particularly considering the links to several areas. Nevertheless, the COVID-19 global pandemic has hindered the provision of relevant services and the total fulfillment of related tasks for a long time. The current day reveals that plentiful measures have been lifted for the COVID-19 pandemic, vaccination has become a part of everyday routines, and countries worldwide have begun to adjust themselves to the "life after the pandemic." However, it is worth reiterating that the pandemic does not only have impacts related to health. The struggle with the permanent traces left by the pandemic on students, teachers, educators, higher education organizations, and other institutions remains highly visible.

The study found that specific challenges were more prevalent among high school students during the post-COVID-19 pandemic. Regarding the motivational variables, this research shows that high school students can adapt to life after the pandemic, and the variables of depression and anxiety impact students and instructors; motivation (at any level) under all circumstances. The pandemic affected individuals at different levels and on different subjects cognitively, psychologically, and motivationally, creating several overall challenges.

Teachers' Perceptions of Their Preparation and Support from Their School Districts and Principals

A qualitative study was conducted by Menchaca and Garcia entitled *K–12 Teacher Support During the COVID-19 Pandemic* (Chapter 10) with forty-two K–12 teachers who are also graduate students enrolled in the Master of Education Principal program in a Texas Hispanic Serving Institution. This qualitative study aimed to discover teachers' perceptions of their preparation and support from their school districts and campus principals during the COVID-19 pandemic. This study is based on the theoretical framework of social support systems. Studies on social support theories and models have been prevalent in academic studies since the 1980s, and social support is the perception and actuality that one is cared for, has assistance from other people, and is most popularly part of a supportive team or network. This study used a qualitative research design that gives meaning to social phenomena and makes it understandable for the readers.

After analyzing the focus group interview data, Menchaca and Garcia identified the following three themes: inadequate preparation for online teaching, technological support, and social/emotional support. *Inadequate Preparation for Teaching Online:* indicates that having an adequate understanding and command of all the tools teachers use in the classroom is essential. Effective professional development for teachers should be sustained over time and connected to classroom instruction while requiring active teacher participation. Online teaching teacher training ranges from official certification courses to professional ones. Districts knew the urgency of creating workshops for teachers and determining their technological gaps to determine how to proceed. The need for sustained training in both the pedagogical and technical areas is essential for effective teaching. *The Need for Social/Emotional Support:* regarding social or emotional support, sources of support can be informal, such as with families or close friends, or more formal, such as with colleagues or community organizations. The source of social support is essential in coping with different or demanding situations, like the pandemic. Of the different relationships studied, teachers' and school personnel's support is more vital than other support relationships. This could be because teachers and school personnel spend at least 7 to 8 hours a day in the same environment for about five days a week. Consequently, these relationships tend to be more stable than relationships with family. *The Need for Technological Support:* teachers require a support system for learning modern technologies such as Learning Management Systems. Online learning has been a concept that has profoundly affected K–12 students. Since the early 1990s, distance teaching via the Internet has become a global trend, and software, hardware, and educational training have been evolving. "Nouns related to e-learning have emerged, such as online learning, distance teaching, digital learning, mobile learning, and more recently, massive open online courses (MOOCs) have shown a trend of learning via the Internet."

Menchaca and Garcia concluded that all stakeholders must remember that the duty of teaching students with technology does not solely rely upon the classroom teachers. A support network of instructional trainers, instructional technology support staff, and principals must be in place for instructional, technical, and social/emotional support during a crisis, such as a pandemic. Any new or existing technologies will require adequate and sustainable professional development from support staff who are teachers. Professional development must be ongoing and available throughout the school year and be made available to teachers before frustration sets in. The same can be said about technical support for teachers. School districts must ensure that both hardware and software are running optimally and that networks are properly functioning and kept so that instruction can be conducted without downtime. Finally, social/emotional support should be provided by peers and leaders. Leaders should be available to listen empathically and to empower teachers. Teachers can be motivated and supported by listening empathically and empowering teachers. Messages that empower teachers will often result in self-confidence and inspire teachers and other staff to take the initiative in moving forward with online learning.

A LITERATURE REVIEW ON ATTACHMENT, ATTENTION, AND ACHIEVEMENT DURING THE COVID-19 PANDEMIC

In Banks et al's. (Chapter 11) chapter entitled *Attachment, Attention, and Achievement During the COVID-19 Pandemic: A Conceptual Literature Review*, the overarching goal of this conceptual literature review was to investigate and synthesize the existing body of empirical research at the intersection of attachment theory and cognitive load theory. This research aimed to identify theoretical relationships between attachment styles, attention mechanisms, and academic achievement, specifically focusing on how these dynamics manifested during heightened stress and uncertainty, such as the COVID-19 pandemic.

The authors' objectives were to provide a comprehensive overview of attachment theory, emphasizing its development, various attachment styles, and its foundational role in shaping individuals, emotional responses, and interpersonal relationships. Also important was to explore cognitive load theory and its implications for attentional processes, emphasizing how cognitive load and attachment styles might impact an individual capacity to focus and sustain attention,

This process included reviewing and synthesizing empirical studies linking attachment styles and attentional mechanisms, particularly during periods of heightened stress and uncertainty, such as the COVID-19 pandemic, to assess the influence of attachment styles and attentional processes on academic success, aiming to uncover patterns and potential mechanisms through which attachment may impact learning outcomes and identify potential areas for intervention and propose strategies that can be employed to mitigate the negative impact of insecure attachment styles on attention and academic success during stressful times, contributing to both enhanced well-being and improved educational outcomes.

Based on the literature review, the authors summarized the following implications:

a. Cognitive load theory provides a framework for predicting relationships between attachment and attention during stressful times, including the COVID-19 pandemic.
b. Cognitive load explains demands on individuals' attention capacity. Additional demands on cognitive capacities reduce the ability to attend to non-relevant stimuli, including coursework and course concepts.
c. Evidence from other universities demonstrates that offering social support opportunities for individuals who may not be securely attached creates engagement and a sense of belonging, particularly during stressful

times, including potentially for students that COVID-19 has impacted; and

d. High stress may make Marginalized groups more susceptible to cognitive load.

SUMMARY

The COVID-19 pandemic has dismantled and disrupted many long-established societal systems, most notably the school and learning system. Distance learning has hastily replaced traditional classes in school. At the beginning of the pandemic, almost all educational institutions were closed first to contain COVID-19 transmission when the number of cases started to rise, causing a massive adverse impact on education and students' psychological well-being. Unfortunately, students of lower socioeconomic status dealt with the worst consequences of schooling, as they cannot afford online resources, including computer equipment and internet services.

Despite evidence of direct impacts of coronavirus disease since 2019, school closure measures are taken on children's health. Almost all educational institutions in low- and middle-income countries (LMICs) have been physically closed for exceptionally long periods, ranging from several months to years. Such a long-term absence from schools and colleges has not only caused worse learning outcomes that are causing intergenerational inequalities but also induced multiple physical and mental health issues and even crises among students at all levels. Different countries launched online education through various media, including television and the Internet. However, due to the lack of resources in many LMICs, this alternate education system could add minimal value to students' learning. Most importantly, it failed to capture the students' attention. Consequently, students felt unmotivated and lost interest in learning, which resulted in an increased dropout rate and more frequent child marriages in these countries. At the same time, the extent of mental distress had increased, causing more burdens and suicidal ideation among students.

Many recent studies indicate that students admit that they did not study as much for their finals as compared to years prior to the pandemic. Online classes through Zoom or similar applications allow direct student-teacher interaction. However, students may remain muted for extended periods in class to allow the teacher to be heard correctly. Many students, much less impressed by online lectures than in real life, take advantage of common internet connection problems and rarely turn on their webcams. As a result, online classes are rarely interactive.

Other issues for policymakers, school administrators, and stakeholders to consider are that many rural residents cannot afford to get smartphones or laptops, which are integral to online classes, and even if they do, the internet bandwidth in those areas is not ideal. Also, the resistance from students against school reopening is inevitable because having had no proper schooling for nearly two years, as observed, some primary and university students expressed incredible unwillingness to sit and take exams at school. The reason for this is apparent: cheating is exponentially more difficult when taking a test in a classroom setting.

Challenges and Opportunities

One challenge for school districts is ensuring adequate planning, training, and support for teachers' and students' digital literacy and online teaching and learning readiness. The COVID-19 global pandemic provided teachers and administrators with a chance to evaluate the readiness of their schools for distance education as well as readiness for future emergencies. Working in crisis mode is not a practical long-range solution for districts, campuses, and teachers, although many districts successfully implemented virtual learning during the pandemic. A second challenge is for teachers to adapt their online lessons so student interactions may occur between the teachers and their peers. Fostering this interaction may be challenging for some teachers, whether they are teaching synchronously or asynchronously.

A more vital interaction is tied directly to the potential opportunity for creating a more substantial instructor presence. Building a stronger instructor presence facilitates student learning, aims to connect with students in the classroom, creates shared experiences, establishes mutual comfort, and is responsive to students. These vital skills require preparation, training, and support for teachers and educators.

Additional Effects of COVID-19 and School Closures on K–12 Students

School closures can also be expected to have consequences for children and adolescents' socio-emotional and motivational development. The psychological strain on families generated by the COVID-19 shock affected students' development in these areas and may adversely affect economic potential. Empirical evidence has linked school closures to several factors, including rising mental health concerns, lower levels of engagement, reports of violence against children, rising obesity, increases in teenage pregnancy, rising levels of chronic absenteeism and dropouts, and overall deficits in the development of socioemotional skills due to social isolation from networks and peers. Retrieved from https://www.richmondfed.org/publications/research/economic_brief/2023/eb_23-29

CONCLUSIONS

School closures and sudden switches to hybrid/virtual learning due to the pandemic adversely affected student achievement through several channels, including a decline in skill accumulation and a disruption of peer effects and peer-group formation. Preliminary evidence suggests that losses occurred early in the pandemic and that there has not been an apparent recovery. Also, the impact on students has been far from uniform, as economic and academic losses tend to fall more deeply on younger students and students from disadvantaged backgrounds.

Simply returning schools and instructional practices to where they were prior to 2019 will not avoid such losses. A wide range of remediation policies has been suggested, and evidence suggests that instructional practices—such as tutoring and individualized small group instruction—appear to be effective. Retrieved from https://www.richmondfed.org/publications/research/economic_brief/2023/eb_23-29

The impacts of COVID-19 and related policy responses may have broad, long-lasting, severe negative effects on students. Students experiencing adversity lose out on their potential the most. If this situation continues, the future generation will endure more severe consequences. With the constant geo-political, socio-psychological, and economic changes and the threat of global warming that may cause other potential man-made and/or natural disasters, we must prepare an educational system based on science and evidence-based research studies to cope with and endure these potential challenges. We will be able to continue to provide the optimal educational experience to our students, who will be the leaders of the next generation.

Lastly, the overarching theme of this book is to provide evidence-based research information and a comprehensive literature review to the readers on how to best support learners, teachers, parents, school administrators, and stakeholders, especially the more marginalized population, concerning technological training and psychological and emotional support during crises, when an alternate form of learning is essential for the learners and the teachers to succeed.

REFERENCES

Ayyildiz, P. & Yilmaz, A. (2025). Researching the entangled: Post-COVID-19 cognitive, psychological and motivational States. In J. D. Salisbury-Glennon, C. H. Wang, & D. M. Shannon (Eds.), *Instructional survival in the midst of the perfect storm: The experiences of K–12 teachers during the COVID-19 Global pandemic*. Emerald Publishing.

Banks, R. F., Campbell, M. B., Dillard, D. M., & Torres, J. A. (2025). Attachment, attention, and achievement during the COVID-19 pandemic: A conceptual literature review. In J. D. Salisbury-Glennon, C. H. Wang, & D. M. Shannon (Eds.), *Instructional survival in the midst of the perfect Storm: The experiences of K–12 teachers during the COVID-19 global pandemic*. Emerald Publishing.

Camp, A. M., Zamarro, G., & McGee, J. (2025). Educators' job burnout and intentions to leave during the COVID-19 pandemic. In J. D. Salisbury-Glennon, C. H. Wang, & D. M. Shannon (Eds.), *Instructional survival in the midst of the perfect storm: The Experiences of K–12 teachers during the COVID-19 global pandemic*. Emerald Publishing.

Centers for Disease Control and Prevention. (2024.). How to Protect Yourself and Others. https://www.cdc.gov/covid/prevention/index.htmlCenters for Disease Control and

Prevention. (n.d.). *Coronavirus disease 2019* (COVID-19). https://www.cdc.gov/coronavirus/2019-ncov/prepare/children.html

Child Mind Institute. (2020). *Supporting families during COVID-19.* https://childmind.org/coping-during-COVID-19-resources-for-parents/ "https://childmind.org/coping-during-COVID-19-resources-for-parents/

Cohen, S., Kamarck, T., & Mermelstein, R. (1983). A global measure of perceived stress. *Journal of Health and Social Behavior, 24*, 386–396.

Conley, S. M. (2025). Teacher self-efficacy during COVID-19: A qualitative study on experienced high school teachers. In J. D. Salisbury-Glennon, C. H. Wang, & D. M. Shannon (Eds.), *Instructional survival in the midst of the perfect storm: The Experiences of K–12 teachers during the COVID-19 global pandemic.* Emerald Publishing..

Demerouti, E., Bakker, A. B., Vardakou, I., & Kantas, A. (2003). The convergent validity of two burnout instruments: A multitrait-multimethod analysis. *European Journal of Psychological Assessment, 19*(1), 12–23. https://doi.org/10.1027/1015-5759.19.1.12

EdWeek Research Center. (2025). https:// www.edweek.org/research-center/

Federal Reserve Bank of Richmond. (2025). *The pandemic effects on children's education.* https://www.richmondfed.org/publications/research/economic_brief/2023/eb_23-29

Jones, D., Kramer, B., & Broadbent, C. (2025). A perfect storm: COVID-19 as a demotivating factor contributing to teacher stress, burnout, and mental health. In J. D. Salisbury-Glennon, C. H. Wang, & D. M. Shannon (Eds.), Instructional survival in the midst of the perfect storm: The Experiences of K–12 teachers during the COVID-19 global pandemic. Emerald Publishing.

Kroenke, K., & Spitzer, R. L. (2002).The PHQ-9: A new depression and diagnostic severity measure. *Psychiatric Annals, 32*, 509–521.

Ladendorf. K. (2025). Instructional survival: A qualitative case study of elementary teachers' experiences teaching remotely and concurrently during COVID-19. In J. D. Salisbury-Glennon, C. H. Wang, & D. M. Shannon (Eds.), *Instructional survival in the midst of the perfect storm: The experiences of K–12 teachers during the COVID-19 global pandemic.* Emerald Publishing.

Menchaca, V. D., & Garcia, A. (2025). K–12 teacher support during the COVID-19 pandemic. In J. D. Salisbury-Glennon, C. H. Wang, & D. M. Shannon (Eds.), *Instructional survival in the midst of the perfect storm: The Experiences of K–12 teachers during the COVID-19 global pandemic.* Emerald Publishing.

Marshall, D. T., Pressley, T., Schoettler, N. M., Trammell, D. L., & Smith, N. E. (2025). Elementary teacher morale and mental health following the COVID-19 pandemic. In J. D. Salisbury-Glennon, C. H. Wang, & D. M. Shannon (Eds.), *Instructional survival in the midst of the perfect storm: The experiences of K–12 teachers during the COVID-19 global pandemic.* Emerald Publishing.

Mosley, K. C., McCarthy, C. J., & Gupta, A. (2025). Social support and COVID-19: How U.S. K–12 Teachers were impacted by gratitude and mentoring during the COVID-19 pandemic. In J. D. Salisbury-Glennon, C. H. Wang, & D. M. Shannon (Eds.), *Instructional survival in the midst of the perfect storm: The experiences of K–12 teachers during the COVID-19 global pandemic.* Emerald Publishing.

NASP. (n.d.). *COVID-19 Resource Center.* https://www.nasponline.org/COVID-19

Sultana, F., Bari, R., & Munir, S. Impact of school closures due to COVID-19 on education in low-and middle-income countries. *Journal of Global Health Reports, 6,* e2022034. doi:10.29392/001c.36902

Wong, D. W., Hall, K., & Wong Hernandez, L. (2021). *Counseling Individuals through the lifespan* (2nd ed.). SAGE Publications, Inc.

Wood, J. N., & Wood, A. (2025). Impact of COVID-19 on students with special needs and parent involvement. In J. D. Salisbury-Glennon, C. H. Wang, & D. M. Shannon (Eds.), *Instructional survival in the midst of the perfect storm: The experiences of K–12 teachers during the COVID-19 global pandemic*. Emerald Publishing.

BIOGRAPHIES

ABOUT THE EDITORS

Jill D. Salisbury-Glennon, Ph.D. is a Professor of Educational Psychology at Auburn University. Her research focuses on student motivation and achievement. Her specific research interests include: college students' learning and study strategies, self-regulated learning, metacognition, motivation, attachment, and academic achievement; as well as creating learner-centered contexts at the university level. More recently, she has been involved in a fairly large-scale research project that investigates the effects of the COVID-19 global pandemic on college students' parental and peer relationships and how these impact college students' learning, motivation, resilience and academic performance. She is currently co-editing two books on the COVID-19 global pandemic entitled: *Examining the cognitive and psychological effects of the COVID-19 global pandemic on high school, undergraduate and graduate learners*; and *Instructional survival in the midst of the perfect storm: The experiences of K–12 teachers during the COVID-19 global pandemic* both to be published by Emerald Publishing.

Instructional Survival in the Midst of the Perfect Storm:
The Experiences of K–12 Teachers During the COVID-19 Global Pandemic, pages 233–343.

Published under exclusive licence by Emerald Publishing Limited
ISBNs: 978-1-83708-502-6 HB, 978-1-83708-503-3 PB,
978-1-83708-504-0 EPDF, 978-1-83708-505-7 EPUB

Chih-hsuan Wang, Ph.D. is a Professor in Educational Psychology at Auburn University. She teaches research methods and data analysis courses. Dr. Wang's work focuses on enhancing learning using technology as well as motivation assessment and learning outcomes within an online learning environment and its impacts on the teaching and learning process. Her other research interests include K–12 STEM education and evaluation, factors that influence international students' motivation and learning, and topics related to health psychology and nursing education.

David M. Shannon is a retired Professor Emeritus in Educational Research at Auburn University. His research interests are focused on issues related to quantitative research methods, program evaluation, and broadening participation in the STEM disciplines. He has research publications in top educational research and evaluation professional journals and he has served as the lead researcher or evaluator, or investigator for over 30 funded projects while at Auburn University. Current funded projects are focused specifically on low-income students, students with disabilities and other underrepresented populations in STEM.

AUTHOR BIOGRAPHIES

Pinar Ayyıldız, Ph.D. is an interpreter, sociologist, teacher trainer and holds MA/Doctor of Philosophy degrees in Educational Management as well as the Cambridge Diploma in Teaching English to Speakers of Other Languages. She has worked as a head teacher, academic coordinator, dean of students and director of English preparatory school in higher education institutions. She has various academic memberships and is the editor of international journals like Participatory Educational Research (PER) and Philosophy and Theory in Higher Education Journal (PTHE). She is an assistant professor of Management Information Systems and the coordinator of instructional processes in Ankara Medipol University, Türkiye.

Romona "Felicia" Banks, Ph.D. is an accomplished educator and researcher specializing in organizational psychology and distance education. As an Associate Faculty member at the University of Arizona Global Campus's College of Arts & Sciences, Department of Behavioral Sciences, she has dedicated her career to fostering an inclusive and stimulating learning environment. Dr. Banks believes in individualized education and employs diverse teaching methods, including technology integration, case studies, and group projects, to help students thrive intellectually and socially. With a Ph.D. in Organizational Psychology, she brings a robust academic background to her instructional roles. Her passion for education and student success is evident through her commitment to enhancing student research and writing skills, providing personalized feedback, and facilitating critical discussions. Dr. Banks' research interests are learner-centered teaching as a predictor of student retention and success in distance/online education; sustain ability of nonprofit organizations; transformational leadership as a predictor of Positive Youth Development; manager-employee relationships as a predictor of retention, effectiveness, and well-being; and Feng Shui as a predictor of work-place performance.

Clint Broadbent, Ph.D. is an assistant professor in the College of Education and Human Development at Southern Utah University. He received his doctorate from Oklahoma State University in Human Development and Family Science with a focus on Advanced Statistical Analysis and Methodology. His research interests center on improving outcomes for underserved family populations, primarily families that have a child with a disability and Latino immigrant adolescents and their families.

Andrew Camp, Ph.D. is a Senior Research Associate in the Annenberg Institute at Brown University and affiliated researcher with the Department of Education Reform at the University of Arkansas. His research focuses on the teaching profession, particularly teacher labor markets, teacher quality, and school staffing challenges. Camp has extensive experience working with state education agencies and advocacy organizations in leveraging quantiative analyses to inform timely policymaking. Much of his research focuses on the challenges facing teachers and policies that schools and states are using to better support then following the COVID-19 pandemic.

Mahaliah Bowman Campbell, Ph.D. Dr. Mahaliah Bowman Campbell holds the position of Assistant Professor of Psychology in the Social Science Department at Claflin University. Additionally, she serves as a part-time Associate Faculty member at the University of Arizona Global Campus, specializing in the Department of Behavioral Sciences. Before transitioning to higher education, Dr. Bowman Campbell dedicated over two decades to public service, holding various roles within the South Carolina Department of Social Services. Her extensive experience includes leadership positions such as Director of Parenting Education and Facilitator for Parenting and Anger Management Programs. In her dual career path, she has seamlessly integrated academia and government service, actively teaching as an adjunct professor at the college and university levels for twenty-two years. She holds a Ph.D. in Psychology, a master's degree in psychology, and an MBA in Management. Additionally, she is certified in Applied Behavior Analysis and as a grant writer and reviewer. Dr. Bowman Campbell's research interests span a broad spectrum, including ADHD, dual stigma, and mental health among athletes at Historically Black Colleges and Universities (HBCUs). Most recently, her research focuses on the effects of vaping among HBCU students aged 18–24 and its implications for their academic success.

Sarah M. Conley received her Bachelor of Science in Secondary English Education from Slippery Rock University in 2015. Moving to Virginia to pursue her teaching career, she has been working in public-school systems since January of 2016. She has taught English in both middle and high school, with specific experience teaching grades 6, 7, 8, 9, 10, and 12. In Fall of 2020, she began a master's program at George Mason University to receive her Master of Science in Educational Psychology. Sarah conducted original research for her master's thesis on the impact of COVID-19 on educator's self-efficacy and graduated in December of 2022.

Yan Dai is a doctoral student in the Educational Psychology program in the Department of Educational Foundations, Leadership & Technology (EFLT), Auburn University. Her research interests focus on motivation (particularly on self-efficacy and self-regulation), resilience, online learning, and cross-cultural compassion research. She also works under a critical theoretical frame using ethnographic and auto-ethnographic methods.

Dana M. Dillard, Ph.D., is an expert in stress. Dr. Dillard has focused her work on stress theory and science, including authoring articles and chapters on psychoneuroimmunology, stress, mindfulness, nutrition, fertility, epigenetics and intergenerational transmission of health risk, evidence-based practices, and more, all of which is rooted in health psychology – the intersection of behavior and wellbeing. As a certified holistic stress management instructor, she is unwaveringly curious about the evidence of stress management practices. In addition to her focus on stress science through a health psychology lens, Dr. Dillard is a program chair and associate professor for the psychology programs at the University of Arizona Global Campus and teaches dual-credit psychology courses through Highland Community College for local high schools. In her previous occupational life, Dr. Dillard was a police dispatcher, which fostered an understanding that we will never know what someone else is experiencing or how they are experiencing it and that all we can do is hold on and be their partner through the moment that their world shatters. These experiences have combined to shape Dr. Dillard's teaching and life philosophy that the unique lived experience of every individual is an opportunity to learn from one another and to grow together.

Alejandro Garcia, Ph.D. is an Associate professor in the Organization and School Leadership department. Dr. Garcia has taught both at the elementary and secondary levels and has served as a Technology Training Specialist for McAllen ISD, Edinburg CISD and Region 1. In addition to being a Technology Specialist, Dr. Garcia's administrative experiences include being Technology/Library Services Coordinator for Mission and Edinburg school districts. Dr. Garcia's research publications and interests are about Technology leadership, Teaching in Higher Education and Distance Learning.

Aradhita Gupta is a Master's Student in the Counselor Education Program at UT-Austin. She completed her B.A. in Psychology and Post Graduate Diploma in Advanced Studies and Research through Ashoka University in India, and has worked as a Teaching Fellow for psychology statistics courses and as a research assistant for the Public Health Foundation of India before coming to the US to complete her masters. Her research interests center on college student mental health, and specifically Non-Suicidal Self-Injury (NSSI). She is interested in exploring a developmental framework for NSSI using the attachment framework, and identifying intervention targets at individual and contextual levels, focusing on parent-child relationships as a central environmental factor.

Lucy Wong Hernandez has been a university faculty, frequent speaker, presenter, and trainer at national and international conferences and seminars for over twenty years. She has authored and contributed to numerous articles on disability rights, social policy, and multicultural issues and coauthored books. She has a Master of Science degree with a concentration in aging and disability and graduate studies in social welfare policies. She taught at York College, City University of New York (CUNY); Hofstra University, New York; the University of Hawaii at Manoa, Hawaii; East Carolina University, North Carolina, Mississippi State University; and most recently, at the University of Maryland Global College. She was the Executive Director of Disabled Peoples' International (DPI) from 1996 to 2002. During her tenure with DPI, a non-governmental organization with consultative status with the United Nations (U.N.), she contributed significantly to the inclusion of disability issues in the United Nations policy agendas related to vulnerable populations, where she also promoted the protection of human rights, social inclusion, and the equalization of opportunities for all persons with disabilities worldwide. Mrs. Wong Hernandez received the Americans with Disabilities Act (ADA) Award in 1990 for her leadership role and contributions to enacting and promoting the ADA in the United States. In 1998, she was inducted into the National Hall of Fame of Persons with Disabilities for her work and contributions to the disability field nationally and worldwide.

Denisha Jones, Ph.D., J.D. is Faculty in the Art of Teaching program at Sarah Lawrence College. She teaches first- and second-year Master's courses, including Foundations of Education, Children, Families, and Identity, and Emergent Curriculum. She earned her Ph.D. in Curriculum and Instruction from Indiana University. Her research interests include pedagogy and practice of teachers participating in social movements, the teacher's role in supporting development through play as pedagogy, and critical perspectives on teachers' work.

Brianne Kramer, Ph.D., is an Assistant Professor of Education in the College of Education and Human Development at Southern Utah University, where she teaches Social Foundations of Education courses and coordinates the Educational Foundations and Policy emphasis for the Masters of Education and Masters of

Interdisciplinary Studies programs. She holds a Ph.D. in Social Foundations of Education from the University of Toledo. Her research focuses on issues of privilege, identity, and resistance in teacher education programs, educational policy, and teacher activism.

Karen Ladendorf, Ph.D. is an Assistant Professor of Education and Co-Chair of the Education Department at College of DuPage in Glen Ellyn, IL. She teaches foundations of education, instructional technology integration, special education, and instructional psychology courses. She also coordinates pre-service teacher clinical placements throughout the Chicago area and is the Kappa Delta Pi honor society college advisor. Karen holds a Masters of Arts in Educational Leadership and a Masters of Arts in Educational Technology. She earned her Ph.D. in Instructional Technology from Northern Illinois University. Her research focused on remote learning experiences with elementary students, virtual reality as an instructional tool, and bringing the younger student voice to the forefront of research. Karen spent 20 years in K–12 setting as a teacher, instructional coach, professional development provider, curriculum writer, and Director of Innovation and Technology. She brings her background of classroom instruction and teacher support to the college classroom to better prepare pre-service teachers for their future careers.

David T. Marshall, Ph.D., is an assistant professor of educational research in the College of Education at Auburn University. His research has focused on the impact that the COVID-19 pandemic has had on K–12 education and charter schools. His first book, *COVID-19 and the Classroom: How Schools Navigated the Great Disruption*, focused on the impact that the pandemic had on K–12 stakeholders, education policy, and teacher preparation from March 2020 through June 2021. Previously, Dr. Marshall worked with teacher residency programs in Virginia for seven years, serving in several capacities. He began his career in education as a middle and high school social studies teacher in Philadelphia, Pennsylvania. He recently served two terms as the chair of the Alabama Public Charter School Commission.

Christopher J. McCarthy, Ph.D. is a professor in the Department of Educational Psychology at the University of Texas at Austin. Dr. McCarthy's professional specialization is in Counseling and he teaches courses in career development, counseling skills, and group counseling. His research interests include stress and coping in educational contexts, group counseling, and career development. Dr. McCarthy's current scholarly focus is on researching factors that cause stress for K – 12 teachers and developing interventions to help teachers thrive. Dr. McCarthy is a member of the American Counseling Association, the Association for Specialists in Group Work, and the American Educational Research Association.

Josh B. McGee is an economist who is an associate professor in the Department of Education Reform at the University of Arkansas, where he holds the 21st Century Endowed Chair in Education Accountability and Transparency. He is also a faculty affiliate of the Office for Education Policy, which is a leading research-practice partnership focused on improving Arkansas education outcomes. He prioritizes policy-relevant questions and collaboration with governments and nonprofits to help them use data and evidence to make informed decisions. His research investigates critical issues in retirement policy, P–20 education, and economic development and has appeared in numerous popular media outlets and prominent scholarly journals. He has extensive experience working in leadership roles in education, government, nonprofits, and philanthropy.

Velma D. Menchaca earned a Ph.D. from Texas A&M University in Curriculum & Instruction with a minor in Educational Administration in 1991. She is currently a professor and department chair for the Department of Organization and School Leadership at the University of Texas Rio Grande Valley. She has previously taught at the University of Texas Pan American, Texas State University and Tarleton State University and has been a university professor 29 years. She taught in the public schools for eleven years. Her research focuses in the areas of cultural responsiveness, English Learners, mentoring leaders and rural school leaders. Dr. Menchaca teaches in the areas of sociocultural issues, school and community engagement and special populations. She teaches in the master's and doctoral programs and has chaired several dissertations. She has made state, national, and international presentations. She has also served on national and state boards, in addition to providing service to her community. She served as principal investigator for a $12,000 grant to recruit and retain high quality teachers in small, rural districts. She has recently received the Mentor Award presently by the College of Education.

Kristen C. Mosley, Ph.D. is a former K–12 public school teacher, administrator, and district researcher and evaluator. She serves as an Academic Affiliate at the University of Texas at Austin, through which she studies teacher stress and coping, and she is also the Director of Research and Evaluation for the Texas Higher Education Coordinating Board's community college finance team. Dr. Mosley has earned degrees from Vanderbilt University (B.S.), Southern Methodist University (M.Ed.), and the University of Texas at Austin (M.Ed., Ph.D.). Dr. Mosley's research and evaluation spans quantitative, qualitative, and mixed methods designs, and her focal areas are teacher stress, coping, and retention, particularly among high-need schools. She has presented her research at multiple international conferences as well as published several chapters and manuscripts in peer-reviewed journals. She is a current member of the Journal for Trauma Studies in Education Editorial Board and a prior member of the Teach For America Austin Alumni Board.

Tim Pressley, Ph.D., is an assistant professor of psychology at Christopher Newport University. Additionally, he is a faculty member for the university's master's in teaching program and the Center for Education Research and Policy. He received his Ph.D. in Educational Psychology from Florida State University and has a background in elementary education. Prior to receiving his Ph.D., Dr. Pressley was an elementary school teacher, which has been a driving force behind his research. His current research focuses on teachers' lives, specifically the impact of COVID-19, teacher effectiveness, well-being, and development. He hopes his research gives teachers a voice on aspects impacting teachers' lives.

Jill D. Salisbury-Glennon, Ph.D. is a Professor of Educational Psychology at Auburn University. Her research focuses on student motivation and achievement. Her specific research interests include: college students' learning and study strategies, self-regulated learning, metacognition, motivation, attachment, and academic achievement; as well as creating learner-centered contexts at the university level. More recently, she has been involved in a fairly large-scale research project that investigates the effects of the COVID-19 global pandemic on college students' parental and peer relationships and how these impact college students' learning, motivation, resilience and academic performance. She is currently co-editing two books on the COVID-19 global pandemic entitled: *Examining the cognitive and psychological effects of the COVID-19 global pandemic on high school, undergraduate and graduate learners*; and *Instructional survival in the midst of the perfect storm: The experiences of K–12 teachers during the COVID-19 global pandemic* both to be published by Emerald Publishing.

Natalie M. Schoettler is a doctoral student in the Educational Psychology program at Auburn University. Natalie received her Master of Science in Educational Research, Measurement, and Evaluation, as well as a Graduate Certificate in Program Evaluation from Auburn University. Before coming to Auburn, Natalie worked as a research assistant for Emory University in an inclusive preschool lab school at the Marcus Autism Center, where children with and without autism learn together and from each other. Currently, Natalie serves as a graduate assistant in Research and Instruction Services at Auburn's Ralph Brown Draughon Library. Her research interests encompass school choice for parents of children with special needs, including charter schools, and the academic and social inclusion of children on the spectrum.

David Shannon, Ph.D. is a retired Professor Emeritus in Educational Research at Auburn University. His research interests are focused on issues related to quantitative research methods, program evaluation, and broadening participation in the STEM disciplines. He has research publications in top educational research and evaluation professional journals and he has served as the lead researcher or evaluator, or investigator for over 30 funded projects while at Auburn. Current funded projects are focused specifically on low-income students, students with disabilities and other underrepresented populations in STEM.

Natalie E. Smith is a native of Waynesboro, Pennsylvania, and is currently pursuing her Ph.D. in Instrumental Music Education at Auburn University, with certificates in Program Evaluation, and College and University Teaching. She serves as a Graduate Teaching Assistant for the Department of Music teaching courses, performing administrative tasks, and working with the athletic bands. Prior to beginning at Auburn, Smith served as an elementary instrumental music teacher for Baltimore County Public Schools. During this time, she also served as the Pep Band Coordinator and Director at Mount St. Mary's University in Emmitsburg, Maryland, where she built a new band play at their Division I Basketball games. Smith holds a Bachelor of Science degree in Music Education from Indiana University of Pennsylvania and earned a Master of Music degree in Flute Performance from East Carolina University. While at ECU, she served as a Graduate Teaching Assistant for the University Athletic Bands, and as a graduate instructor for the Flute Studio. Smith is also an active performer, studio teacher, clinician, and adjudicator. Her research interests include curriculum development and reformation in collegiate music education, urban teaching, and program evaluation.

Joseph Torres, Ph.D. is a native to Southern California, who has dedicated his career to assisting others and the advancement of students in their academic and life journey. His research and specialization are in chaplaincy, marriage and family systems, parenting, and children and adolescents. He received his Bachelor of Science in Psychology from University of Phoenix, his Master of Science in Psychology: Chemical Dependency and Pastoral Counseling from California Southern University, his Master of Arts in Marriage and Family Therapy from Touro University, and his Doctor in Philosophy in Counseling and Psychological Studies from Regent University. He serves as faculty in multiple universities; in multiple departments and disciplines as well as serving as a committee chair and member for doctoral dissertations. He also is a healthcare and police chaplain as well as a therapist. Dr. Torres is a member of the California Practical Chaplains Association, Ontario Critical Incident Stress Foundation, American Association for Marriage and Family Therapy, Association of American Educators, and Christian Educators Association International.

Deja' L. Trammell is a native of Montgomery, Alabama who has dedicated her career to the advancement of students of color in higher education through academic and professional supportive services. She received her Bachelor of Science in Psychology from Alabama State University, her Master of Social Work from Clark Atlanta University, and her Master of Science in Education Research, Measurement, and Evaluation from Auburn University. She is a third-year doctoral student at Auburn University pursuing her degree in Educational Psychology with a focus in Higher Education Administration. Her research focuses on the identities and experiences of Black students throughout academia and how culturally responsive practices in education can foster student agency and success. She is committed to enhancing the growth and development of students of color in education by providing diverse, equitable access to institutional resources and programming.

Chih-hsuan Wang, Ph.D. is a Professor in Educational Psychology. She teaches research methods and data analysis courses. Wang's work focuses on enhancing learning using technology as well as motivation assessment and learning outcomes within an online learning environment and its impacts on the teaching and learning process. Her other research interests include K–12 STEM education and evaluation, factors that influence international students' motivation and learning, and topics related to health psychology and nursing education.

Daniel W. Wong, Ph.D. is the Department Chair and Professor of the Department of Counselor Education at the University of Southern Maine. He is a professor emeritus at Mississippi State University (MSU), where he served as the Department Head of the Department of Counseling and Educational Psychology from 2009 to 2018. From 2004 to 2009, Dr. Wong was a Professor and Director of the Doctoral Program in the Department of Rehabilitation Studies, College of Allied Health Sciences, and an Adjunct Professor in the Department of Physical Medicine and Rehabilitation, Brody School of Medicine at East Carolina University (ECU). He also served as department chair of the Department of Counselor Education at the University of Hawaii -Manoa (2001–2004) and at Hofstra University from 1986–2001. He received the 1992 Research Award from the American Counseling Association (ACA) and the 2005 Research Award 3rd Place from the American Rehabilitation Counseling Association (ARCA). He has published over sixty (60) articles in refereed and professional journals and numerous position and policy papers for disability and rehabilitation issues nationally and internationally. Dr. Wong published a book with his colleagues entitled "Counseling Individuals Through the Lifespan" (January 2015) by SAGE Publication Inc. The second edition of this book was published in October 2020.

Amanda Wood, Ph.D. grew up in Springfield, Missouri where she attended Springfield Public Schools and Drury University graduating with a B.A. in Education. She taught elementary school for five years during which time she obtained her MA in Profession Counseling, M.A. in School Counseling, and her psychological examiner certification. She received her M.S. in Educational Administration and her principal certification in 2015. She completed her certification as Director of Special Education, her Ed.S., and her PhD in Educational Leadership from Saint Louis University. She continues to work as a school psychological examiner in the Wentzville R-IV School District.

Jody Wood, Ed.D. worked 31 years in public education during which time she was a public-school teacher prior to becoming a curriculum director. While working in the curriculum arena, she supervised all secondary content areas. She became an assistant superintendent for curriculum and instructional services at Wentzville School District prior to joining the Educational Leadership Department at Saint Louis University. She is now in her 18th year at SLU where she serves as an associate professor of educational leadership where she teaches district curriculum, professional development, teacher evaluation, and administration of special education.

Adem Yilmaz, Ph.D. is an academic, analyst, educational researcher, and a measurement and evaluation specialist. He holds a PhD in Measurement and Evaluation. His fields of expertise are as follows: teaching and learning of science, science education, scale development, measurement and evaluation, SPSS, LISREL, AMOS, EFA/DFA analyses. Dr. Yilmaz is a Measurement, Learning & Evaluation (MLE) Specialist and is the editor of several international books on Measurement and Evaluation. He is currently a faculty member and is working as an associate professor of education in Kastamonu University, Türkiye. He is also a member of several committees in the same university.

Gema Zamarro, Ph.D. is a Professor in Education Reform and Economics at the University of Arkansas and 21st Century Endowed Chair in Teacher Quality at the Department of Education Reform. Her research is motivated by policy-relevant questions and the use of rigorous methods to help inform policy. Dr. Zamarro has performed research in the areas of education and labor economics. Her work includes studies of the relationship between teacher quality and student performance, teacher recruitment and retention issues, the gender and educational effects of the COVID-19 pandemic, the effect of school closing policies on student outcomes, and the effect of dual-language immersion programs on student outcomes, among other topics..

Printed and bound by CPI Group (UK) Ltd, Croydon, CR0 4YY

13/09/2026

14961030-0003